A School Through Time

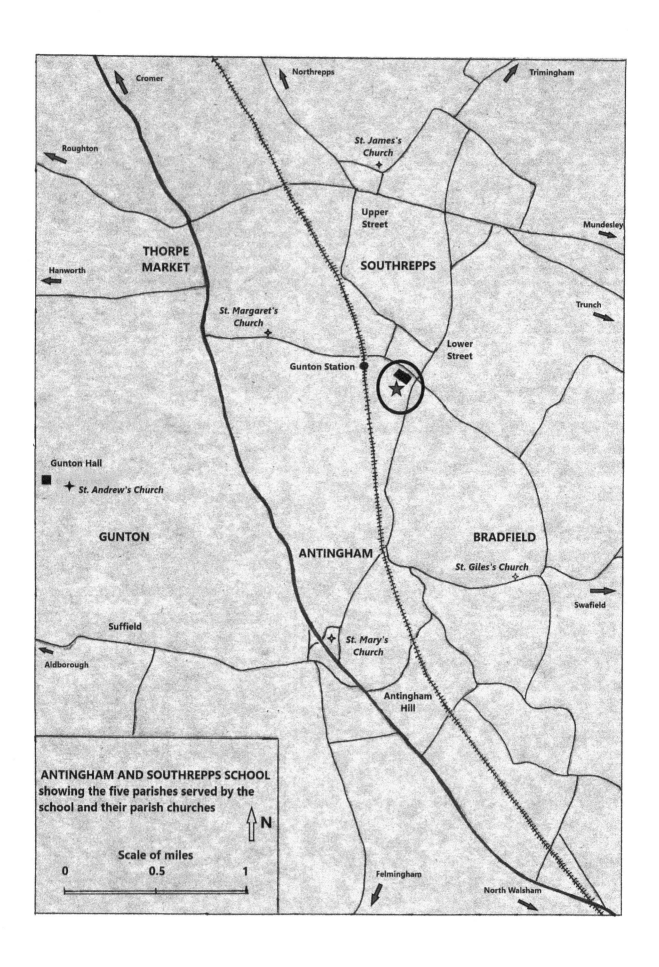

Cromer

Northrepps

Trimingham

St. James's
Church

Roughton

Upper
Street

Mundesley

THORPE
MARKET

SOUTHREPPS

Hanworth

St. Margaret's
Church

Trunch

Lower
Street

Gunton Station

Gunton Hall

St. Andrew's Church

GUNTON

BRADFIELD

St. Giles's Church

ANTINGHAM

Swafield

Suffield

Aldborough

St. Mary's
Church

Antingham
Hill

ANTINGHAM AND SOUTHREPPS SCHOOL
showing the five parishes served by the
school and their parish churches

↑N

Scale of miles

0   0.5   1

Felmingham

North Walsham

A School Through Time

200 years in the life of
Antingham and Southrepps School
and its people

Margaret Dowland

POPPYLAND
PUBLISHING

First published 2021 by Poppyland Publishing, Lowestoft, NR32 3BB
www.poppyland.co.uk

ISBN 978 1 909796 79 9

Typeset in Frutiger Light 9.5/12.5pt
Proofread and edited by Duncan and Sarah Westlake
Indexed by Duncan Westlake
Design/page layout by Pauline Hull

Front cover: School photograph 1906.
Southrepps Society collection

*Frontispiece: Map of Antingham and Southrepps School showing the
five parishes served by the school and their parish churches.*

Back cover: Mr Baldwin and his class 2006.
Dave and Janine Spanton

Contents

Introduction   1

Social History in the late 18th and 19th centuries   3

A History of Primary Education in England   5

The Suffield family and the school   11

How the changes in education influenced the school   14

Educational resources available in the late 19th century   20

Finance and funding   25

The school buildings   31

Occupants of the school house   44

The Headmistresses of the Girls' school   57

The Headmistresses of the Infants' school   60

Attendance   67

Holidays   75

Punishments   77

Vocational subjects   80

Recreation and sport   86

Diseases and health care   90

The school and agriculture   98

The school and the two World Wars   100

150th Anniversary   112

Appendix   114

   HMI School reports transcribed   116

   Timeline   126

   Staff of the school   133

   Pupils   137

Index   160

Acknowledgements

This book has been many years in the research and writing with so many people giving help and support along the way. So in the best traditions I apologise to those who I may not mention.

My thanks go to those who attended the school or worked there, and who were so generous with their time and memories. Ann, Betty, Bill, Derek, Emma, Heather, John, Meg, Sara, Sarah, Steph, Fiona, Freja, Dave and Janine. Lynne, the school secretary, deserves her own thanks.

Neil, thank you for your encouragement.

Carol and Colin for all the help with the Southrepps archive and Chris with the details of the World War One soldiers.

Megan Denis at Gressenhall Museum for hunting out artefacts I did not know existed. The staff of the British Schools Museum in Hitchin, Hertfordshire, who generously gave me a copy of their book *Joseph Lancaster, The Poor Child's Friend*, by Joyce Taylor. I recommend a visit.

An extra special thanks must go to Gloria, who I have never met, but thanks to her I have the photograph of the gallery steps invented by Samuel Wilderspin, the grandson of her eight times great grandfather. She helped a complete stranger and I am humbled by her generosity.

Pauline Hull who is the graphic designer of this book. She has brought her many years of expertise to the project and transformed it.

Sarah and Duncan Westlake who have helped with the research as well as proof reading and editing. I hope they enjoyed it, I certainly did.

John who without a shadow of doubt made this book happen and to whom no words can express my gratitude you were and are truly amazing.

Finally to my two lads David and Gavin.

Introduction

This is the history of a North Norfolk school built in 1826, which has seen the reigns of eight monarchs from George IV to Elizabeth II.

It is the story of an exceptional school built very early in the development of education for the masses. It originally served the tenants of Lord Suffield's estate and, on becoming a Board School, educated the children of five parishes: Antingham, Bradfield, Gunton, Southrepps and Thorpe Market. It has always educated girls as well as boys, and was built through the largesse of one family; a family who believed in the need for education, and were prepared to pay for it. It covers the changes in education over the centuries as well as through social and medical advances.

The contents of this book are the result of research, reading the log and minute books, visits to the National Archive Kew, the Norfolk Archive Centre Norwich, Gressenhall Museum and the five parish churches. It is my interpretation, highlighting areas of particular interest to me.

There are few records available about the early days of the school. It appears that from 1826 to 1878 it operated as one unit with two schoolrooms, the Headmaster, and an assistant teacher. Once it became a Board School it was split into three entities: The Infants' school, the Girls' school, and the Boys' school, with the Headmaster of the Boys' school in overall charge. The log books date from 1878, at first in three separate volumes – one for each School. By 1925 they are all combined in one; the final entry is 1989. There are five volumes in total.

The managers' minute books, also consisting of five volumes, cover the period from 1875 when the school became a Board School, until 1986. There are also a few entries in a punishment book. All these volumes are held at the Norfolk Archive Centre.

The main focus of the book is the period covered by the log books; there are references to later events as they are relevant to each chapter.

It was the small details in the log books that sparked my interest and fascination; unfortunately, these are no longer recorded in a simple accessible form. It was handling the actual documents and visualising the person as they wrote the day's account that made me want to share their story.

So much of what we now take for granted occurred during the life of the school: better health care, the welfare state, greater job and career opportunities, improving gender equality, opportunities in sport and recreation and thankfully now a prolonged period of peace. These things are no longer recorded as they are all around us and are what we expect.

Education has improved. We know that every child matters, that to improve our society we need to give our children the best education we can. This was not always so, and it is good to recognise what a groundbreaking school this was.

Our teachers are now trained professionals, but it has taken over a hundred years to reach this state. Children now go to school five days a week, education is free, there is a broader curriculum and numerous school trips. In 1939 a trip to London would have been a major undertaking, not a quick spin down the motorway.

The building itself has its own tale to tell as is reflected in its Grade II listing; it is certainly a striking building that demands to be noticed. Stand and look at it and you can hear the voices of the children who have played in its grounds and sat

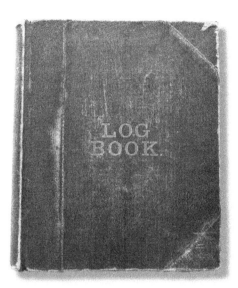

The Infants' log book, start date 1878.

The minute book from 1903, when the school came under the control of the Norfolk Education Committee.

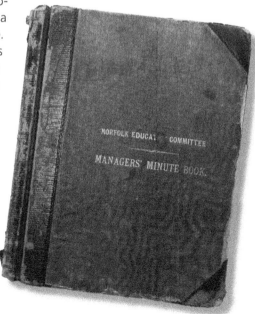

shivering in its school rooms. Children who have walked across the tops of hedges as snow drifts have filled the roads, to those who today arrive by car; they have all walked through those gates thanks to Lord Suffield.

Let me put Antingham and Southrepps School in context. Using data collected by the Norfolk Historic Buildings Group, we see that 200 rural Norfolk schools were built before 1870. The oldest purpose-built rural primary school for the general population was built in Dickleburgh near the Suffolk border in 1814, and is now used as the church rooms.

Antingham and Southrepps school is one of the oldest rural Primary schools in Norfolk still open in its original building. Hockering near Dereham would appear to be the oldest, with some of its original 1815 building still being visible. The others are St. Augustine's in Costessey (1820), Carleton Rode (1821) and Blakeney (1824), with Antingham and Southrepps (1826) in fifth place.

Within a radius of five miles of Antingham and Southrepps, 11 other schools were built in the 1800s. Of the 12 schools, six are still active, and four are still using the original buildings. (*Norfolk Historic Buildings Group Journal volume 5* (2013)).

Antingham and Southrepps 1826 still a school in its original building

Overstrand 1830 now an art gallery. The school is in new premises behind the original buildings

Suffield *c*1830 now a private house

Gimingham 1834 now a private house

Knapton 1839 now the village hall

Mundesley 1840 now the public library. The school is still open in new premises elsewhere in the village

Trimingham 1847 now a private house

Swafield 1852 now the village hall

Trunch 1853 demolished

Roughton 1871 still a school in its original building

North Walsham Infants 1874 still a school in its original building

Northrepps 1879 still a school in its original building

School photograph from the 1900s
Southrepps Society collection.

Social history in the late 18th and early 19th centuries

This was a period of social and political unrest throughout the kingdom. It was the early stages of the Industrial Revolution when large numbers of people began to move from rural areas to towns.

In 1800 the majority of the population still worked in agriculture or related industries. Most goods were made by hand and many craftsmen worked on their own with perhaps a labourer and an apprentice. In 1801 only about 20% of the population lived in urban areas; by 1851 this had risen to over 50% and by 1881 it had further increased to about two-thirds of the population. By the late 19th century factories were common and most goods were made by machine.

This industrialisation was much less widespread in Norfolk, with agriculture remaining the main occupation. There was also an oversupply of labour forcing down wages and increasing discontent amongst the workers. Changes in agricultural practice to a four-year rotation to include a turnip crop, which had been introduced by Norfolk farmer and statesman 'Turnip Townshend', increased the need for agricultural labourers. There was still considerable seasonal unemployment. New enclosures of common land were rife with owners fencing off large areas, thereby depriving the commoners of their traditional rights. The Corn Laws were also enacted, which increased the price of a loaf of bread, a staple food for the less well off. Increasing poverty led to 'bread riots' such as those in Ely and Littleport, which resulted in the hanging of 5 men at Norwich Castle.

Mechanisation in farming was also in its infancy, but was slow to gain a foothold in Norfolk due to the abundance of labour. Some tenancy agreements actually forbade the use of machinery. In the 1830s there were serious attacks on new machinery and buildings, known as the 'Swing Riots' as the affected farmer would receive a letter of warning signed 'Swing'. Lord Suffield was warned of an intended attack on his saw mill at Gunton, which fortunately was averted.

The French Revolution, which began in 1789, was still exerting its influence, with fears that a similar uprising could occur in Britain. The Norfolk-born Thomas Paine in his book *The Declaration of the Rights of Man* (1791) stated that, 'Men are born and remain free and equal in rights. Social distinctions may be founded only upon the general good.' A mass meeting was held in Manchester in 1819 demanding universal suffrage; the violent military suppression of the protest resulted in what became known as the 'Peterloo Massacre'. The outcome of these events and others meant that there was increasing hostility towards the ruling class. It was also a time of minimal education for the poor. Indeed, one attitude to education was that the poor should be taught just enough that

Farm worker from the 1920s at Hall farm, an unchanging image of the time.
The Southrepps Society; Tyler collection.

they would know their place in society. Many objected to any education occurring at all in case it gave the poor ideas above their station.

The case against educating the poor

In a debate in the House of Commons in 1807 on the Parochial Schools Bill, a Tory MP Davis Giddy said:

> However specious in theory the project might be of giving education to the labouring classes of the poor, it would, in effect, be found to be prejudicial to their morals and happiness; it would teach them to despise their lot in life, instead of making them good servants in agriculture and other laborious employments to which their rank in society had destined them; instead of teaching them subordination, it would render them factious and refractory, as is evident in the manufacturing counties; it would enable them to read seditious pamphlets, vicious books and publications against Christianity; it would render them insolent to their superiors; and, in a few years, the result would be that the legislature would find it necessary to direct the strong arm of power towards them and to furnish the executive magistrates with more vigorous powers than were now in force. Besides, if this Bill were to pass into law, it would go to burthen the country with a most enormous and incalcu-

lable expense, and to load the industrious orders of society with still heavier imposts. (*Hansard* House of Commons 13 June 1807 Vol 9 Cols 798-9 with minor corrections).

Those in favour of universal education

Fortunately, there were more enlightened people who saw the importance of education and campaigned to make it universally available. Tom Paine's *Age of Reason* (1794-5), Mary Wollstonecraft's *A Vindication of the Rights of Woman* (1792) and William Godwin's *Political Justice* (1793), viewed education as part of the search for a fair social order and the pursuit of human rights. It was Adam Smith (1723-1790) who, in *The Wealth of Nations* (1776), first advanced the demand for popular education as essential for the growth of factory production (Gillard D (2018) *Education in England: a history*. www.educationengland.org.uk/history).

The literacy rate in England at this time was very low: it was probably less than two thirds for men and less than a half for women, and England was already lagging behind some other European countries which had introduced compulsory elementary education.

The labour of children made a vital contribution to a family's financial well-being, either directly through wages, or in rural areas as physical help with all aspects of farming. Any attempt to introduce formal education would reduce this contribution and may have been seen as detrimental to the family economy. The prospect of school fees having to be paid, however small, would have compounded this problem. The immediate need to feed the family may have been seen to outweigh the long-term advantages that would come with education.

The founding of the school

It was in this climate of antipathy towards education of the poor that the 3rd Lord Suffield founded Antingham and Southrepps School in 1826. It was built at his own expense for the children of his tenants. Its position in the middle of the estate meant that it could be reached by all and although fees were paid by the families these varied according to their rent. He also provided a school house and paid the Headmaster's salary. This was a school far ahead of general views on the need for education of the poor.

c1910. Pit Street Lower Street – Hill House is to the right. The view would have been much the same one hundred years earlier.
The Southrepps Society collection

A History of Primary Education in England

Before the late 1780s education was mainly the preserve of the rich and there was little formal education for the general population. The aim of the Sunday School movement of the 1780s was to teach the poor to read the Bible and to train them in the habits of hard work and piety. These schools, as the name suggests, held lessons on a Sunday and sometimes in the evenings after the day's work was done. There were also Dame schools run by women who were probably illiterate themselves, that catered for younger children. They did teach needlework to girls but basically it was childminding. There was no state interest or funding for education at this time. Educational reforms tended to start in the cities where the large numbers of ill-educated children were more obvious.

Monitorial System

The aim of the Monitorial System was to teach as many children as possible as cheaply as possible basic literacy and numeracy. It was not compulsory and fees were payable.

In the late 18th century two people, Dr Andrew Bell, and Joseph Lancaster, both separately founded the Monitorial System, and their systems were to dominate popular education for many years. Dr Bell was a Church of England Clergyman and Joseph Lancaster a Quaker. Dr Bell's developed as the National Schools and Joseph Lancaster's as the British and Foreign Schools. One of the main differences between the ideas was the importance of the teaching of established religion. Both used the Bible as the main and in some cases only written text. Joseph Lancaster wanted to educate the poor and improve their lives, whereas the National system could be said to be more interested in teaching the poor to know their place in society. Both systems started with high ideals and principles but as they were expanded across the country standards declined. This may well have

been because both systems were dependent on the drive of their instigators and as more schools were built their personal input decreased, and no system was in place to help to maintain the original principles or to look to the future.

The layout of the classroom varied depending on which system was used but the principle was that all the children were taught in one large room under the scrutiny of the Headmaster, who sat at a raised desk at one end of the room. The children were then divided into groups, usually of 10, and instructed by a monitor, a child of 10 or 11 who had been given-out-of-hour's tuition by the master. What they were taught by the Headmaster they in turn taught their fellow pupils. They were taught the basics of reading, writing, arithmetic and needlework. In the Lancastrian method the children stood for these lessons, in semicircles around the room with the lesson being taught pinned to the wall in front of them. As their learning progressed so would they move to the group next

This shows the last remaining Lancastrian monitorial classroom. Not visible are the red semi-circles that were marked on the floor around the classroom where the small groups were taught.
British Schools Museum, 41/42 Queen Street, Hitchin SG4 9T.

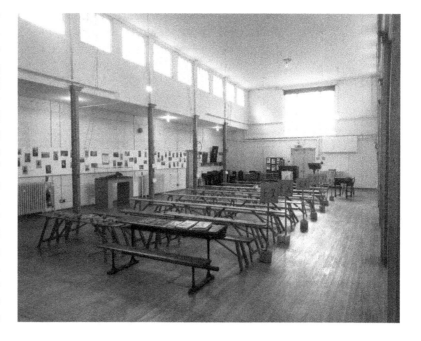

to them. They would return to simple benches and tables in the centre of the classroom in front of the Headmaster's desk for writing. The youngest and least able were closest to the dais. These tables had sand trays for the children to practice their letters whilst the more able progressed to using slates. They might be summoned to the Headmaster to be tested on their learning. The learning process was regulated by punishment and reward.

In the Bell system the arrangement was reversed with the writing desks to the sides of the room and the children standing in the middle for their lessons. The lesson being taught was attached to standard posts in the middle of the room, around which the small groups of children gathered.

This was the 'ideal' but the monitor could be younger than 10 and may have received minimal tuition. Monitors were paid a small sum. The British and Foreign Schools and the National Schools both trained teachers but sometimes it amounted to nothing more than how to implement the system. The aim was to teach the poor good and orderly habits and train them to read God's word.

Samuel Wilderspin

At the same time Samuel Wilderspin, a pioneer in infant education, was advocating that children of seven years and under should be taught separately from the older children. The infants would be taught directly by the teacher. He made extensive use of pictures, writing: "Whatever children can see excites their interest, and this led to the idea of grouping them together to receive what are called 'object lessons'". (*Early Discipline Illustrated; Or, The Infant System Progressing and Successful.* By Samuel Wilderspin)

He considered it important that if possible, there should be a smaller room where each class could be taught in turn. It is likely that this is where the term 'classroom' originated from. He then developed the galleries in the 1830s so that all the children could see the teacher; this was raked seating as in a modern lecture theatre. Sometimes the galleries were built into the smaller 'classroom'.

His system became known as the simultaneous method. He also promoted play and playgrounds as an essential part of education. He believed that undirected 'free' play was a way of "developing character and moral behaviour through co-operation and shared play".

1833 Education Act

The Government's attitude to education slowly changed. In 1833 the first Parliamentary grant for education gave £20,000 (equivalent to £2,350,000 in 2020), to be distributed amongst the National and British and Foreign Schools, but this was for the building of new schools, not financial support for existing ones. In 1839 the Committee of the Privy Council was set up to inspect schools and distribute the grants. They also took responsibility for approving building plans and produced 'ideal' plans incorporating the monitorial and simultaneous systems.

These ideas were introduced into Antingham and Southrepps when the school was enlarged in 1877.

Pupil Teachers

In 1846 a pupil teacher scheme was introduced with the aim of replacing the monitors with apprentices, who would then become teachers. Children from 13 years would be apprenticed to a school as pupil teachers, teaching fellow pupils in the day and being taught themselves before school or in the evening by the head teacher. The indenture would last 5 years. On completion of their five years the pupil teacher could either become an uncertificated teacher or they could sit for the Queen's Scholarship exam, which would qualify the holder for a place at a training college. They were then trained for anything from one to three years, being awarded a first class, second class or third-class certificate, with 3rd class being the highest.

The children were taught by rote. In the gallery lessons there would be discussion about

This is a copy of an 1851 government plan for a school of 120 pupils, showing how schools were encouraged to adopt a combination of the monitorial and simultaneous methods. Adapted from diagram in Seabourne 1971.

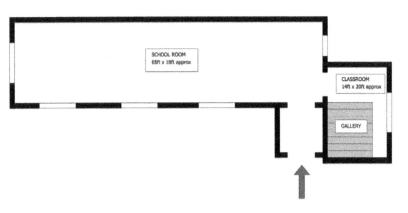

SCHOOL ROOM 65ft x 18ft approx

CLASSROOM 14ft x 20ft approx

GALLERY

the objects they had to learn about, then they would return to their desks and copy out 20 questions and the corresponding answers, and it would be on these that the inspectors would test the learning of the pupils. Sadly, a government report of 1861 concluded that:

Before the attention of Government had been directed to the subject of popular education, many schools conducted on the monitorial system had been established in different parts of the country, but the first important result which was obtained from the inspection of the state of education in the years 1839-46 was proof of the inadequacy of the monitorial system, and of the inefficiency of the teachers who were then in possession of the schools. The unanimous testimony of the inspectors was that the teachers were bad, and that the monitors, from their extreme youth, were of little use. They were fit only for the discharge of routine duties, and even these they discharged without interest, without weight, and without authority. They were frequently untrustworthy, and almost always ignorant.

The consequence of this was that the schools were generally in a deplorable state in every part of England.
(Gillard D (2018) *Education in England: a history.* www.educationengland.org.uk/history)

The 1862 code resulted from this report. The unforeseen outcome was to narrow the curriculum as the teachers taught only what was necessary to get the grants.

1870 Education Act

The 1870 Education Act was very important as it demonstrated for the first time a commitment to provide good quality education on a national scale. It established a system of Board schools which were locally managed by elected boards and drew their funding from local rates. It made provision for Board schools to write local bye-laws making education compulsory for children aged five to ten, but it wasn't until the Education Act of 1880 that education became compulsory nationwide for all children between the ages of five and ten. More pupil teacher training colleges were also set up to cope with the increasing number of pupils.

In 1872 the revised Code of Education stipulated that every scholar be examined according to 6 standards in reading, writing and arithmetic. Standards I to VI, roughly corresponding to ages seven to 12

	Reading	Writing	Arithmetic
Standard I Age 7	Read one of the narratives next in order after monosyllables in an elementary reading book used in the school	Copy in manuscript character a line of print, and write from dictation a few common words	Simple addition and subtraction of numbers of not more than four figures, and the multiplication table to multiplication by six
Standard II Age 8	A short paragraph from an elementary reading book	A sentence from the same book, slowly read once, and then dictated in single words	The multiplication table, and any simple rule as far as short division (inclusive)
Standard III Age 9	A short paragraph from a more advanced reading book	A sentence slowly dictated once by a few words at a time, from the same book	Long division and compound rules (money)
Standard IV Age 10	A few lines of poetry or prose, at the choice of the inspector	A sentence slowly dictated once, by a few words at a time, from a reading book, such as is used in the first class of the school	Compound rules (common weights and measures)
Standard V Age 11	A short ordinary paragraph in a newspaper, or other modern narrative	Another short ordinary paragraph in a newspaper, or other modern narrative, slowly dictated once by a few words at a time	Practice and bills of parcels
Standard VI Age 12	To read with fluency and expression	A short theme or letter, or an easy paraphrase	Proportion and fractions (vulgar and decimal)

The effect of the revised code was to create a minimum education; no rewards were available for expanding the pupil's knowledge so only the minimum was taught.

Mundella code

In 1880 Anthony Mundella became the equivalent of today's Secretary of State for Education in the Gladstone government. He introduced the Mundella code to address some of the deficiencies of the education system. It introduced the merit grant designed to promote more intelligent teaching rather than teaching for inspection. Schools were to be classified as 'fair', 'good' or 'excellent' for the purpose of allocating the grant, and inspectors were provided with instructions to guide them in their assessment. The grant would be payable on the average attendance of the school, not on individual pupils. It also introduced new subjects such as science, and for the girls, cookery. Grants would also be paid for these. The standards system was finally abandoned by 1900.

Religious teaching in the board schools was to be 'non-denominational'. The schooling was not free, except in proven cases of poverty.

1891 Education Act

Fees remained payable until a change in the law in 1891. The Act provided for ten shillings (50p) a year to be paid as a 'fee grant' by Parliament for each child over three and under fifteen attending a public elementary school. Further legislation in 1893 extended the age of compulsory attendance to 11, and in 1899 to 12. There is a complicated amendment to the act:

The parent of any child may at any time after such a child is 11 years of age and has passed 4th Standard give notice to the Local Authority that such child is to be employed in agriculture.

The minimum age for exemption for school attendance in the case of such a child shall be 13yrs. Such a child shall be required to attend School between the ages of 11 and 13, 250 times in the year from the 1st Sept to 15th June. Any such child as soon as it has made the number of attendance required for the above mentioned period shall whilst employed in agriculture be exempt from further obligation until the succeeding period mentioned.

(Gillard D (2018) *Education in England: a history* www.educationengland.org.uk/history)

1902 Education Act

In 1902 Parliament passed a new Education Act, drafted by AJ Balfour (who became prime minister later that year), which radically reorganised the administration of education at local level. It abolished the school boards in England and Wales. All elementary schools were placed in the hands of Local Education Authorities under the control of the County Councils and County Borough Councils which had been established in 1888. It also made provision for voluntary extended secondary education to the age of 16.

Changes began to be made to pupil teachers' education. In 1900 almost one quarter of all teachers were pupil teachers, so to increase the quality of education the minimum age for a pupil teacher was raised from 13 to 15, except where Her Majesty's Inspector (HMI) authorised a younger age, usually in rural areas. Pupil teachers continued to be examined annually by the HMI. They also could not teach for more than 5 hours a day or 20 per week. In 1904 the minimum age was increased to 16 and the number of hours they could work further reduced with compulsory training at pupil teacher centres. Further changes meant that the role of pupil teacher had almost ceased to exist by the outbreak of the First World War.

1918 Fisher Act

The 1918 Fisher Act (named after Herbert Fisher, President of the Board of Education) raised the school leaving age to 14 and Local Education Authorities were required to ensure:

That public elementary schools included 'practical instruction' in the curriculum and offered advanced instruction 'for the older or more intelligent children';

That they attended to 'the health and physical condition of the children;

That they cooperated with other Local Education Authorities to prepare children for further education 'in schools other than elementary', and to provide for the supply and training of teachers.

However, austerity after the war forced the provisions of the Act to be postponed as cuts were made to the education budget, and the compulsory age increase did not occur until the 1921 Act.

1944 Education Act

The 1944 Education Act raised the compulsory age for leaving school to 15. This came into force in 1947. It also made all secondary education free and established Secondary Modern Schools and Technology Schools alongside Grammar Schools. The 1944 Act also aimed to provide a comprehensive School Health Service by requiring the provision of school meals, free milk, medical and dental treatment. The Government quickly realised that there would be insufficient accommodation for the extra pupils so they designed a rapid construction

The senior school c1920.
The Southrepps Society collection

temporary building, the HORSA, an acronym for 'Hutting Operation for the Raising of the School leaving Age'.

With the raising of the school leaving age there was a shortage of teachers, so an emergency training scheme aimed at older people with a wealth of experience and ex-services people came into force. They would not have to have specific academic qualifications but the selection process would be rigorous. It would be a one-year course and two years' probation.

The 1960s

In the 1960s progressive teaching methods became more popular, with integration of the curriculum and greater creativity for the children. The eleven plus was being abolished and attention was becoming focused on the need of the individual child.

There was to be flexibility in the curriculum, use of the environment, learning by discovery and evaluation of the child's progress. Until this time streaming had occurred in primary schools.

There was also an aim to reduce class sizes to a maximum of 40 in primary schools.

1988 Education Reform Act

The Act provided a basic curriculum to be taught in school. It set out attainment targets and introduced 'key stages'; primary schools having key stages one (Infants) and two (Juniors). There were three core subjects of English, mathematics and science, plus six foundation subjects of history, geography, technology, music, art and physical education. The national curriculum testing regime came into force in 1991 and became known as Standard Assessment Tests or SATS.

2010 Academies Act

In July 2010, the Government introduced the Academies Act. This allowed not-for-profit organisations to run schools. They continue to receive funding from Government and are still inspected by Ofsted. The Act had in effect removed most schools from Local Education control.

Senior pupils c1950 with Mr Hare.
The Southrepps Society collection

The Suffield family and the school

The Harbords were a local family who played a significant role in the development of Cromer and its surrounding areas.

Harbord, 1st Lord Suffield

Harbord Harbord (1734–1810) owned the Gunton estate and was Member of Parliament for Norwich; he was raised to the peerage as the first Lord Suffield in 1786. He married Mary Assheton in 1760. Their contributions to education began when she, in a codicil to her will dated 1814, left £600 to endow a school in the village of Suffield for the education of the poor. She died in 1823, and by 1833 the school had been built. The 3rd Lord Suffield continued to support the school after it was built and paid for the construction of the school house. It was originally a school for 22 girls only, and is thought to have closed by 1925.

William, 2nd Lord Suffield

On the death of his father in 1810 William Harbord (1766–1821) became the 2nd Lord Suffield. He was the second son of Harbord and Mary, the first son Charles having died in infancy. William married Caroline Hobart in 1792. They lived at Blickling Hall, only coming to the Gunton estate for the shooting. Lady Caroline Suffield, like her mother-in-law, was also a believer in education. In 1831 a school was built in Oulton on land given by the dowager Lady Caroline Suffield; she also paid for the building and endowed the school with £2,230. That school closed in 1964. Lady Caroline Suffield also supported a Sunday school for boys and a separate school for girls, both in Blickling. William was succeeded by his brother Edward (1781–1835).

This simplified tree shows the order of succession. John Harbord and Harbord Harbord are both included as they were managers of the school. John Harbord was also rector of St James Southrepps.

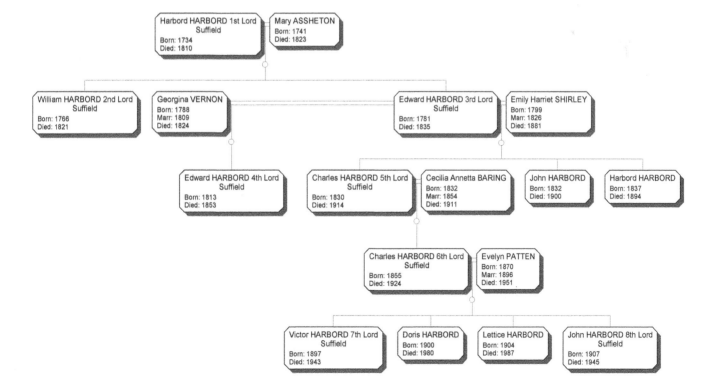

11

Edward, 3rd Lord Suffield

Prior to succeeding to the title in 1821, Edward was MP for Great Yarmouth (1806–1812) and for Shaftesbury (1820-1821)

He was a radical Liberal (Whig), who campaigned strongly for the abolition of slavery and for prison and electoral reform. His obituary also cites an interest in general education and the relief and benefit of the poor, and this is certainly reflected in his personal letters. His son Charles wrote in his memoirs about how his father had built "a handsome school for boys and girls", as well as "a schoolhouse all made of flint". This is the Antingham and Southrepps School we know today. From his personal correspondence, it is evident that he played an important role in the selection of the school's Headmasters. Their terms of employment were generous by the standards of the time and, in order to encourage the attendance of his tenants' children, free places were available for larger families.

Edward died in July 1835 aged 54, following a fall from his horse. He was succeeded by his eldest son Edward Vernon Harbord, 4th Lord Suffield (1813–1853).

Edward, 4th Lord Suffield

Edward was an absentee landlord. His brother Charles remarked in his memoirs that his brother was not interested in his duties, later recalling what poor condition the church and school were in.

Edward married Charlotte Gardner. They had no children, so on his death in 1853 he was succeeded by his half-brother Charles (1830–1914).

Charles, 5th Lord Suffield

Charles Harbord, 5th Lord Suffield, was a great favourite with the Royal Family, being first Lord-in-Waiting to Queen Victoria and then to her son Edward, the Prince of Wales. The Prince, and later as King, visited the Gunton estate.

Charles married Cecilia Annetta Baring in 1854. They moved into Gunton Hall and set about restoring the estate to its former glory.

The *Norwich Mercury* records on the 1st August 1857 that nearly 200 children belonging to Lord Suffield's schools were entertained in a "most munificent fashion" at Gunton Park.

On the 15th December 1877 Lord Suffield gifted the school buildings and land to the managers of Antingham and Southrepps Board School. In recognition of the role played by Lord Suffield the managers agreed on the 22nd September 1876 that the School seal should be the crest of the Rt. Hon Lord Suffield. The family

133 *closed as a fair attendance could not be expected. H.R.H. was shooting at Thorpe Market.*

Oct 1st *Board meeting in the Board room. Lady Suffield visited the school.*

17th On Friday afternoon the children were taken to Gunton Park to join in a public Welcome to Lt. Col. Hon. C. Harbord on his return from S. Africa.

Nov. 21st on windy days. Lady Suffield visited the school and watched children at work.
" 23rd Miss ...

involvement with the school did not end there. Lady Suffield was a member of the first Board of trustees of the new Board School, as was the Hon. Harbord Harbord, Charles's youngest brother. Both of them served on the Board for many years, as did another brother, the Rev. John Harbord, rector of St James Southrepps.

Philanthropy seems to have run in the family as his niece Rachel, the daughter of Rev John Harbord, wrote to the Board in 1895 asking if they could furnish her with a room in which to store books for the use of the residents in Lower Street. Their reply was that the coffee room in Lower Street would be a more suitable place to house the books. This was later deemed to be unsuitable; sadly it is not recorded what happened to the books but it seems unlikely that they were given room in the school.

Lady Cecilia died in 1911, followed 3 years later by Charles in 1914. He was succeeded by his son, also Charles (1855–1924).

Charles, 6th Lord Suffield

Charles Harbord, the 6th Lord Suffield, married Evelyn Patten and she keeps up the family links and responsibilities, and is recorded as visiting the school on many occasions.

Following the 1902 Education Act the school came under the control of Norfolk Education Committee and the school board ceased, being replaced by a managing body.

Charles's daughter Doris was the last member of that branch of the family. With the death of her brother John without issue, the succession continues through the 5th Lord's brother, John, who was the rector of St James Southrepps, to today's 13th Lord Suffield, John Harbord-Hamond. After the death of Doris Harbord, Southrepps Commons were passed to Southrepps Village. It is perhaps fitting that today's pupils still use the Commons for some of their lessons.

How the changes in education influenced the school

The system of education first used in 1826 when the school was founded was the monitorial one, the first Headmaster Mr Birt having been trained at the National System of Education School in London. This was Dr Bell's system. The school has always had two separate class rooms, so a second teacher would have been required, and the probability is that this would have been Mrs Birt, despite her having no known qualifications. In 1829 Mr John Wortley was appointed Headmaster, and both he and his wife were qualified in Dr Bell's system. Many educational changes occurred nationally between the opening of the school in 1826 and it becoming a Board school in 1875, but how many of these were introduced into the school is unknown. Some will have been, in order to access the grant money that came with improving standards. It was an endowed school and very much under the control of its benefactor. During the time of the 4th Lord Suffield (from 1835–1853), who was very much an absentee landlord, the school fell into disrepair and his input into the welfare of the school and its pupils was minimal. When Charles Harbord inherited the title in 1853 its fortunes greatly improved.

Board School

With the school becoming a Board School in 1875 and expanding in 1877, a separate Infants' department was built, as popularised by Samuel Wilderspin. Galleries were installed in the Infants' school room, and in the extra classroom at the west end of the Boys' school.

The large school rooms remained unaltered. The 1851 government plan recommended dimensions of 65ft by 18ft for the school room and 14ft by 20ft for the classroom. The dimensions of the Antingham and Southrepps schoolroom are 41ft by 19ft and the classroom 12ft by 19ft. There were also two playgrounds, one for the boys and the other for the girls and infants. In the 1835 plan and in the pre-1877 photograph of the school there appears to be no differentiation of playgrounds for the pupils.

The log books make it clear that monitors were employed by the school, and in the Infants' they appear to have been as young as eight.

So by 1878 both Dr Bell's monitorial and Wilderspin's systems were in use in the school. The first recorded pupil teacher was Elizabeth Amies in 1881, and monitors continued to be employed as late as 1905.

The Minute books from 1875–1903 record the school's expansion and transition from Estate School to Board School and then Education Authority School. Boards were locally elected bodies financed by a local precept. In the case of this school five parishes paid towards its running costs: Antingham, Bradfield, Gunton, Southrepps and Thorpe Market. The first meeting of the School Board was held in 1875, the Board members being:

Rev Dolphin, vicar of Antingham and
   rector of Thorpe Market (Chairman)
Lady Cecilia Suffield
Hon Harbord Harbord, brother of Lord Suffield

The Wilderspin National School Museum, Barton-upon Humber. It gives a good idea of what the Infants' classroom at Antingham and Southrepps School may have looked like. It shows the gallery and the post in the foreground with the day's lesson on it. The lighting at Antingham and Southrepps was from paraffin lamps, not gas as in this case. One interesting point concerning Antingham and Southrepps is that one of the Her Majesty's Inspectors' reports from 1888 recommended that the schoolroom walls should be coloured, not whitewashed. No record of what colour was used has been found.
Courtesy of Gloria, a descendant of Samuel Wilderspin.

Feb. 1st The Rev. J. Dolphin visited the school on Friday afternoon, and promised to pay school fees for children Farrow. Readmitted Edith Botwright

15th Rev. J. Dolphin promised to pay fees for

For some families the compulsory nature of education would have caused severe financial hardship and in those cases their fees were paid by the Board or local Poor Law Union.

Boys' Log 1st February 1884.

Rev Gwyn, rector of St James Southrepps
John Burton
George Clarke
George Ives, farmer at Bradfield Hall

It was those who were in positions of power and influence that ran the school; these were the people who ran the Poor Law and work-house and were the major employers in the district. The clerk was James Spurrell Plumby, a Poor Law clerk who lived in Southrepps. James worked in this role right up to his death in March 1893 at the age of 87. Fairfax Davies, a solicitor, took up the post of clerk in April 1893.

The 1870 Education Act authorised the managers to pass their own local bye-laws, making school attendance compulsory in their district, and there is evidence that Antingham and South-repps had such bye-laws. They are referred to in the minutes but no copies of them have been discovered. Parents were summoned before the Board and even prosecuted for the non-attendance of their children, and an attendance officer was employed by the Board for this purpose.

Norfolk Education Committee School 1903

The last meeting of the Antingham and South-repps School Board was held on 25th September 1903. When the school came under the control of the Norfolk Education Committee, the social mix of the managers was much the same as it was for the Board's first meeting 28 years earlier:

Earnest George Owles, farmer at Gimingham (Chairman)
Rev Sullivan, rector of St James Southrepps
Rev Frederick Thew, vicar of St Nicholas Swafield (does not attend a single meeting)
James Harrison (address given as Southrepps)
Charles Learner, farmer at Hill House Southrepps
Clement Owles, farmer at Thorpe Market
Rev Davies, vicar of St Mary's Antingham and St Margaret's Thorpe Market, attends from 1904
Mr W Moulson, clerk and attendance officer.

1906 School photo.
Southrepps Society collection.

Children up to 14 years continued to be taught at Antingham and Southrepps School, even though the national school leaving age was 13.

In 1936 the managers received a letter from Norfolk Education Committee discussing the possibility of withdrawing all children over the age of 11, in order to build up the numbers in the Central school to be formed in North Walsham. The managers objected and the plan was not carried out.

1944 Education Act

With the passing of the 1944 Education Act children had to stay at school for another year, so the school was now taking children from the age of 5 to 15. This meant that the pupils could stay at Antingham and Southrepps School, or move on to a Grammar School or one of the newly created Secondary Modern or Technical Schools.

Mr Edward Meatyard was one of the teachers employed under the emergency teachers' scheme to help accommodate these extra numbers caused by raising the school leaving age.

In 1950 Roughton School decided that they no longer wished to take the older pupils; they wanted to be a primary school only. As Cromer School was full, the Education Authority asked if Antingham and Southrepps School would accommodate them. In discussion with the Headmaster the managers agreed to take the 17 older pupils from Roughton. This brought the number on the school roll to 150. In consequence, it was decided that Mrs Hare should increase her hours as school secretary from six hours a week to half time.

In 1957 the Norfolk Education Authority reorganised all its schools, and Antingham and Southrepps was designated as a Primary, so all the children over 11 left in the July of that year.

Whole school photo c1950.

Antingham and Southrepps School

Children I propose putting in for
Scholarship are Doris Hunt,
Phyllis Earle, Winnie Gray and
Leslie Bane. I scarcely think
Charles Gotts & John Reynolds would
do well enough.

Some children took scholarship examinations for Grammar schools. Disappointingly, it is not recorded if they were successful.
Boys' log 9th March 1921

The managers protested against
such withdrawal on the grounds that
1st. The distance from Southrepps to
N.Walsham School — 3½ to 6 miles
2nd The parents will refuse to send their
children so far.
Also   3. We have everything we need at
this School
4. This has been a District School

The managers were unhappy with the proposed changes to remove the older pupils to North Walsham and protested in the strongest terms.
Minute book 8th December 1936

Friday Aug 3

School closed at 3.45 pm to day for
the Harvest Holidays. 134 scholars
are on the registers
5 children left for the Secondary
Grammar School and 6 for the
Modern Secondary School, both
at North Walsham. Four others
left having reached the school-
leaving age, two went to other schools
& four were admitted

This was the first year that children over 11 without scholarships had the option of moving to other schools to continue their education.
Boys' log 3rd Aug 1945.

June 2nd

School re-opened after one weeks holiday.
Mr Edward Meatyard (Reg. no. 45/1023) one-
year trained under M of E. emergency scheme
commenced duty today.

Mr Meatyard taught at the school for four years, moving to Sprowston in 1951 to be nearer to his home. The pupils remember him as having a withered arm and having served in the war.
Boys' log 2nd June 1947

6 infants admitted and one 11+ boy (David Turner re-admitted from North Walsham Secondary Modern) Number on roll now 146. No. present 144

3rd Sept | School re-opened this morning. 30 children have gone to North Walsham Sec. Modern School, 1 child has left at 15+ for work 1 child to the Paston Grammar School and 1 other to Sutherland House (Private) School. Total left 33. 8 children aged 5 admitted. No. on roll 107, attendance 104.

Until then the numbers transferring to secondary school had been relatively small.

There were plans in the late 1970s for the school to become a First School, effective from 1984, but they did not come to fruition. In 1985 the school joined a Federation of small Schools; Northern Area Group, consisting of Antingham and Southrepps, Aldborough, Bodham, Colby, Erpingham, Gresham, Northrepps, Overstrand and Roughton. The Federation bought two minibuses that allowed the children from different schools to share lessons. They had joint sports fixtures and projects on subjects such as science and music, as well as craft, design and technology. It enabled them to access £4000 of resources from the Eastern Arts Association, and they also shared school trips. In May 1987 12 pupils from Aldborough School and 21 from Antingham and Southrepps went on a joint field trip to Yorkshire, which was declared a great success. The teaching staff shared training days and expertise. They employed a group coordinator, Mrs Pollard, based at Aldborough, who also acted as a supply teacher, allowing more sharing of resources between the schools.

Forest School

In 2007 Norfolk County Council funded a Forest School course for primary school teachers in Norfolk. Emma Harwood, the reception and year one teacher at Antingham and Southrepps, took up the opportunity to attend the level 3 course.

The ethos of the Forest School movement is that learning should be led by the children in a natural environment, preferably woodland. It is a long-term programme that promotes independence, resilience, self-confidence and self-esteem. It promotes the social, emotional, and physical wellbeing of the child and connects children with the natural world.

Under the Headship of Mrs Day, the teachers (now at the expense of the school) were gradually trained as Forest School level 3 practitioners. With the amazing resource of a wood immediately opposite the school, the infants would spend at least half a day a week learning in the wood. They learnt independence, making dens and climbing trees, use of tools, fire safety and cooking food on the open fire. In time all

Far left: The school badge changed to reflect the change in emphasis of the school. A competition was held amongst the pupils and the new badge was based on a design by Anderson Down.

Left: The original badge dates back to 2002 when a simple school uniform was first introduced of red sweatshirt, white polo shirt and grey trousers or skirt.

the classes would spend half a day across the road on the common, with activities suitable to their age. The year six pupils even smelted their own pewter using syrup tins. The PTA paid for all outdoor all-weather wear so that the children went outside come rain or shine. This meant that even the most reluctant child relished the outdoors. An added bonus was that it increased parental involvement in the children's education, particularly that of the fathers who were keen to be involved in den making! Some parents even took the level one course themselves. The school gained Forest School registration and became a centre of expertise.

During this time, the number on the roll had risen to 110. When the new block was built a drying room was included to dry out the all-weather clothing.

Life goes in a full circle and once again the school children were using the common during the school day.

The school continued as a Community Primary School until 1st October 2014 when it became part of the North Norfolk Academy Trust. This consists of Sheringham High School, Stalham High School, Gresham Village School and Nursery, as well as Antingham and Southrepps School.

A completed den in the foreground constructed with the help of eager dads. It is covered with reeds that the children had collected from the reed bed on the common. In the background is the ring of tree stumps for the children to sit on around the camp fire on which they toasted marshmallows and made dough sticks. 2008

Educational resources available in the late 19th century

This extract is from an exercise book of 1874. It appears that it may be a book for recording test answers, as the questions seem unrelated to each other, and on one occasion the whole exercise is repeated later in the book.

Southrepps Society; Hewitt collection

Fortunately, some books and exercises used in the school in the 19th century have survived, allowing us an insight into the material available at that time.

The way the children were taught in the early days of the school was by rote and by their peers; it would have been very basic. The lessons were attached to standard posts in the middle of the classroom and books would have been scarce, mainly the Bible. As education pro-

gressed more books became available, but the children were not allowed to take them home for fear of them becoming soiled.

An exercise book from 1874 survives; it shows how the children learnt the question and the answer, and it was this that the inspectors tested them on. In the English history section, it is doubtful that any average adult today has heard of Robert FitzStephen, who laid siege to Wexford in 1169. In the same exercise is

---

Ans. He was king of Epirus and a man of great courage?

Ques. How did Virginius hear of his child's position at Rome.

Ans. By his friends who intercepted the letter?

Laura Hewitt
November 19th 1874

English History.

Ques. Where was General Wolfe killed

Ans. He was killed at the storming of Quebec?

Ques. How long did Stephen reign

Ans. He reigned from 1135 to 1154.

Ques. What knights landed in Ireland and laid siege to Wexford.

Ans. Robert Fitz?

Ques. Why did Sweyn king of Denmark invaded England?

Ans. To revenge the massacre of the Danes, he invaded England with a large fleet?

Ques. What was the death of Richard 3?

Ans. The body of Richard was discovered covered with wounds he was the only monarch since the conquest who has died in battle?

Ques. What was the fate of the Duke of Northumberland?

Ans. He was executed.

Laura Hewitt
November 30th 74

Roman History.

Ques. Of what did the Senate consist in the time of Romulus?

Ans. They consisted of a hundred citizens who acted as counsellors to the king

Ques. Who was chosen by the Senate to succeed Romulus?

Ans. Numa Pompillius?

Ques. What were the augurs.

Ans. They were soothsayers or diviners of future events?

Ques. By whose order was Servius Tullius slain

Ans. By the order of Lucius?

a question about General Wolfe's death in Quebec in 1759.

The section here on Roman history will have had no relevance to the pupils at all; Who was chosen by the Senate to succeed Romulus? The handwriting is however excellent.

In both log books there are numerous entries through the years of the gallery lessons to be taught that year.

Unsurprisingly, the same topics appear most years. The items would be shown to the pupils and they were meant to make observations about them. There is a later record of a pupil teacher giving a lesson to the whole infant school on the 'lead pencil'.

The textbooks of the time were thin and small in size. Of the three geography books illustrated here, all published before 1900, only

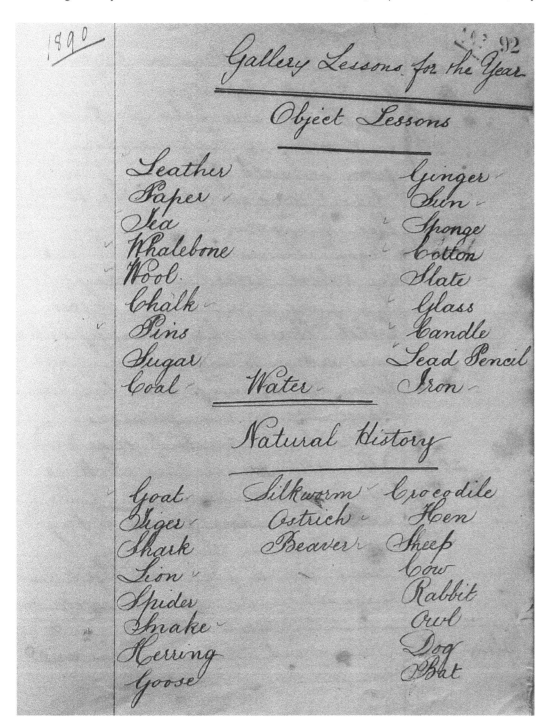

A gallery lesson from 1890. The others are all similar, in that they are just a list of objects or animals.

This Hutchinson's Geography *dates from post 1871. Again, the question and answer method was used. None of the books shown here exceed 16 cms × 14 cms in size (6½ inches × 4 inches).*
Southrepps Society; Bird collection.

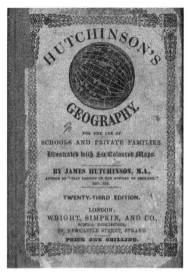

Mr Watson's copy of Geography of Great Britain and Ireland *is slightly larger, but has only 48 pages. Mr Watson was a pupil teacher at the school from 1890 until 1895.*
Southrepps Society; Bird collection.

The Academic Geography book dates from between 1871 and 1899 and has suggested lessons in it.
Southrepps Society; Bird collection.

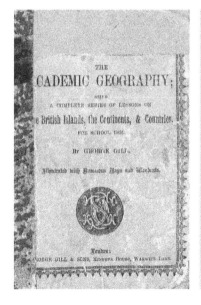

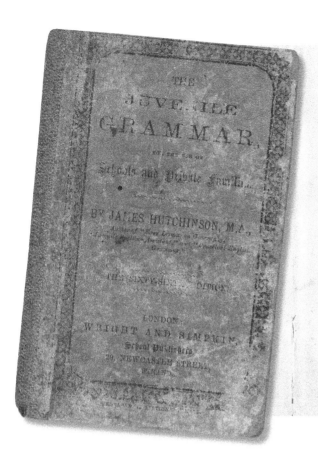

THE

JUVENILE GRAMMAR.

WHAT does Grammar teach us?
To express our ideas with propriety.
What do you mean by "with propriety?"
I mean that it teaches me to speak as
well-educated persons speak.
Do all well-educated persons speak cor
rectly?
They do in general, if they move in good
society.
How is Grammar usually divided?
Into four parts.
What part of Grammar do we first notice?
Or-thog-ra-phy.
Which the second?
Et-y-mol'-o-gy.
The third?
Syn-tax.
The fourth?
Pros-o-dy.

A Juvenile Grammar from 1886 with its opening page. This would not make many children turn to page two!

Southrepps Society; Bird collection.

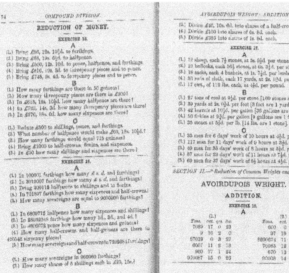

The Combined Lesson Book for Standard IV (10-year-olds). This extract is of a suggested Maths lesson.

Southrepps Society; Bird collection.

one contained any illustrations, and those were six hand-drawn basic maps of the continents.

The topics were clearly very dry and more about limited facts and figures, rather than the rounded subject we know today.

Mr James Hutchinson M.A. produced a wide range of books, including this one on grammar for use in school, or the private home if it could be afforded.

The final book is a combined volume on English, geography and arithmetic. It too is small, thin and un-illustrated.

For the decimalised child of today the monetary calculations expected of a 10 year-old are daunting; for example, "How many sovereigns and half crowns in 7292684 farthings?" In exercise 17 no. 5. "69 men work for 37 days of 8½ hours at 4½d. per hour: how much does it cost?"

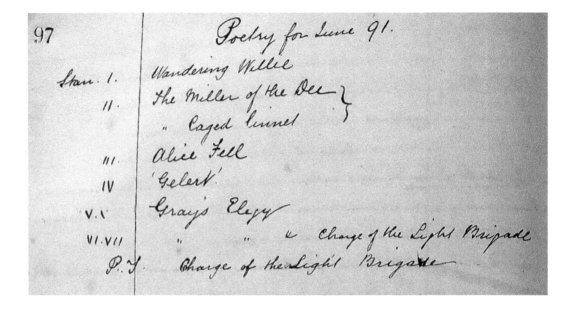

Not only do the log books record the gallery lessons, but the Boys' log lists the poetry that the pupils are to learn that year. The children had to learn these by rote. The inspector would listen to them recite the work and would expect meaningful expression. This example lists "Wandering Willie" by Robert Burns for Standard I; this is for 6–7 year-olds to learn. The only advantage is that they may not have had to read it or write it down as it would have done nothing for their spelling. The pupil teachers (PT) were also given a poem to study.

Gressenhall Museum also holds copies of the following books that had been used at Antingham and Southrepps:

Common Sense English, The Water Babies, Stories from Hiawatha, and *Gulliver's Travels.*

Displays around the school would have been minimal. Following the coronation of King Edward VII, Mr Amies sought permission to buy pictures of the King and Queen for display, and in 1903 Messrs Colman donated a parcel of pictures to the school (the Colman family lived at Southrepps Hall).

Wandering Willie by Robert Burns

HERE awa, there awa, wandering Willie,
Here awa, there awa, haud awa hame;
Come to my bosom, my ain only dearie,
Tell me thou bring'st me my Willie the same.
Winter winds blew loud and cauld at our
*   parting,*
Fears for my Willie brought tears in my e'e,
Welcome now the Simmer, and welcome,
*   my Willie,*
The Simmer to Nature, my Willie to me!

Rest, ye wild storms, in the cave of your
*   slumbers,*
How your dread howling a lover alarms!

Wauken, ye breezes, row gently, ye billows,
And waft my dear laddie ance mair to my arms.
But oh, if he's faithless, and minds na his Nannie,
Flow still between us, thou wide roaring main!
May I never see it, may I never trow it,
But, dying, believe that my Willie's my ain!

Finance and funding

At the time the school was built education was not funded by the state. So how was it funded? Lord Suffield built the school at a cost of £3000 (around £300,000 in 2020). He also paid the Headmaster's salary, and the parents were charged fees, as shown by The House of Commons Education Returns of 1833:

Antingham parish (pop 248) – One daily School (commenced 1826), contains 62 males and 58 females, and is supported primarily by Lord Suffield, who allows a salary of £50 per annum to the school master and his wife, together with six acres of land rent free, and four chaldron* of coals annually, and partly by small payments from the parents of the children varying from 1d to 6d per week for each child, according to the rent paid by the parents, but a less sum where two are sent; and nothing extra for all of the same family above two; those who are tenants of Lord Suffield pay rather less than those who are not; this school was instituted for the instruction of the poor of the parishes of Thorpe Market, Antingham, Bradfield and Lower Street of Southrepps; but the poorer inhabitants of the Upper Street will be admitted until the number from the other places shall be considered sufficient by Lord Suffield.

(*Accounts and Papers of the House of Commons*, Volume 42)

*A chaldron is a measure of volume equivalent to about 2½ tonnes

Although there is no evidence to support this, the school may have received some funding from the parishes, as it is described as an Estate/National school. National Schools were set up under the auspices of the Church of England.

The first time that funding became available from the Government was in 1862, with the revised Education Code, the sum of four shillings per scholar per year being paid, based on the average number in attendance throughout the year. Each school would receive a further eight shillings per pupil if satisfactory standards were achieved in reading, writing and arithmetic. This rigid payment-by-results system was gradually relaxed over the next thirty years because of its detrimental effects on the breadth of education. There are several references over the next 20 years to show that the school was

Report for '85.
"Mixed School". The work done in this big school is barely fair, and the Discipline is not good. The Grammar is so weak in the third and fourth Standards that the Grant cannot be recommended as the Recitation is also poor. The list of representation is very large, but it does not appear that the children are fit for higher work. The Merit Grant is recommended with some hesitation.

Grants were available for different subjects. This report shows that the English Grant could not be paid as the standard of work was not good enough. However the Merit Grant would be paid, but only with hesitation. The school was on notice that standards needed to be improved or they would not get the Merit Grant next year. The report for 1886 was not a lot better but they did manage enough improvement to be paid the lower English Grant.

Boys' log 1885.

denied part of the payment, the first one being recorded in the Minute book in June 1879, when the infant grant was reduced by 20%.

Board Schools

The 1870 Education Act set up Board Schools and empowered school boards to frame bye-laws making attendance at school compulsory for children between the ages of five and thirteen; it did not however require them to do so. Nor did it make education free. It was following this Act that the school became a Board School in 1875 with its first board meeting being held on the 25th October. In March 1878 the board agreed to advertise the School bye-laws in the Norfolk News. An attendance officer was appointed and the first prosecutions for non-attendance were recorded in December of that year. He was also responsible for collecting arrears of fees.

The Act also set out how schools could raise money:

> 53. The expenses of the school board under this Act shall be paid out of a fund called the school fund. There shall be carried to the school fund all moneys received as fees from scholars, or out of moneys provided by Parliament, or raised by way of loan, or in any manner whatever received by the school board, and any deficiency shall be raised by the school board as provided by this Act.

> Deficiency of school fund raised out of rates.

> 54. Any sum required to meet any deficiency in the school fund, whether for satisfying past or future liabilities, shall be paid by the rating authority out of the local rate.

The school board may serve their precept on the rating authority, requiring such authority to pay the amount specified therein to the treasurer of the school board out of the local rate, and such rating authority shall pay the same accordingly, and the receipt of such treasurer shall be a good discharge for the amount so paid, and the same shall be carried to the school fund.
(Gillard D (2018) *Education in England: a history.* www.educationengland.org.uk/history)

The amount received in fees from the parents in the same quarter in 1876 was £8 13s 8d

The board had set the fees payable by the parents at 2d per child per week, not exceeding 6d per family. This was higher than they had been paying under Lord Suffield. This, and the fact that education was now compulsory, caused some difficulty for the poorer families, and they could apply to have their fees paid by the Board of Guardians. These payments counted as Outdoor Relief, to prevent very poor families from having to enter the Workhouse through debt. In 1876 it became enshrined in law that:

> The parent, not being a pauper, of any child who is unable by reason of poverty to pay the ordinary fee for such child at a public elementary school, or any part of such fee, may apply to the guardians having jurisdiction in the parish in which he resides; and it shall be the duty of such guardians, if satisfied of such inability, to pay the said fee, not exceeding three pence a week, or such part thereof as he is, in the opinion of the guardians, so unable to pay.
(Gillard D (2018) *Education in England: a history.* www.educationengland.org.uk/history)

Table showing the amount paid by the five parishes in two separate quarters 1876 and 1886.

Parish	Rateable value in pounds 1876	Amount payable to School in pounds 1876	Amount payable to School in pounds 1886
Antingham	2363	10	19
Gunton	1408	6	14
Southrepps	4017	17	28
Thorpe Market	1708	7	14
Bradfield	1246	5	9
Total		45	84

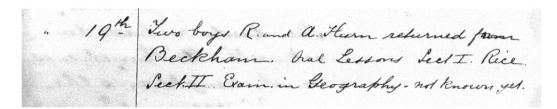

The Union would pay significant amounts of money to the school until 1891, when school fees were abolished.

In 1875 Lord Suffield gifted the school and its grounds to the board, although the legalities of the transfer were not completed until 1876. In order to extend the building, the managers took out a loan of £1356 from the Public Works Commissioners.

In 1876 the Managers were notified that in order to receive the maintenance grant a certified teacher had to be employed. Neither the Headmaster Mr Elden, nor the school mistress Mrs Earl, were qualified, and in August 1877 both were removed from their posts.

The board had been paying Mr Elden £70 per annum, and Mrs Earl had received £30 as school mistress. Under the new staffing arrangements Mr Amies received £130 as Headmaster of the Boys' school, and Miss Allen was paid £70 as Headmistress of the Girls' school. The Head of Infants', Miss Maguir, received £45. The staffing bill had therefore increased by 145%.

The attendance officer, appointed in 1878, also had the important job of pursuing arrears of fees. He would check the circumstances of the parents' ability to pay the fees and report this to the board for their consideration. Sometimes the parents were allowed to pay the arrears in instalments.

In 1879 the school received £130 14s 5d in grant money from the Government for the Boys' and Girls' school, but the amount paid for the Infants' school was reduced by 20% for poor educational achievement.

In 1880 49 children were in arrears, which was about 16% of the school roll. The amounts owing varied from 4d, which was two days of schooling, to 7s 8d; this was over six weeks' worth of unpaid fees. The total amount of outstanding fees was £14 11s 4d. All of the families were asking for their fees to be remitted. In May the amount of fees remitted was £11 14s 6d. In 1884 the board decided that every child not bringing the school fee at its first attendance should be sent home for it. Children who were sent home for fees were marked with a cross in the class register. The log records "two children stopped at home for whole week" as a result of this new ruling.

Compulsory Education

The Elementary Education Act 1880 made education compulsory from five years to the age of ten, but it was still not free.

A Minute book entry for July 1881 states that proceedings were to be taken against 11 parents for non-payment of fees, of whom eight were taken to the County Court.

In August 1882 the Managers published a circular. Mr Amies received copies on 6th October, when it was given to all the parents:

1   No child under any circumstances to be refused admission or be sent out of school for non-payment of fees.

2 When a child is entered or re-entered on the books of the school, the parent is to be furnished with a paper stating that as long as the child attends school the parents will be liable for the school fees paid each week in advance, that if under any circumstances the parent becomes unable to pay the fee an application must be made to the teacher for remittance who will submit application to the school board.

3 When the school fees of any child are two weeks in arrears notice be sent to the parent to be informed that if such parent has any application to be made for remittance upon the form on the back of the notice but if fees are not paid and no application is made parents will be liable to be sued in the County Court.

4 All applications for remission of fees to be sent to the teacher who will report to the parent whether the school board will remit the fees or not.

5 All cases where the parents do not pay the fees;
   (i) Where they do not apply for remission
   (ii) Where they apply for remission and are refused to be dealt with in the County Court.

6 The cases defined in paragraph 5 to be submitted to the teacher whose department it occurs to report them to the school board

7 The school board to give instruction to an officer of the board to take the necessary procedures that may be required.

Further Government funding became available in 1882 with the Mundella code, which introduced merit grants. These would reward excellence in teaching and it also introduced grants for more subjects such as science, geography, art, cookery and laundry.

One curious thing to note is that in 1889 Mr Amies had his contract renewed, but his salary was reduced from £130 to £100 per annum. The number of pupils was reduced but not by a significant amount and the Girls' school had been amalgamated with the Boys'. No explanation is recorded for this reduction.

Abolition of school fees

The Elementary Education Act 1891 abolished parental fees, and the Government paid 10 shillings for every child over three and under 13. As a result of free education there was no longer any need for Outdoor Relief, and the school received its final payment for pauper's fees from the Erpingham Union on the 3rd August 1891, a sum of £3 8s 4d. It would seem that there was then a shortfall in funding for schools, and the Agricultural Rates Act was passed in 1896. This Act had its origins in the tithe system, by which a tax was levied on agricultural land in order to finance the Church. With the development of the Poor Law, the Church became increasingly responsible for education. Although it was not a Church school, under the terms of the 1896 Act Antingham and Southrepps School was able to levy a rate on agricultural land of the five parishes that it served, in order to meet some of its costs. In some half-years the sum went as high as £98.

Breakdown of the agricultural levy as paid by each parish in 1896.

Antingham	£10 5s
Gunton	£ 9
Thorpe Market	£ 8
Bradfield	£ 5 15s
Southrepps	£20 10s

As with the parish levy, Southrepps paid the most and Bradfield the least.

January 1889. It was decided by the board that several families should be removed from the non-paupers list. This listed those whose fees were paid for by the poor law. The non-paupers list was paid for by the parish and was influenced by the school board, as the vicars were members of it. In February of that year the board was asked to reconsider its decision, and three families were reinstated on the non-paupers list. The Headmaster recorded that "several attendances had been lost due to this matter". The families could not afford to pay.
Boys' log January 18th 1889.

The 1901 census returns for Southrepps parish list the board school on Station Road or part of it. The census return for Antingham parish of course lists the Amies family, who were resident in the school house.

With the passing of the 1902 Education Act the funding of schools changed. There was no longer a direct charge on agricultural land, nor were the parishes charged; all funding came from the Local Education Authority. However the grants were still subject to inspection and in 1913 the school had £3 6s 8d deducted due to staff shortages. They received £329 13s 8d.

Another grant was paid depending on the size of the population of the parish in which the school was situated. Antingham and Southrepps School was on the border of two parishes. The managers claimed that the school consisted of a Mixed school and an Infants' school. Both buildings are in the same enclosure, but one stands in Southrepps parish and the other in Antingham parish. Their interpretation was that, under the 1902 Education Act, Antingham's small-parish status meant that they could claim the small-population grant for the Infants'

school. This was refused in 1904 but paid from 1906–1909. There then followed lengthy correspondence as to whether the two departments could be considered separate schools, not least as they were in the same building, and whether the schools were available for the education of all the children of both parishes. Tax returns and rateable maps were consulted and eventually it was agreed that the entire school (with the exception of the front porch!) was actually in Antingham parish, and therefore the small-population grant could be claimed for the whole school. From 1902 onwards the school was funded from local and Government taxation.

It has come to light that as a result of the 1902 Act the school was renamed Southrepps and Antingham, but was altered back to Antingham and Southrepps in 1905. This name change has not been found in any other document.

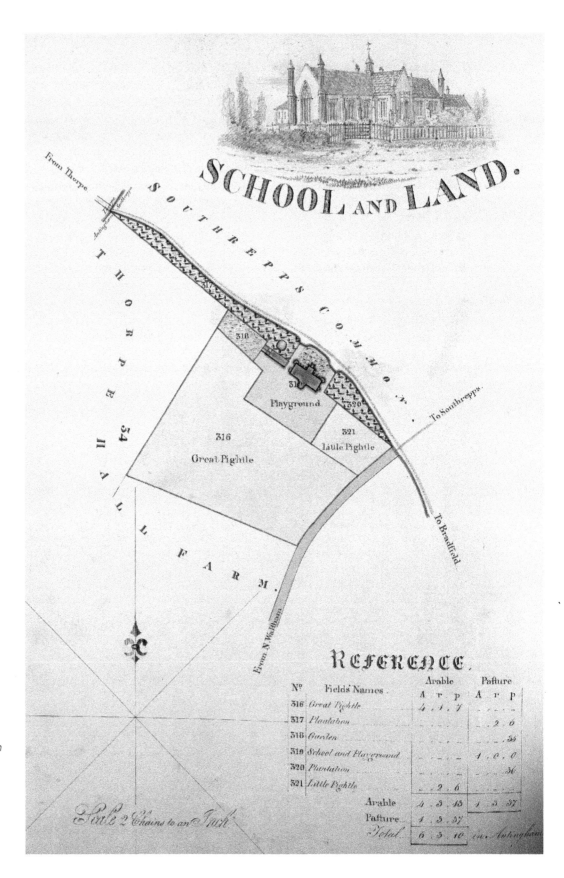

1835 image of Antingham and Southrepps School from an album of maps of the Suffield Estate. It is the oldest known image of the school.
Norfolk Records Office. gtn 3-5-1-2_001.

The school buildings

Enlarged image of pen and ink drawing on the 1835 plan. The building to the rear is the school house. There are three windows to the left-hand side of the porch rather than the four that are there today.

Below: St Margaret's, Thorpe Market 2020.

Bottom: Front of the school 2021.

The school was built on Lord Suffield's land on the boundary of Antingham and Southrepps parishes, midway between Thorpe Market and Bradfield. It was surrounded by farmland on three sides, with Southrepps Common to the North. This remains the case today. .

What is striking, if one is familiar with the building, is the size of the end window. It also looks very ecclesiastical. This may well be explained by looking at St Margaret's Church in Thorpe Market, c1796. Both buildings were built for Lord Suffield, and it is assumed to be by the same builder, who is believed to be a Mr Wood. Little is known of him except that he is thought to have been involved in the construction of the Pyramid mausoleum at Blickling.

The design is described as Gothic and the materials used are stone and flint. This was a prestigious building, far above a simple flint cottage. Not only are the flints knapped but those on the pinnacles are squared as well; this would have been time consuming and expensive of resources. This suggests that Lord Suffield was sending a message with this school. It has been built to the same high standards as the church; it is perhaps saying this is an important building, education matters. If you look at other buildings in the villages from the same period this one really stands out.

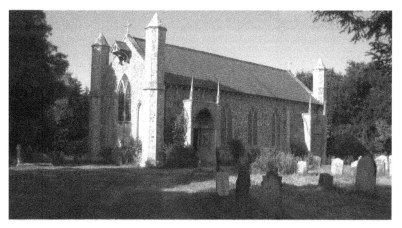

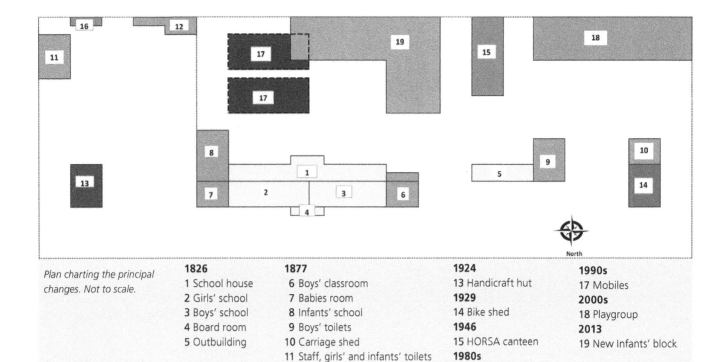

Plan charting the principal changes. Not to scale.

1826	1877	1924	1990s
1 School house	6 Boys' classroom	13 Handicraft hut	17 Mobiles
2 Girls' school	7 Babies room	**1929**	**2000s**
3 Boys' school	8 Infants' school	14 Bike shed	18 Playgroup
4 Board room	9 Boys' toilets	**1946**	**2013**
5 Outbuilding	10 Carriage shed	15 HORSA canteen	19 New Infants' block
	11 Staff, girls' and infants' toilets	**1980s**	
	12 Coal shed and girls' play shed	16 Temporary toilets	

The school clock, dated 1826, has two faces – one in each of the original school rooms. Unfortunately, it has not worked for many years; indeed the hands on the other face are missing.

1826

The original buildings were: the school consisting of two school rooms, the school house, the board room or porch, and an outbuilding.

The school consisted of two large school rooms. There was no internal access between the school and the school house. The outbuilding shown on the old photograph was probably a storehouse.

1877

In 1877 the school was extended. The original end walls were taken down and rebuilt further out, adding an extra bay at each end of the building. The octagonal pinnacles were painstakingly replicated.

This end of the building was the Boys' school, opening into their playground. The building in the foreground, which is the original outbuilding, was also extended to become the boys' offices, as toilets were known.

Opposite the boys' offices was the stabling for the managers' horses and carriages, for use when attending meetings; it also doubled up as the boys' play shed. When the managers applied for a loan to extend the school they were refused money to build the carriage shed,

Rear view of the school taken prior to 1877. It shows the school house. Behind is the school and on the left the outbuilding. On the 1835 plan the rear of the school house is all marked as playground.
Antingham and Southrepps School.

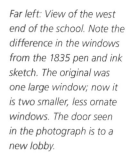

unless it could be used by the children as a play shed at other times.

The main building was divided into the Boys' and Girls' schools. In 1877 the internal arrangement was now two large school rooms and two smaller classrooms, the Boys' school being at the west end.

In the boys' smaller classroom (number 3 on the plan) a gallery was erected. The 1905 plans show its removal, as well as the removal of the internal wall between the large school room and the small classroom. At the same time a full-height folding glass partition was put in, dividing up the now enlarged boys' school room.

The small classroom in the Girls' school remains. It did not have a gallery, and has had many functions over the years: babies' room, cloakroom, toilets, kiln room and library.

At the front of the school are the porch and the board room.

In 1952 the board room was converted into the medical inspection room. The front door was bricked up, and a new door opening to the west side was constructed. An internal partition was built, and the second door into the Girls'

As part of the 150th anniversary celebrations in 1976 the bricked-up doorway was faced with knapped flints with a date inscription above. In 1996 the flints were removed and a door reinstated. The inscription remains. Antingham and Southrepps School.

school was blocked up. In 1976 a new oil boiler was installed in the former medical room.

The Infants' school was built at the south-east end of the main building and the east end of the school house.

The minute books record that the managers employed Mr Matthew Daniel Welden as builder for all the extension work. The timetable for the alterations was that the school would shut on the 20th July 1877 and re-open in the September, an unrealistic timescale considering the amount of work involved. The main school

actually re-opened on the 28th January 1878 and the Infants' school not until the 8th April. As Mr Welden had been unable to complete the works by the agreed date he forfeited £5 for every week's delay. These extensions cost £1350 (the equivalent of about £150,000 in 2020). This was paid for by a loan from the Public Works Loan Commissioners. Unfortunately, due perhaps to the time pressures, the work was not well done. On the 16th July 1880, following a storm, one of the pinnacles was damaged. The managers sent a letter to Mr Chapman, the superintendent of the works, stating that poor materials and bad workmanship had led to the failure of the pinnacle. Eventually Mr Chapman agreed to carry out the repairs at cost price. This was just a precursor of worse to come.

The managers commissioned a survey of the buildings just seven years after the new extended school opened. Here is a summary of its findings, from a letter dated 6th October 1883 from Mr John Pearce of Surrey Street, Norwich:

The new parts of the building are seriously cracked and settled, both in themselves and at the junctions with the old work. The worst section needing the greater portion of the wall to be pulled down, a proper foundation secured and the wall rebuilt in a sound

Infants' school (number 8 on the plan). Although the Infants' school was built in the same style its pinnacles are nowhere near as ornate as those on the main part of the building. The buttresses are also different.

> *"The Teaching continues to be intelligent and the Boys have done their work well. A good deal of the building work seems to have been badly done and to be in a dangerous condition. The Registers should be checked*

and proper manner. The walls of the class-room at the boys' end need underpinning the fractures cut out and refilled. The boys' porch must also be cut out and stopped.

The gutters are inadequate. The walls need repointing, wood work repainted and flashing repaired.

On the inside the walls with the fractures will have to be made good and replastered. All rooms require to be painted and white-washed as well as the window and door frames and stoves repointed.

The South West angle of the Infant school is injured by damp caused by a defect in the roof as well as other areas of the school and the school house.

The boundary wall to the west side of the boys' playground requires to be taken down and rebuilt as well as a portion of the headmaster's garden wall.

Cause of the Failure:

I attribute the cause of settlement and fracture to be insecure foundations, bad material and worse workmanship.

The repairs to the whole school were finally carried out in the harvest (summer) holiday of 1884.

16th Part of the ceiling in the Infant School fell on Thursday morning. Off Friday morning the Gallery was fixed in the Class Room.

23rd Infant scholars worked in the Mixed School and Class Room while the ceiling in Infant School was all taken down and repaired. The 1st Standard all worked together with Miss Trollope, and the 2nd and 3rd class infants with P.T. and Monitors.

30th Infants returned to their own room on Wednesday. The ceiling to be finished during the Harvest holiday. School year ends this week.

September 12th School opened on Monday Sep 8th after 5 weeks holiday. The repairs were not finished in time to begin on the 1st.

The full survey report of the school carried out in 1883 by John B. Pearce.
The hand writing is beautiful even though the contents make dismal reading for the school board. He pulls no punches in identifying who should take the blame for the defects.
National Archive Kew ED 21/12653 1877-1910

Surrey Street Norwich
October 6/1883

EDUCATION
3 NOV 1883
No 160 93

Antingham W.D. School Board

...my
Clerk.

Dr Sir

According to the wish of your Board conveyed to me by your letter of the 14th Sept last I have carefully surveyed the School Buildings situate in the parish of Antingham

I find the new parts of the building added some five years since are seriously cracked and settled both in themselves and at the junctions with old work the worst case is on the North wall of the class room at the East end, it will be necessary for the greater portion of this wall to be pulled down, a proper foundation secured and the wall rebuilt in a sound and proper manner

The walls of the Class room at the end of Boy's School are also settled and cracked, but I am of opinion the wall can be underpinned, the fractures cut out and filled in without rebuilding

Boys Porch has also a settlement, this must be cut out and stopped

The whole of the Eaves gutters require cleaning out fixed to proper fall and additional stacks of down pipe to take the water away, as they are too small & flow over the present down pipes are too far apart, there is also a length of gutter required over Boys Porch and connections must be made to the drains from the new down pipes. ses road

The walls both stone & brick work, strings, all round door & window frames require pointing generally, this also applies to the buttresses — The wood and iron work to be painted & the slates & lead flashings repaired

Interior

The walls of Class rooms will require to have the fractures made good both on the cement blocks and plastering above and when the walls are rebuilt must be replastered,

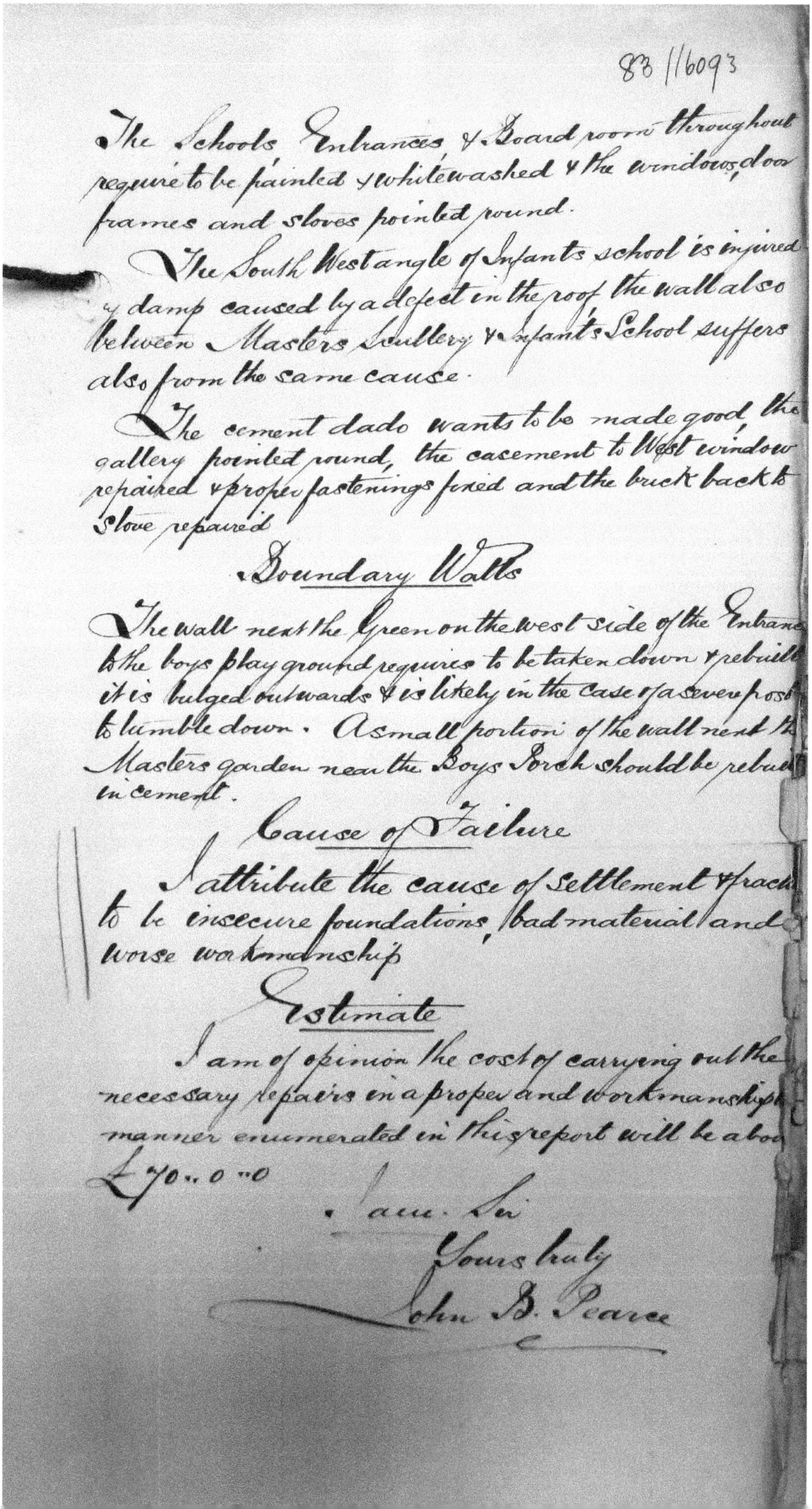

83/16093

The Schools, Entrances & Board room throughout require to be painted & whitewashed & the windows, door frames and stoves pointed round.

The South West angle of Infants school is injured by damp caused by a defect in the roof the wall also between Masters Scullery & Infant's School suffers also from the same cause.

The cement dado wants to be made good, the gallery pointed round, the casement to West window repaired & proper fastenings fixed and the brick back to stove repaired

Boundary Walls

The wall next the Green on the West side of the Entrance to the boys play ground requires to be taken down & rebuilt it is bulged outwards & is likely in the case of a severe post to tumble down. A small portion of the wall next the Masters garden near the Boys Porch should be rebuilt in cement.

Cause of Failure

I attribute the cause of settlement & fracture to be insecure foundations, bad material and worse workmanship

Estimate

I am of opinion the cost of carrying out the necessary repairs in a proper and workmanship manner enumerated in this report will be about £70..0..0

I am Sir

Yours truly

John B. Pearce

Above: The Infants' school was built with one exit, on the east side. This photograph shows where the original door was (as shown on the 1905 plan). The space between the buttresses and the window frame is narrower.

Above right: The lack of fire door was remedied by putting in a door to the Headmaster's garden, on the west side. They did not seem concerned about the red bricks that were used in the construction of the fire door, which are out of keeping with the rest of the building.

The cost of repair was considerable and the managers wrote to the Education Board for advice as to whether they had a case for damages against the builder, architect, or superintendent of the works. The conclusion was that they had no redress from any of them. They then requested financial help so that the cost of the repairs would not fall on the ratepayers. As there had been an underspend on the original loan it was agreed that the difference could be used for the repairs.

In 1954 it was finally drawn to the managers' attention that the Infants' school had only one exit in the unfortunate event of a fire. If there were a fire the children would have to escape through the next classroom and the cloakroom before exiting the building.

View of the west side of the Infants' school before the fire door was installed.
The Southrepps society; Hare collection.

Left: c1930s taken in the girls' playground showing the height of the windows in the Infants' school prior to them being lowered.
The Southrepps Society; Bird collection.

Above: After the windows were lowered, the managers were unhappy with the result and instructed the Headmaster to query it with the builder; the managers then expressed themselves content with the outcome. It is a poor brick match but at least it is better than the red bricks used on the fire door.

At the same time as the fire door was installed the opportunity was taken to lower the window sills in the Infants' school room.

The Infants' school was built with a gallery. This was removed in 1906 as part of the alterations and a partition was installed, which is still in use today. The classroom shown has also had many functions as staff room, part school office, computer room and library.

The last of the 1877 alterations occurred in the girls' playground. In the south-west corner was the coal shed and girls' play shed. There

Left: In 1983 a hatch was made in the wall between the Infants' school and what had originally been the Girls' classroom and then became the babies' room (number 7 on the plan). This was so that parents could talk to the school secretary whose office was now located in the Infants' school.

The ceilings in this part of the school were also lowered in 1983 in the classroom beyond the partition.

> *Tenders* for the Coals (Best Derby Brights) and Coke were sent in from the following firms
>
> Mess.rs Cubitt + Walker — Coke — Coals 22/6
> " Press + Pallett 22/6 22/.
> " Groy + Co. 21/6 21/.
> *It was Resolved* to accept the tender of Mess Groy + Co.

was also a faggot yard where kindling for the fires was stored. This was behind the girls' toilets, which were in the south east corner of the playground, and the last building to be built as part of the 1877 extensions.

The school was heated by open coal fires in all the classrooms, as was the school house. It

was the responsibility of the managers to get the best price for fuel.

More efficient heating using back boilers and hot-water pipes was installed in 1917. In 1966 a new central heating system was installed, but this was still coal fired. It was not until the 1970s that oil central heating was put in.

The need for the scavenger only came to an end in 1960, when septic tanks were installed. Mains drainage did not come until 1979.

1924

The handicraft hut (number 13 on the plan) was a wooden building erected around 1924. The school taught vocational classes in cookery and laundry for the girls and woodwork for the boys, and it was for these lessons that the hut was built. The hut remained in use until 1966, mainly for woodwork; it was eventually removed in 1983.

1929

The cycle shed (number 14 on the plan) was built in 1929 next to the carriage shed. At that time a large number of the children travelled up to three miles to school. Five teachers used bicycles, as well as the student teacher from Trimingham. The boys of Roughton and Northrepps schools also cycled every Friday to attend woodwork classes.

1946

The prefabricated building known as a HORSA (Hutting Operation for the Raising of the School leaving Age) was erected in 1946 in the Headmaster's garden. It was built as result of the 1944 Education Act, which made it the duty of

the Local Education Authorities to provide school meals. It had a fully equipped kitchen.

1990s

The two temporary modular classrooms (number 17 on the plan) arrived separately sometime in the 1990s; the exact date is unknown. They were in use until their removal in 2010 to make room for the new Infants' block.

2000s – Playgroup

The playgroup (number 18 on the plan) was independent of the school. The parents of the children who attended the playgroup were

instrumental in obtaining finance and in constructing the groundworks for the new building. Until then the playgroup operated out of two rooms in the old school house: the parlour (what is now the school office) and the sitting room.

2013

The new Infants' block opened in 2011 (number 19 on the plan).

This is a two-classroom block with toilets and drying room, and is heated by a ground source heat pump. It has interactive white boards and was designed to mirror the shape of the school.

Above left: Canteen (number 15 on the plan). It originally had a corrugated asbestos roof and was fully refurbished in 2018.

Above: The garden was landscaped for Early Years' play, with a veranda to facilitate all-weather outdoor play.

Temporary toilet block (number 16 on the plan). There is no record of its arrival or removal, but it is present in the aerial photograph of the school c1990. The two mobile classrooms can also be seen.
Antingham and Southrepps School.

Plan of the school house as it would have been in 1826.

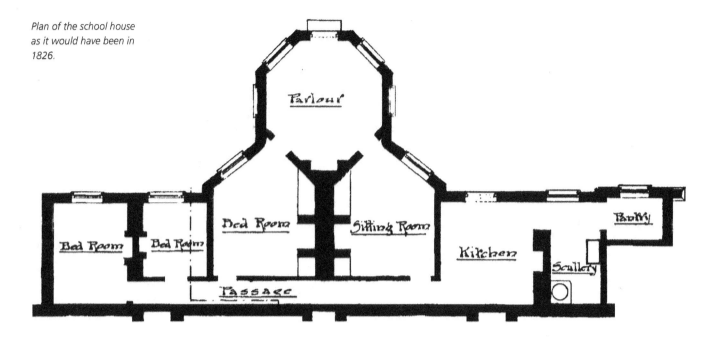

The School House

The school house was the home of every Headmaster until 1971. It had three bedrooms, a parlour, sitting room, kitchen, scullery and lobby. It also had a large vaulted cellar, which is inaccessible today. It is believed to have been largely unchanged apart from the conversion of one of the bedrooms to a bathroom.

After 1971 the house was let to a tenant. In 1982 the house was vacant and the school requested that it became part of the school. This was agreed and a door was knocked through between the Girls' school room and the passage in the school house. The doorway was not completed until 1984. The Parent Teachers Association paid for, and carried out, much of the work, which included new heating. The kitchen became the cookery room. One of the bedrooms, which had previously been converted into a bathroom, became the library.

The rooms in the house have had various uses over the years, with the final configuration occurring in the 2000s when the two smaller bedrooms and the scullery became toilets, all accessible directly from the classrooms. The larger bedroom became the Headteacher's

This extract from the Headteacher's report to Governors illustrates just how much work went into making the school house fit for use by the school.
Minute book 3 February 1985.

Mrs. Marett, Mr. Scargill and Mrs. Pike spent two evenings wallpapering the new school library. Mr. Lewis made and fixed shelves in the school house. Mr. Dinnes made the bookcases for the library. Mr. Todd painted the ceiling. Mrs. Bonney painted the woodwork. Mr. Purdy provided the carpets and Mr. Jeckell fitted them. Mr. Scargill helped Mr. Lewis to remove the bath from the bathroom. Mrs. Marett and Mr. Scargill removed the rubbish from the school house garden and Mr. Pike removed the rubbish from the school playground. This may seem a rather long and detailed list but it illustrates the level of involvement of the parents and the lack of help from County. Despite assurances from the local Councillor that Mr. Wright from County supplies would look into the matter, we had already been told Mr. Wright had no money and could not help us at all.

This gets a special mention as the school was heated by coal and then oil, and it was lit by paraffin. In 1946 the school was sent electric bulbs and shades.
Boys' log13th March 1946.

Mr Hare himself wrote to the Chief Education officer explaining the urgent need for electric light.
School log 24th November 1950.

In 1906 the managers agreed to provide water to the children at break time. They bought galvanised cups that were chained to the school wall.
Minute book 26th July 1906.

office, the parlour the school secretary's office, and the kitchen became the staffroom.

Electricity

In 1948 the Governors wrote to the Education Committee requesting that electric light might be installed in the school as on winter afternoons it was "too dark for the girls' needlework or even for written work by the boys". There was no reply; they wrote again in 1949. The Education Committee replied to say that it was unable to approve of the installation of electric light.

In January 1951, the Education Committee was again approached by the managers as "the need for light is very great". Electricity was eventually installed in the Whitsun holidays of 1951.

The school well

The school had its own well, from which all its water was drawn. It has several mentions in the log and minute books, the first being on the 26th March 1904, when it was agreed that the well should be deepened by three feet. The Master was tasked with finding the cost which was £3 2s 6d (£380 in 2020), the work to be carried out by Mr Mayes.

A year later in February 1905 there was an entry about the misuse of the well by a local family, tenants of the Gunton Hall Estate. The managers wrote to the Estate manager, who requested permission for the family to use the well, but this was declined.

Occupants of the school house

Letter of reference for Joseph Birt, sent by the Central School in London to Lord Suffield. Although it refers to the National School at Gunton it does mean Antingham and Southrepps School.
Norfolk Records Office gtn 5/9/15/8.

The school house came as part of the Headmaster's contract, together with six acres of rent-free land and four chaldron of coal annually. It was attached to the rear of the school, with no internal connection, and was the residence of all the Headmasters, their families, lodgers and servants until 1971.

To the Committee of the

National School

at Gunton.

Gentlemen,

This is to certify that Mr. Joseph F. Birt has had every opportunity of Instruction in the National System of Education which the Central School affords, and has availed himself of the advantages presented to him from ——— He is acquainted with the general principles and practices of the System, and I hope will prove well qualified to model and conduct his School with credit to himself and satisfaction to his employers; but as this depends in a great measure on his own attention and personal application to the duties of his School, it can only be ascertained by Trial.

I have the honor to be,

Gentlemen,

Yours &c.

Wm Johnson

Central School, London.
18 March 1826.

P.S. The above certificate is meant for the information of the Committee only and is not intended to be put into the hands of the Master.

Joseph Flower Birt
Headmaster 1826–1829

Joseph was born in 1797 in Gloucester, where he was a chorister and then organist, playing at several churches in the area. It was here that he met his wife Elizabeth Ford, marrying her in 1824. After his marriage he applied for a post of organist at St Clement Danes in London. His application was unsuccessful, and so he changed his course in life, enrolling at the Central School in London, where Dr Bell's theory of Education was taught. On completing his training he was appointed by Lord Suffield as the first Headmaster of Antingham and Southrepps School.

After less than a year at the school his daughter Elizabeth was born, with Sarah Anne arriving in 1828. Joseph relinquished his post as Headmaster in March of 1829, with the family moving to North Walsham. Unfortunately there is no information as to what post he went to. Then tragedy struck the family as his wife Elizabeth died in March 1830. She is buried at St Margaret's, Thorpe Market in an unmarked grave. Three months later Joseph married Martha Chestlebugh in North Walsham Church. Joseph died 16 years later in North Walsham, where he is buried.

John Wortley
Headmaster 1829–1854

A letter in the Gunton archive from Lord Suffield's agent gives John Wortley as the next Headmaster. He and his wife were both trained in Dr Bell's method and took up their posts in March 1829.

John Wortley was born in Ludham in 1795, marrying Charlotte Parslee on Christmas Eve 1827 at St Peter Mancroft, Norwich. The 1841 census shows them living in the school house with their son, two year old Robert, and 15 year old Mary Anne Cole, servant. Charlotte died in

Gunton Park 21st Feby 1829

My Lord,

Letter from Lord Suffield's estate manager. Both the Wortleys have been trained in Dr Bell's method. Once again the School is mis-named but from other documentation it definitely means Antingham and Southrepps.

One curiosity that should be recorded is that in the 1st edition of the Norfolk Directory of 1836 Nathaniel John Sexton is shown as Headmaster, but in the same year Kelly's directory lists John Wortley as Headmaster. No other reference to Mr Sexton has been found and as can be seen Mr Wortley follows on directly from Mr Birt.

Norfolk Record Office
gtn 5/9/38/18/1.

1850 at the age of 46 and is buried in the churchyard at St Margaret's, Thorpe Market. John continued to live at the school house with Robert and a new house servant, 20 year old Mary Ann Bunn. His retirement from the school was probably in 1854, as there was an advertisement in the Norfolk Chronicle in February of that year for a married couple wanted at Lord Suffield's School.

By 1861 he was a farmer of 40 acres, living in Thorpe Market with his son Robert and their housekeeper Mary Warton. He died in 1863 and is buried next to his wife at St Margaret's.

John Elden
Headmaster 1854–1877

John Elden was born in Aylsham in 1836. Although the 1854 advertisement for the post of Headmaster called for a married couple, John was successful in being appointed as a single man, and only 18 years of age. This seems a surprisingly young age for such an appointment. John lived with his mother Elizabeth, elder sister Emily and Elizabeth Hiscock 21, a school mistress. It is likely that Miss Hiscock also taught at the school. All that can be found about Elizabeth Hiscock is that she was born in 1840 in Royal Tollard, Wiltshire. By 1871 Miss Hiscock had left and John's mother Elizabeth had died. James and Ann Earl now lived with the Eldens in the school house. He was an agricultural labourer and she was schoolmistress at the school.

Born Ann Howes in 1825 in Ecking, Derbyshire, Ann married James Earl, a Southrepps lad, and in 1851 she was in domestic employment, living in Lower Street, Southrepps. By 1861 she was a seamstress and then 10 years later she was a school mistress and working at Antingham and Southrepps School. So the school is now in the care of two unqualified teachers. Both of them had their contracts terminated in 1877 after the school became a Board School,

The graves at St Margaret's, Thorpe Market. John and Charlotte Wortley at the front and those of John and Emily Elden behind to the left.

William and Louisa are seated in the middle. The oldest son George has the moustache; William stands at the end of the row. The girls are; Louisa, Jessie, Edith, Ruth, Mary and Katie. Margaret is standing between her parents. Alice and Elsie are sitting on the ground. The dog is Gyp.
Antingham and Southrepps School.

as in order to receive education grants the school board was required to employ certified teachers.

Mr Elden's sister Emily died in 1877 after he had lost his post as Headmaster. He moved to Trimingham Road, Southrepps as an estate agent's clerk, living on his own. He died in 1888 at the age of 52. He is buried next to his sister, also at St Margaret's, Thorpe Market. The four graves of the Wortleys and Eldens are within touching distance of each other.

As for the Earls, they moved into a house in Lower Street, at first with her mother living with them and then on her death on their own. James continued to work as an agricultural labourer and she has no occupation listed. Ann died in 1903 aged 78, James having predeceased her in 1894.

William Elliot Amies
Headmaster 1877–1913

29 year old William Elliot Amies was appointed Headmaster on the 13th July 1877. He was to become the longest-serving Headmaster. The newly extended school did not reopen until the 28th January 1878; in the intervening time he collected information about all the school-aged children in the district.

William was born in Bacton in 1848, the son of schoolteachers George and Elizabeth, who taught at the National School at East Ruston. His parents later became the managers of the

Smallburgh workhouse. William married Louisa Brummage in 1870.

They moved to Taplow in Buckinghamshire where William was a schoolmaster. Their eldest child George was born there. By 1873 the family had moved to Worstead, where he was Headmaster of the National School. It was here that their next four children were born. The following six children were all born in Antingham, making a total of 11, all of whom survived to adulthood.

The 1881 census shows that the family of seven had Louisa's father James Brummage living with them until his death later that year. They also had a servant, Elizabeth Long.

The school house had only three bedrooms. Not only did the family live there but in 1891 so did William's mother Elizabeth, and also a young lodger Ernest Price, making a total of 14 in the house. The large cellar may have eased the space. William was also a landlord: he was granted a half day from school duties on the 17th October 1904 to collect his rents.

Mrs Louisa Amies

Louisa Brummage was born in Banham in 1846. As Mrs Amies she assisted in the school, teaching needlework or supervising classes when staff could not be recruited or were absent. There are many entries concerning her work in the school logs, but she is never mentioned in any of the inspectorate reports and there is nothing to suggest that she is qualified in any way, or that she was paid for the work she did.

George

Their eldest son George was born in 1871. On the 2nd April 1886 George began as a monitor in the Boys' school, assisting with the first class. By June of 1887 he is listed as a pupil teacher, and in the 1890 school report he is teaching and was to be informed that he is now qualified under article 50, but not under article 52.

On the 31st October 1890 he left to go to Maidenhead, where he had been appointed as assistant Master at St Luke's School. In February 1897 he is shown as teaching back at Antingham and Southrepps for a week, and again just for the day on the 3rd April.

Louisa

The oldest daughter Louisa was born on the 19th July 1872 in Worstead.

On March 19th 1886 Louisa left the school at the age of 13. The 1891 census has her listed as pupil teacher but living in the school house. However, there is no account of her working as a pupil teacher at Antingham and Southrepps; the assumption is that she was working at another local school. She went on to work as a Board school teacher in Surrey.

There are many references over the years to Articles, in this case Art. 50 and 52. These refer to the educational codes of the time which dictated what responsibilities teachers were allowed to undertake. These were frequently amended. No definitions of these articles have been found.
Boys' log July 1890.

It is not recorded if George had been working in the school during the period of April to August, just that he and his sister Jessie left the school on the 11th. George later emigrated to Australia.
Boys' log 11th August 189.7

The 1884 school log entry 25th July shows Louisa at the age of 12 working as a monitress.
Infants' log 25th July 1884.

Jessie

Jessie was born in Worstead on the 15th January 1874. On the 19th March 1886 she replaced her sister Louisa as monitress. By 1889 Jessie was teaching in the Mixed school. She left the school on the 11th August 1897. She married Charles Wigg, who was also a school teacher. It is not recorded if she continued to teach.

Edith

Edith was born on the 6th December 1875. There are no references to her in the school logs at all. In 1911 she was 35, living with her parents in the school house and with no occupation shown.

Ruth

Ruth was the last of the children to be born in Worstead, on the 2nd July 1877. As with Edith there is no record of her in the school logbooks. She married Francis Shepperd.

Mary

Mary was the first of the children to be born in Antingham, on the 22nd January 1879. Like her sisters Ruth and Edith she does not appear to have shown any interest in teaching. She married a school master, William Coad.

Katie

Katie was born in 1881. In 1896, when she was 15, the school log records her as a pupil teacher in the Mixed school.

She left the following year on the 31st May having secured an assistant mistress post in Oxford. Five years later she married Alexander Wyness, who was also a school master.

At 17 Jessie is a pupil teacher in the school, going on to be employed as an assistant teacher in the Mixed school. She was given the opportunity to gain experience in the Infants' school with the resignation of Miss Tilney in March 1897.

Boys' Log 26th March 1897.

In August 1900 Katie is on the staff of the school listed as qualified under Article 68.

Boys' log August 1900.

William

William was born in Antingham on the 23rd May 1882. He took a completely different route in life from the rest of the family. In 1901 he was working in Thorpe St Matthew, Norwich as an electrical engineer, and by the time of the 1911 census he had moved to Sheffield. In 1913 he married Esther Elizabeth Unwin in Sheffield. William founded the Bakelite firm in Sheffield in 1929.

Margaret

Margaret was born on the 16th October 1884. The School log records her as a monitress. By 1902 she is a first-year pupil teacher.

Alice

Alice was born on the 17th January 1887. There is no mention of her in the school log books.

However, the 1911 census shows that she was still living with her parents in the school house, and no occupation is given. It is probable that she moved to Smallburgh with her parents. In 1922 she married a grocer, Alfred George Ribbands, at Smallburgh.

Elsie

The last of 11 children, Elsie was born in Antingham in 1890. She was a pupil teacher at the school.

In 1907 there is an entry in the minute log that the HM Inspector could not approve her appointment at the school. No reason was given, and her services were terminated on the 31st January. In 1911 she was a Council school teacher living with her parents in the school house.

June 1905 Margaret leaves the school to take up a teaching post in Lower Mitcham.
Infants' log 30th June 1905.

This entry shows Elsie is in charge of a class of 38 pupils, when possibly only 15 years old herself.
Boys' log 7th April 1905.

What was William like as a Headmaster?

The HM inspector reported in 1878 that: "The school is orderly and classification careful and a good beginning of work has been made." The rest of the report was about the physical state of the school. This is a recurrent theme throughout his headship. On the whole the school was deemed to be fair.

William remained Headmaster for 35 years, retiring in 1913 to Smallburgh, where he died in 1924. His widow Louisa died in 1929 in Guildford, Surrey, having gone to live with her daughter Margaret. Their servant Elizabeth Long was born in Worstead in 1864. She married Jonah Watts in 1886. Of their lodger Ernest Price no record can be found.

William had a six-month spell of illness, being absent from the school from September 1885 until March 1886. This is reflected in the inspector's report.

Unless he had been sent away to hospital it must have been very difficult being ill and living on the premises with his wife and children working in the school. There appears to have been no reference in the minute book to the Headmaster's long absence. Mr A Farrington from Norwich was responsible for the school in this period.

To read transcripts of all HMI reports see the appendix.

Boys' log July 1886.

Mr Amies appears to have been well thought of, or at least his position as Headmaster was, as he was invited to the rededication of St Andrew's Church, Gunton, the personal church of Lord Suffield. St Andrew's was designed by Robert Adam; it is in the grounds of Gunton Hall.

Boys' log 5th August 1894.

July 26th Received Report "Mixed School" The condition of the School is only just fair. The long illness of the Master has been a great disadvantage owing, no doubt, a good deal to this, the order in the upper half of the School is still unsatisfactory. There was again a very long list of Children represented in the same Standard. The first Standard did poorly in all their work; the other Standards fairly except in Arithmetic, which was below fair in the third, fourth, and sixth Standards English was just good enough for the lower Grant, but the third and fourth Standards did badly in Grammar; Geography was quite below the mark, except in the top class. Needlework and Singing by note were well done."

5th August. H. Master absent for 1½ hours on Wednesday morning to attend opening service at Gunton Church. Examination of P.T. and Monitresses on Saturday 9 & 12. A.M.

Hector Percy Jones
Headmaster 1913–1938

The next resident of the school house was Hector Percy Jones. He was born in 1878 in Aberdare, Glamorgan, taking up his post at Antingham and Southrepps School on the 1st February 1913.

Mr Jones had a keen interest in teaching the children horticulture and allowed the school to use part of the garden as a fruit plot. He was also very vocal to the Ministry of Education in Whitehall about the inadequate arrangements made for the teaching of handicrafts, cooking and laundry. One of his letters accompanying complaints about the barn in which these lessons were taught requested that the officials should not mention his complaints to the land-lady. She was a personal friend and he would not like to offend her.

Following a managers' meeting about the amalgamation of the schools in 1925, Mr Jones wrote an extensive letter with his concerns about how they would deal with staff changes. He was worried that staff would be treated unkindly, and in particular that they would dispense with Mrs Jones's services. He set out in detail Mrs Jones's educational experience and her significant contribution to all aspects of the smooth running of the school, in particular her kindness to the children. It appears from the letter that Mrs Jones was not formally qualified, but that to lose her from the staff would have a profound effect on the success of the school.

Mr Hector Percy Jones.
The Southrepps Society collection.

He suggests a transfer to the Infants, that she might study Miss Bent's methods before she leaves. The managers listened to his entreaty and Mrs Jones was indeed transferred to the Infants, where she continued to work until she tendered her resignation as temporary teacher in September 1938, retiring at the same time as her husband.

Mr Jones helpfully gives a full resume of his teaching career starting in Aberdare in 1895 and finishing at Antingham and Southrepps in 1913
Boys' log November 1921

Mr Jones received many glowing reports from the Inspectors – this one from July 1920. The high standards were maintained and the reports give an interesting insight into what was taught at the school. Mr Jones clearly had a love of geography and seems to have transmitted that to his students.
Boys' log July 1920.

Below: Mr Jones led the school for 25 years, leaving in September 1938. He died in Cromer in 1954. His wife Maud Eliza Hough, whom he had married in 1902, died the same year; they had no children.
The Southrepps Society collection.

GIFT FOR SOUTHREPPS HEAD MASTER

Retiring After 44 Years as a Teacher

After forty-four years in the teaching profession Mr. Hector Percy Jones, of Cromer, yesterday retired from the head mastership of the Southrepps and Antingham School. In the presence of the scholars, school managers, and parents at the school a cheque for £13 15s., with which Mr. Jones is to purchase a greenhouse, was handed to him yesterday. Accompanying the cheque was a plate with a suitable inscription. There was also a book, the work of two of the scholars, Ralph Briggs and Allen Self, containing the names of the subscribers, and a bouquet for Mrs. Jones.

Mr. Jones has been head master at Southrepps for 25 years and his total service with the Norfolk Education Committee is 31 years. He is succeeded by Mr. Thomas Dack, of South Creake.

The chairman of the school managers, the Rev. A. G. Metcalfe (Rector of Antingham), presided. Mr. F. C. Crane (assistant head master), who was responsible for collecting the money, mentioned in his remarks that Sir Frederick Sullivan, rector of the parish from 1901 to 1921, had sent Mr. and Mrs. Jones a silver sweet dish "as a memento of the years we worked together."

The Chairman said that Mr. Jones had put his heart into his work for the school which represented four parishes. The school had progressed under him and at one time it was touch and go whether it should not be a central school, but eventually that honour was awarded North Walsham.

Mr. Hewitt having added his tribute to Mr. Jones, the children gave cheers for Mr. Jones. Mrs. Metcalfe then handed the cheque and plate to Mr. Jones.

Mr. Jones, in returning thanks, said he was proud to see his old schoolboys carrying on with the Southrepps Football Club. He would continue as president of the Football Club and treasurer of the Men's Club at Southrepps. He paid a tribute to his assistant, Mr. Crane, thanked the parents for their support and kindness, and added that he was proud of the fact that in one report the school was described by the inspector as one of the best he had seen. If he had succeeded it was because he had never had a cane in his desk and had aimed at getting the best out of the children. He had never minded mischief in a child, and preferred a mischievous child to a quiet one. He was grateful to all the subscribers and to the old pupils who had written to him.

Barbara Amis having presented a bouquet to Mrs. Jones, the hymn "Through all the changing scenes of life" was sung. Afterwards the teachers entertained the parents and managers to tea.

Government Report.

Inspected on 29th & 30th July 1920.
Report by Mr E. D. Fear

Mixed Department.
General:
There are many praiseworthy features about this School. It is exceptionally well taught and conducted,

347 1920

as a whole, but the following points merit special mention.

The intelligence and wide knowledge of the older Scholars, their industry and legitimate pride in their work, have had their due influence with the parents who take a keen interest in their children's progress and in the School generally.

Map-reading and construction, and the principles of Geography are thoroughly well taught and much in advance of anything usually attempted in a village School.

The use of the sliding Scale in connection with the teaching of Arithmetic is also unique; hence the boys take a keener and more intelligent interest in this subject, and are able to solve more advanced problems expeditiously & correctly than in most Schools.

C. H. Pearson
22/9/20

Mr Jones was an active member of the Masons and very involved in the welfare of the men in the village. With his own money he bought two adjoining rundown cottages in Lower Street in the 1930s which were to be converted into a men's reading room. The work was done by its members. This building is now the Social Club.

Thomas F. Dack
Headmaster 1938–1945

Thomas F. Dack was born on the 17th September 1908 in Walsingham. He and his wife Margaret née Hibbert with their two children were the next inhabitants of the school house. Sadly, their first-born twins died at birth in 1937. Margaret was also a school teacher. He had previously worked at South Creake. Thomas Dack was the Headmaster at the school for seven years from 1938 until 1945, seeing the school through the Second World War.

In July 1939 he took a party of 35 senior children to London Zoo; they went by motor coach, leaving at 6am and returning at 11.15 pm, accompanied by fellow teacher Miss Watts. He was summoned in 1941 to attend a medical examination under the Armed Forces Act, even though teachers were on the reserved list of occupations free from conscription.

He also played the organ and was absent on one occasion to play at a funeral at Antingham Church. Mr Dack left to be Headmaster of Reepham School, and is fondly remembered by his former pupils. His last day was the 29th June 1945. The school house then stood empty for three months while Mr Crane was acting Headmaster. Mr Dack died just short of his 100th birthday in 2008, at Wells-next-the-Sea.

The 1939 England and Wales Register shows that a Mr Frost, who was born in 1897, lived with the Dacks in the school house. He was Head teacher at Dagenham County High School, whose children had been evacuated to the area during the war and were attending the school at that time.

John Robinson Hare
Headmaster 1945–1969

Mr Hare took up his post on the 1st November 1945. He was born in September 1904 in Shardlow, Derbyshire, son of a relieving officer. He married Mena Holliday in 1929; she disliked her name, so she was always known as Paddy. He worked in Whittlesey, Cambridgeshire, where their two sons were born. In 1939 he was Headteacher in Hindley, Lancashire.

Some former Antingham and Southrepps pupils had a hard time with him and remember him as being very strict, but one recalls how he went out of his way to order a special left-handed pen for her to improve her handwriting. Her report went from adequate to very good under his teaching.

Mrs Hare was not only the school secretary from 1948 onwards, but also helped with music and dance in the school – she was an

Mr Dack took up his post on the 1st November 1938.
Boys' log 1st November 1938.

As with all the wives before her, Mrs Dack also worked in the school as a temporary teacher. She was even prevailed upon to cook the school dinners for two days when Mrs Gotts was absent.
Boys' log 10th July 1942.

Above: Mr Hare is the teacher standing at the end of the middle row. 1951.
Antingham and Southrepps School.

Mr Hare was a keen bird watcher and enjoyed taking the older pupils on an annual trip to Blakeney.
The Southrepps Society; Hare collection.

21ᵗ March | Telephone message received last night that Miss Stone's mother (aged 99 9/12) died yesterday so Miss Stone will not be able to come to school this week.
Mr Grace still absent.
Mr & Mrs Hare in charge of whole school.

On one occasion in 1960 a combination of staff illnesses and family problems meant the school of 109 pupils was in the sole care of Mr and Mrs Hare.
Mixed log 21st March 1960.

30ᵗʰ April 51. | Mr. Richards (County Bee Expert) delivered one colony of bees at this School at 4.45pm. this afternoon.

He also kept bees and his granddaughter remembers that there were several hives in the Headmaster's garden. An annual report about the bees had to be submitted.
Mixed log 3rd April 1951.

28ᵗʰ Feb. | found everything satisfactory. School closed for Easter Holiday. John Robinson Hare relinquished his post as Headteacher today

The Hares lived in the school house for 24 years, leaving in Febuary 1969.
Mixed log 28th February 1969

accomplished pianist. She is recorded on several occasions as teaching when other staff were absent. She was also an extra pair of hands on school trips.

They retired to Upper Street. He died in 1982, and Mrs Hare in 1988. Both were laid to rest St James's Church, Southrepps.

Mr Harold Gladwin
Headmaster 1969–1980

Born in Stockport in 1920, Mr Gladwin came to the school from a teaching post in Matlock, Derbyshire. He oversaw a period of uncertainty, as the Education Authority rearranged the local schools. He also organised the 150–year celebration, when children put on a gymnastic display, a concert and dressed in period clothes. Various local people and businesses donated money to the cost of the flint panel.

Mr Harold Gladwin.
Antingham and Southrepps School.

Mr Gladwin (Headmaster) informed the managers that he had removed from the school house and was now living at 'Woodlands,' Mill Lane, E. Runton, Cromer. After some discussion the correspondent was instructed to inquire of the Education Committee what use the house was to be put too, mentioning the possibility of deterioration if not in use.

Mr Gladwin was the last Headmaster to live in the school house, having tried unsuccessfully for many years to get the managers to modernise it and install central heating.

There is one entry in the minute book about how he had led a school trip to Paris, and that it was a great success. It was whilst he was Headmaster that the French language and culture formed an important part of the curriculum. He is described by his former pupils as a lovely man. They tell a vivid story with much affection about him smoking in school. They even remembered the brand being Carlton cigarettes in a maroon box. He would be smoking whilst marking work in an adjacent room and when called on for assistance he would come through with the cigarette cupped in his hand behind his back.

Mr Gladwin left at the end of the summer term in 1980. He and his wife retired to Bradfield Road, Antingham, and he died in June 1993.

Tenancy

Mr Gladwin may have been the last Head teacher to occupy the school house but he was not its last resident. A Mr MacDonald rented the house from October 1971. It proved to be an eventful tenancy. Chickens were straying onto school land, mice were in the school, said to be attributable to the school house, and there were too many unruly dogs. The fence was mended between the garden and the playground and the tenant warned regarding restraint of his pets. After further incidents with his animals Mr MacDonald finally left in 1982.

1977.
28th Feb.   Mr. R. J. Bone (Mr. Juniors) found two ponies from the school house in the infants playground. These were eventually removed.

Headmistresses of the Girls' school

The school educated boys and girls from its inception. It had two classrooms, and the job description for the Headship was for a married couple. As far as can be ascertained from the documents found, there have always been male and female teachers at the school. It may well be that the youngest children were taught with the girls; certainly this was the case when the expanded school reopened in January 1878, before the new Infants' department opened in the April.

From 1878 the school was split into three separate parts: the Infants' school, the Girls' school and the Boys' school. Each school had its own log book and was responsible for collecting its own fees. The Headmaster was in overall control, and he lived in the school house. He was answerable to the managers for the running of the entire school.

The first Headmistress of the Girls' school was Louisa Allen. She was appointed on the 13th July 1877, to commence work in the September on completion of the extension. Her pay was to be £70 per annum and she had to find her own accommodation. For some reason her pay was increased to £75 per annum in the October, even though she had still not taken up her post as the work on extending the school

had overrun. No other information about her has been found.

The work on the school was eventually finished, and the Girls' school opened on the 28th January 1878.

An assistant teacher, Lydia Rix, was appointed in February 1878, but she resigned in March due to ill health, having rarely been in attendance. In April the infants left the Girls' school, as all the delayed building work had been completed and their own school was at last ready for use. Maria Hammond was engaged as a monitor in April, but left in May. With a class size of 93 this was greater than could be managed by one teacher and, despite the inspector calling for more assistance, it took until October to employ Mary Butler.

Whilst still at the school Mary took her exams to become a certified teacher, qualifying in December 1880. She was lodging with the Woods family at Laburnum Cottage in Lower Street. She worked at the school until June 1881, when the Girls' school was amalgamated with the Boys'. She continued to work as a teacher, becoming the Headmistress of an elementary school in Thanet, Kent.

Miss Allen left the school in January 1879, to be replaced by Emily Brett. Emily was only 20

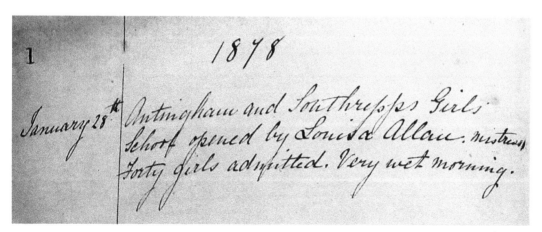

The first entry in the Girls' log book.
Girls' log 28th January 1878.

57

HM Inspector Francis Synge records the need for extra staff and more books.
Girls' log 28th May 1878.

> 1878
> May 28. School visited by me Francis Synge. Some efficient help is much needed without delay. I do not see how it can be managed under present circumstances except by an assistant teacher qualified under Art 79.
> More Bks needed.

17

> Girls' School "The School is orderly, the classification careful, and a good beginning of work has been made. The help of an Assistant Teacher is needed for the present and Monitors who will ultimately be apprenticed are needed also for a future staff. The supply of reading-books will be insufficient for the coming year.
> The windows open inconveniently and the weights of the ventilators are dangerous and should be altered
> I am to request your attention to Article 32 (c) in the case of the Girls' School.
> The staff is at present insufficient.
> General improvement will be expected in all Departments next year if a deduction is to be avoided under Article 32 (b)"

The HM Inspector is highly critical of the poor staffing level and warns of a reduction in the grant if not resolved. He also highlights the ventilation, an on-going obsession of the inspectors
Girls' log April 1879.

when she took up the post. She was born at Downham and she too lodged with the Woods family. At the time of her appointment there was no Infants' teacher so she had to teach the girls, and have the infants in the classroom as well. On one day there were 84 girls and 42 infants, and this state of affairs continued for three months until April, when a new Infants' teacher was appointed.

This is the second time that the staffing levels had been found inadequate, just a year after the first, but no record can be found of any extra teachers or monitors being appointed. Despite this the school appeared to run in a satisfactory and orderly manner until 1881, when Miss Brett resigned. She continued to work as a teacher, returning to the family home in East Dereham.

There is an interesting entry in the managers' book from October 1879, that the girls had been taking books home, and this was to be stopped as the books were becoming dirtied and spoiled.

Following the resignation of Miss Brett, the managers, at their meeting on the 26th May 1881, decided to amalgamate the schools. This would save money by not having to pay Headmistress wages. They also felt that by rearranging the teaching staff the children would get better attention and therefore the school would be eligible for a higher grant. It would be acceptable for the boys and girls to be in the same classroom as long as they did not share desks with the opposite sex, and that there was no indiscriminate mixing of children. The Girls' school closed on the 9th June 1881.

The current school hall, originally the Girls' school room.

It is the room in the school which best gives a flavour of what it would have been like in 1878, with its high ceiling, single fireplace and original clock. The panels on the lower walls are also probably original. The door on the left-hand wall was added in the 1980s.

The Headmistresses of the Infants' school

The separate Infants' school opened in April 1878 with the extension of the original school. The first mistress was Rebekah Jane Maguir; she was to be paid £45 per annum.

Unfortunately she did not retain her post for long, as the managers received a letter in July 1878 informing them that she was not a certified teacher. This was now a requirement in order to receive the education grants. It is not clear if there had been a misunderstanding or a deception, but the managers decided it was not desirable to continue with her services. She remained at the school on reduced pay until the beginning of the harvest holiday, and then left. The only report of her time at the school was not very complimentary.

There was no immediate replacement Headmistress. The outcome was that, from September 1878, the older infants were taught with the boys, and the younger ones with the girls. From 13th January to 28th April 1879 all of the infants were taught with the girls.

Miss Mary Balle

Miss Mary Balle was appointed mistress of the Infants in April 1879. She was born in 1860 in Montacute, Somerset. In the 1871 census, when she was 11, she was recorded as a boarder at a Wesleyan school in Cornwall. On her appointment to Antingham and Southrepps School at the age of 19, she lived with her widowed mother in Lower Street.

She left the School in November 1882. In the 1891 census she was teaching in Snowhill, Gloucestershire. She married David Hart in 1892 and they emigrated to Canada in 1894, taking her mother with them.

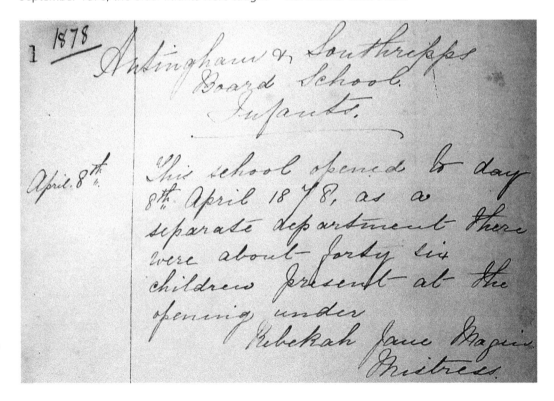

The new Infants' school opened with 46 pupils transferring from the Girls' school.
Infants' log 8th April 1878.

1878

Infants' School. "Neither discipline nor instruction in this school are as yet satisfactory. A gentler manner and the help at least of some efficient Monitors are needed.

Blinds are wanted. The weights of the ventilators are dangerous and should be altered. A 'urinal should be provided for the Boys'"

4

Miss Maguir's only HM Inspector's report and it is not very encouraging. The issue of ventilation is a recurrent theme over the years.
Infants' log August 1878.

May 14th

'Infant School. The school has been little more than a month under the present Teacher. The children are very backward and the order is not yet as good as it ought to be. The help of efficient monitors is much needed. Blinds have not yet been provided and will be much needed when hot weather comes"

Miss Balle's first HM Inspector's report shows that she has a lot of work to do. When inspected again in 1880 the school had improved.
Infants' log 14th May 1880.

Below: Photograph from 1890.
The Southrepps Society, Bird collection.

The reports for Miss Trollope are not good; there were difficulties with both discipline and attainment.

Infants' log January 1885.

> "Infant School"
>
> "Discipline & attainments are still poor in this school. The work of the first Standard was especially poor. The pupil teacher has as yet everything to learn as to the teaching and management of her Class.
>
> E.M. Ames has passed fairly but should attend to Teaching.
>
> The issue of a Certificate to Miss Trollope is deferred for a more favourable report. Amount of Grant = 140 . 13 . —

1885

Miss Inez Trollope

Miss Inez Trollope was born in Syderstone in 1861. She trained to be a teacher at the Diocesan Training Institution, St George's Plain, Norwich, and took up her post on the 27th November 1882 at the age of 21.

She resigned in September 1885. In 1891 she was living with her parents in Heigham and teaching in an elementary school. In 1901 she was living in the school house at Newton Flotman, where she was Headmistress. By 1911 Inez was described as a governess pensioner (at the age of 49) and foster mother at a poor law girls' home at 55 Botolph Street, Norwich, where she was head of the institution. She died in Norwich in 1949.

Miss Eleanor Soames

Miss Eleanor Soames started at the school on the 14th September 1885; despite being on the school staff in 1891, no census record can be found for her. The HM Inspector's reports are satisfactory, although the inspector reports that she is hard pressed with insufficient help, and

children starting at an older age than would be expected. The logs show that, despite this, her assistant is often taken away to assist in the Mixed school.

Miss Soames led the Infants' school for eight years, leaving on the 18th November 1893 before her replacement was appointed.

Miss Harriet Louisa Tilney

On the 8th January 1894 Harriet Louisa Tilney became the next Headmistress of the Infants' school. No census returns have been found for Miss Tilney. Her reports however show her to have been a competent teacher. She left the school in March 1897.

Miss Naomi Bent

Naomi Bent was the longest-serving and last Headmistress of the Infants' school. She started at the beginning of the September term in 1897. She was born in Leicestershire in 1863, and at 34 she was the oldest Mistress to start at the Infants' school. She had previously taught at an endowed school in Hatton, Warwickshire. She lodged with the Watson family at Rectory Farm,

Infants School.
"There are a great many children over seven in this school who are not up to the work of the first Standard. This is partly due to their late admission, and partly to the want of efficient help. If the children were really Infants, the work might be considered very fair. As it is, the Merit Grant is recommended with a good deal of hesitation, and only because the mistress has done her work satisfactorily. Children over eight should not be retained in the Infant school.

_ _ _ Thynne
Clerk to the School Board

HM Inspector's report. He remarks on the late age of the children starting school. This is a recurrent theme, as is the need for efficient help.
Infants' log August 1887.

1896

Infant's School.   158

Good methods are employed, the children are interested and the instruction continues to improve. The order is satisfactory. Additional pegs are wanted in the cloak room for the Infants.
R. E. Thain is recognised under Article 50 of the Code.
B. Watson. - - Spelling*

Staff A.L.Tilney mistress.
       Bessie Watson. Pupil Teacher
                            2nd year.

The HM Inspector is pleased with the work that Miss Tilney has achieved.
Infants' log September 1896.

*Letter sent by Miss Bent
to the managers; she also
listed the starting ages
of the children when
admitted:
Ivy Gray
  6 years 3 months,
Olive Mayes
  6 years 2 months,
Ernest Hurn
  6 years 2 months,
Marjorie Gaze
  6 years 8 months,
Ivy Reynolds
  6 years 2 months,
Dorothy Hewitt
  5 years 9 months,
Edith Craske
  5 years 7 months,
Ethel Risebrow
  5 years 8 months,
Dorothy Jordan
  5 years 9 months,
Alfred Lubbock
  5 years 9 months,
Theophilus Gray
  5 years 9 months,
Kathleen Gray
  5 years 9 months,
Florence Bane
  5 years 9 months,
Harry Jeffries
  5 years 5 months,
Antony Vergerson
  5 years 4 months,
John Stanley Futter
  5 years 9 months.
Infants' log 10th April 1902.*

Antingham.

The problems that the previous Headmistresses faced had not been resolved. There remained a shortage of staff and she was very concerned about the late age at which the pupils started school.

Miss Bent was clearly struggling with the late admission of children to the school; it is interesting to note how many were over the age of six. The issue of the late starting age remained unaddressed, with her returning to the subject in 1908.

Not only were the children above the usual age for starting school; there continued to be a shortage of staff and the schoolroom accommodation was challenging. The 1906 HM Inspectors' report recorded that she had to teach 54 children in two classes, which were necessarily seated at either end of the main room. This was compounded by the fact that the gallery had still not been taken down and was using up valuable space, despite this having received adverse comments from the inspectors over the previous seven years.

After 28 years at the school Naomi Bent retired, on the 31st March 1925. She return-

1911
Jan. 16th

Copy of Report -
Infants.

Owing to the great happiness of the children, their ready response, and interest in their work, a visit to this school is an unmixed pleasure. The Head Mistress directs her Assistant, or Assistants, wisely, and her own work is invaluable. I saw nothing but genuinely good work either at this visit, or at the visit paid a year ago. Naomi Bent C.T. Elizabeth Wright. S.

Despite all these problems, by 1911 Miss Bent receives a glowing report from the Inspector.
Infants' log 16th January 1911.

Infants' c1920.
The Southrepps Society, Bullimore collection.

ed to the county of her birth and died in Leicester in 1954 at the age of 91. With her retirement the Infants' school as a separate entity ended.

Following the stipulation of the Education Board that a female teacher should be given general charge of the Infants, Miss Mabel Agnes

Stone was appointed. She held the post for the next forty years, retiring in 1965. Her involvement with the school did not end there as she continued as a supply teacher for many years. She is fondly remembered by past pupils as a lovely lady

Miss Bent was clearly much respected, and the records show her development as a kind and effective teacher.

This was reflected in fulsome comments in the Minute book, as well as the generous collection made for her retirement gift of a watch, £16 2s 6d, a substantial sum at the time.

Minute book 9th January 1925.

The Resignation of Miss Bent upon her retirement was read & accepted. The thanks of the managers for her long & valuable services were directed to be sent to her with good wishes for her future health & happiness

The Infants' school was to be amalgamated with the Mixed school but permission for this action had to be sought from the Board of Education.

Norfolk Record Office gtn 68/12 2/3.

All communications should be addressed to— "The Secretary."

BOARD OF EDUCATION.

WHITEHALL, LONDON, S.W.1.

Please write at the head of any further communication—

1. Norfolk.
2. Antingham and South Repps Council School No.8.

E. 27/8/3.

16th February, 1925.

Sir,

With reference to Mr. Davis's letter of the 26th ultimo (H.B.) I am directed to state that the Board agree to the Authority's proposal to amalgamate the Mixed and Infants' Departments of Antingham and South Repps Council School under the present Head Master of the Mixed Department as from 1st April 1925 on condition that a woman assistant teacher is given general charge of the Infants under the supervision of the Head Teacher.

I am, Sir,
Your obedient Servant,
Robert R. Campbell

To the
Local Education Authority.

Attendance

With the passing of the 1870 Elementary Education Act it became a legal requirement for children between the ages of five and ten to attend school. The School Boards set up under that Act became responsible for ensuring that children attended school, and local bye-laws could be passed extending the upper age. Such bye-laws were adopted by the Board, but the details of these are unknown. In 1893 the leaving age was raised nationally to 11 years, and in 1899 to 12 years.

Antingham and Southrepps appointed its first attendance officer in 1878: William Peacock, who was born in Wymondham in 1836. Before applying for this job he had been a police inspector in Lambeth, retiring from the force in 1874 with an "infirmity of the body", and he returned to his native Norfolk. His task was to ensure the attendance of the pupils and enforce the payment of school fees. The Headmaster would give him a list of absentees, irregular attendees and those in arrears. He would send out notices and visit homes and, if required, the Board would give him permission to take the offending parents to court. The Boys' log of 1878 records that on the 23rd September he was given a list of 27 poor attenders; he then sent notices to the parents warning of the consequences, and by 3rd October several boys had returned to school.

The number of pupils actually attending is difficult to know, as the registers have not survived and the recording of the figures in the log books is erratic. In 1879 the total number of children on the school books was 303, made up of 216 in the Boys' and Girls' and 93 Infants. The Board defined regular attendance as seven attendances a week, or 28 in four weeks. A whole school day counted as two attendances, the morning session and the afternoon session. With an average attendance in that year of 41%, this was very poor. At every monthly Board meeting, the attendance officer was reporting on arrears in payment of fees and irregular or non-attendance. To assist the attendance officer in his task the school requested from the five parishes a list for the last ten years of all children registered.

This photo is believed to be from about 1890. The average attendance for that year was 53%. This photo will have been of those who turned up on the day. In 1896 the number on the school roll was 296, in comparison with 2012 when the roll was about 110.
The Southrepps Society; Bullimore collection.

The attendance figures recorded in the logs are erratic with three sets of data available for one month and none for the next so this is an average for the Infants' only. In 1879 the number of pupils on the roll was 93 so the attendance was very poor with a huge seasonal drop at harvest time.

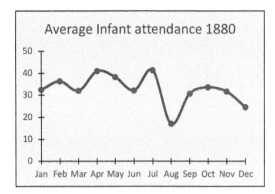

Again the figures have been averaged out. Now that education is free the number attending is better: there were about 80 infants on the roll at this time. In May there was almost full attendance. The average figures do not show the huge drop in the week 19th February due to heavy snow fall

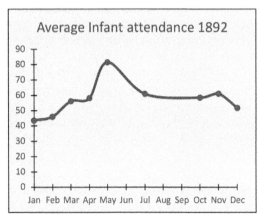

Children were often an essential source of income for these families. The average agricultural wage in 1882 had gone down and was only 13s 7½d (68p) a week. Poor attendance could be the result of a number of factors.

While seasonal variations are repeated throughout the data, there is no apparent pattern to the peaks and troughs. A major cause of absence was illness, which is covered elsewhere. Others were the need to help at home, in the fields and with the harvest. The weather played its part: one entry in the Infants' log records that there were "Only 13 children at school. Roads are unfit for little children to cross and nearly all of them have one to two miles to come to school". Even in 1917 poverty was still a factor: for example in January of that year it was reported in the Minute book that two families

cited the lack of boots as the reason that their children were unable to attend school.

There are many documented instances of parents being taken to court for the absence of their children, some examples being:

1877: Mr James Brooks, a sheepshearer and widower, was prosecuted for disobedience of an order to ensure his child attended school. The court fined him 4s (20p) or 11 days imprisonment with hard labour. The average wage in 1877 was 14s 1½d (71p, the equivalent of about £43 in 2020). This was a harsh punishment; he may have had no-one to look after his children and would struggle to pay the fine.

1889: Seven parents were prosecuted for non-attendance of their children.

1903: George Reynolds' parents were prosecuted. George was one of four children and his father was a farm labourer.

1904: Proceedings were taken against the parents of Henry Jordan of Bradfield; they were fined 7s 6d (37½p).

The Norfolk Chronicle would regularly report on these prosecutions.

Miss Malson's School

The Board was also responsible for ensuring that all children in the five parishes attended a school deemed to be adequate. In 1879 several children had left Antingham and Southrepps to attend a private school run by Miss Malson in Upper Street. Few details of this school are known, but it clearly caused the Board concern, and Mr Peacock was tasked with investigating. He reported to the Board that 'she had more children than she ought as there was not sufficient cubic feet in the room for each child in accordance with the 1870 Act'. The outcome is not recorded. However, in April 1906 it was reported in the Minute log that the small private school in Upper Street had closed. Whether this is the same establishment is not clear but it would seem likely. The attendance officer

The bad weather, combined with poor heating at home and at school, may well have caused the children to suffer from chilblains. These cause the feet to swell and become red, itchy, and painful, making the wearing of boots very difficult.
Infants' log 3rd January 1890.

1890
Jan 3rd | The attendance has been poor the whole week. this is partly owing to the weather and to the fact that some of the children have bad feet and are unable to get their boots on.

was instructed to see that those children from the private school were attending a school somewhere; four of them were admitted to Antingham and Southrepps School.

Illegal employment

The school board also checked on the employment of children who should be in school. In 1880 they cautioned Mr Robert Woods of Upper Street, a cattle dealer, that he would be prosecuted if he continued to employ Robert Moy of Southrepps, aged ten. Master Moy was the youngest son of a widowed mother and the income from his employment would no doubt have been very welcome. The outcome of the warning is not recorded. It is interesting to note that a lodger in the Woods household at the time was Emily Brett, a teacher at the school.

With the death of Mr Peacock in 1884, Mr H Hewitt was appointed attendance officer. He was also a farmer and lived in Church Street with his wife and four children (They went on to have a total of fourteen, four of whom died). He does not appear to have been as scrupulous as his predecessor, as in 1897 the Board had to fine him 2s 6d (12½p) for the employment of James Hewitt (who was not his son), who should have been at school.

Legal Employment

Children could leave school early if they had made a sufficient number of attendances and were going into employment.

The Board had to be satisfied that the employment was sound, and the certificate could be cancelled if the job was lost or changed. In 1910 Edith Ward and Grace Gray, both of Thorpe Market, applied for labour certificates and both were turned down as the proposed home employment was not deemed beneficial. Edith left school the following year to become a domestic servant. Grace continued to attend her local school after the family had moved to Foulsham.

Special Needs

Children could be excused school if they had a medical condition that was deemed to make them too frail or ill to attend or, in those less enlightened times, "uneducable". The medical officer would grant them an exemption certificate. This would appear to allow the family to

not send the child to school, and also absolve the school of having to try and teach them.

One family, the Thurstons, who lived in Lower Street, tried to take advantage of this and when taken to court in 1893 over the non-attendance of their son James, they produced a medical certificate, supposedly signed by a Mrs J Shepherd. It transpired that Mrs Shepherd had never even seen the child and that the certificate had been signed by the office maid servant. It was decided that no further action would be taken.

Abolition of School Fees

In 1891, with the passing of another Elementary Education Act, all school fees were abolished. The removal of this financial burden on poor families almost certainly helped to raise attendance, with the average in 1894 being 79%.

Norfolk Education Committee produced certificates giving permission to leave school. The child had to have had at least 350 attendances at school since the age of five and to be aged not less than 13.
Norfolk Museums Service (Gressenhall Farm and Workhouse).

FORM 146a (1).

NORFOLK EDUCATION COMMITTEE.

LABOUR CERTIFICATE.

Permission to Leave School.
UNDER BYE-LAW 5 (b).

I Certify that *Robert William Hilton* residing at *Roughton* is not less than THIRTEEN years of age, having been born on the *16* day of *November 1901*, as appears by the Registrar's Certificate now produced to me, and has been shown to the satisfaction of the Local Education Authority for this district to be beneficially employed by *Mr Ernest H Winger* and has made **350** attendances after 5 years of age in not more than two Schools during each year for five years, whether consecutive or not, as shown by the Certificate furnished by the Principal Teacher of the *Gt Massingham* School.

Dated this *Thirteenth* day of *March* 1915.

Secretary to the above-named Committee.

The Child named in this Certificate is exempt from School attendance before the age of 14 years only so long as the Child continues to be beneficially employed to the satisfaction of the Local Education Authority in the above employment.

Below: The Regulations for the prize scheme were displayed in the school.
The children would also receive a card with their attendance on one side and the rules on the back.
Norfolk Record Office gtn C/ED 3/3.

However, this improvement was very erratic and unsustained. In 1896 it was brought to the board's attention that there was a great falling off of attendance on Friday afternoons, so it was decided that instead of having a morning and afternoon session there would be one continuous session of four hours, starting at 9.00 with a half hour break.

Even though the legal starting age had been five years since 1870, there were still some children starting school in 1902 as old as six years and eight months. This would have had a significant impact on their learning, as stated by Naomi Bent (the Infant mistress) to the managers.

No action appears to have been taken on the late admission of children, so Miss Bent raises the issue again in April 1904. This delay in addressing the concerns of Miss Bent may be due to the changes in management that occurred when the school became a Norfolk Education Committee school in 1903.

However, there is no reference in the minute book to the starting ages of the children, so her concerns remained unaddressed. Indeed in 1919 she is still recording the ages of children admitted to the school as old as five years and eight months.

Prizes for Good Attendance

The abolition of fees was not having enough effect on attendance throughout the school. The average attendance was dropping again so the Board decided action was required, and in December 1899 a prize scheme was introduced. The regulations were very specific and were displayed in the school.

If the monthly average was good a half-day holiday was awarded. The average attendance

Ornate certificates of attendance were also given for full attendance over the year, with the design changing every year.

Medals were given nationwide to pupils for attendance, with each authority producing their own. A silver-coloured medal celebrated one year's full attendance, and for three years a gold-coloured one. They came complete with black, red and yellow ribbon and a date bar. The name of the recipient could be engraved on the reverse. It wasn't just medals and certificates awarded; for those children with exceptional attendance, possibly of either six or seven years, there would be the prize of a watch, awarded by Norfolk Education Committee. An example

Embossed cards were used to encourage attendance. They were colourful scenes, such as farmyards, for the youngest, and for the older children black and white images of famous or local places.
Norfolk Museums Service (Gressenhall Farm and Workhouse).

for the first year of the scheme had gone up to 85% from 71% the year before. One of the first actions by the new managers in 1903, when the school became a Council School, was to approve the continuation of these half-day attendance holidays. Other incentives were introduced, such as reward cards for the infants.

In 1911 Frank Bullimore of Thorpe Market was awarded this certificate for full attendance.
The Southrepps Society; Leveridge collection.

Gilt medal with ribbon.
Norfolk Museums Service (Gressenhall Farm and Workhouse).

held by Norfolk Museums Service is a small pocket watch in a steel case fastened by a spring clip to a brooch in the form of a ribbon bow.

The last reference to an attendance officer was in March 1917, as the responsibility for enforcing attendance then passed to the County Education Committee.

Certificates continued to be issued by the Education Committee to every child, recording their attendance and progress.

On this occasion the watches went to Ella Baker of Upper Street and Chas Cossey of Lower Street. Chas was not the only member of the Cossey family to receive a watch. In 1911 his brother Sam did as well, and his sister received a white medal.
Boys' log 8th October 1910.

8. VII. '10

> Wednesday was so wet a day that only 52 children came - no attendances were reckoned - On Thursday the Chairman with Messrs Learner & Harrison, handed the prizes to the children, Ella Baker & Chas. Cossey received watches, Sam. Cossey Girls Medal, Walter Bullimore, Bea. Mayes, Walter Briggs, & Herb. Briggs white Medals. there were also 43 book prizes. Miss Jane Gibbons left the school on Friday having resigned her situation as UC. Ass.t

This letter of 1908 to the managers came from Mrs Martha Paul, wife of Walter, a farmer and dealer, who had eight daughters. Their address changed over the years. In 1891 they were living in Bradfield, when Charlotte and Susan would have been attending the school. In 1901 when Lucy, Alice, Gertrude, Kathleen, and Martha were at the school the family was living in Trunch, which makes the full attendance even more remarkable as they had to walk about two miles to school. In 1911 they were at Jublies Farm in Bradfield. Dorothy was the last one to go to the school. Unfortunately, there is no record as to whether her appeal to the managers was successful.
Minute log April 1908.

> A letter was read from Mrs Paul stating that owing to the outbreak of Scarlet Fever her two girls would lose the Attendance Prize of a Watch offered by the Committee. One girl had made 6 years perfect attendance and the other 7 years and two sisters had made 5 or 6 years of perfect attendance and she hoped the managers would recommend these

> cases for consideration by the Committee
> The Clerk was instructed to forward the information to the Committee and state the Managers trust they may favourably consider it as they should think that 4 girls in one family making 24 years perfect attendances must be a record

The Clerk was instructed to draw the attention of the Com.tee to the record of seven years' perfect attendance made by Chas. Whitwood and to strongly recommend that the Committee give a special reward. It was noted that the record was all the more unique owing to the fact of the child living nearly 2 miles from the school.

Charles Whitwood would have been 13 years old and had walked every day from Antingham Hill, where the family lived. It is not recorded if the request was successful and, if so, what the reward was. He is not mentioned in the prize-giving list for that year, but he may have left the school by then. He went on to become a furnishing salesman.
Minute book May 1911.

Norfolk Education Committee.

REPORT OF ATTENDANCE, CONDUCT, PROGRESS, ETC.,
OF

Gracie Snelling STANDARD or CLASS I Southrepps SCHOOL.

for the Quarter ending _____ Harvest

Number of times School Opened _____

" " Present _____

" " Absent _____

" " Late _____

" " Lessons Lost _____

MARKS.

	Gained.	Possible		Gained.	Possible
Conduct			Drawing	32	36
Reading	30	30	Grammar		
Writing	10	10	Geography		
Spelling	15	15	Mapping		
Composition	20	20	History		
Arithmetic	45	45	Obj. Lessons		
Mental Arithmetic			Recitation	12	12

TOTAL MARKS 164   POSITION IN STANDARD 1st

18.

H. P. Jones.
Head Teacher

The date for this one given to Gracie Snelling is unknown, but it is after 1913 as it is signed by Mr Jones, the Headmaster. She was obviously a good student as she came 1st in her class as well as having full attendance.
The Southrepps Society; Young collection.

Boys from many families were helping in the hayfields to bring in the harvest as there was a shortage of men due to the war. On this occasion no action was taken.
Minute book July 1916.

In the case of these two families in March of 1917 a different outcome occurred, perhaps because it was clear that they were not helping the war effort.
Minute book March 1917.

Photographs from the Millennium.
Dave and Janine Spanton

During the First World War there were more absences as children were needed in the fields. The managers' attitude to this varied from case to case.

The official returns to the Department of Education show that from 1920-1953 attendance was over 88%, the highest being 94%.

Maintaining good attendance will always be the goal of a school, and today this school achieves about 98%. Parents can still be prosecuted for non-attendance of their children. Today's Academy runs a breakfast club and after-school activities to help working parents to get their children to school.

Holidays

As a result of their dependence on agriculture rural schools took a much more flexible attitude to holidays than those in towns. Holidays were decided by school managers and none of them were for a fixed duration. At first there were only three holidays a year: Christmas, Easter and Harvest, with no half-terms. From 1880 it was not uncommon to also have a Whitsun break, which could be anything from two days to a whole week. The harvest holiday could be shortened as a result. Holidays were also decided at short notice; for example, the managers' meeting on the 26th March 1904 decided that the Easter holiday would run from the 30th March until the 11th April, giving parents just four days' notice. The harvest holidays were very dependent on the state of the crops and changed from year to year, as well as being variable in length.

When the spring half-term holiday first started has not been found, but it was perhaps about 1939. The first mention of an October half-term is 1947. Holidays were given for other events, in addition to the half days earned for good attendance. The last reference to setting the dates of holidays was in 1954, when the managers agreed to align the Antingham and Southrepps holiday dates with those of North Walsham.

Feast Days

In the early days the log books show that the school closed for religious occasions such as Shrove Tuesday and Ash Wednesday, when the children were expected to attend church. Sometimes a half day's holiday was recorded, but it was not initially given on every occasion. It then became a yearly event, as the attendance figures were recorded as rather low. These holidays dwindled as religious observance decreased and had mainly ceased by 1913, although Mr Jones kept up the tradition of granting a half day holiday for Shrove Tuesday for many years.

Half Days

The most frequent reason for a half day holiday was the Southrepps Fair, which was held every June. In some years the children were given a half day holiday and sometimes two consecutive half days. Flower shows held by the different villages were another excuse for a half day

By 1946 holidays were slightly more organised and two-day half-terms had been introduced. It is interesting to note that the length of the harvest holiday is not specified. The holidays were still set by each individual school. Boys' log 13th February 1946.

holiday. Various church treats resulted in a half day, such as the ones held by the Methodist church in Lower Street, the Southrepps Sunday School treat, or the Wesleyan Sunday School treat.

In the early days of the school, before the log books began, the Suffield family held treats for the children at the Hall.

All these treats continued for the whole time that Mr Amies was Headmaster.

The half day holidays for village or Church School treats continued until 1935. The Southrepps Fair ceases to be mentioned after 1916, and the half days for good attendance very quickly disappear. Half days for flower shows were also discontinued.

There were half day holidays for all royal occasions: coronations, jubilees, weddings and inaugurations. There was even one for the Queen's birthday, combined with the relief of Mafeking in May 1900, and one on the 29th October 1909 for the visit to Norwich of King Edward VII.

Polling Station

The school was closed so that it could be used as a polling station for local and general elections. This was not unusual; schools today often close for the same purpose. The first date recorded for polling closure was 1885.

At the next general election, in 1886, the school was closed on the Friday afternoon to prepare for polling on the Saturday. The next three elections were held on either a Saturday or Monday.

The 1918 Reform Act gave the vote to all men over 21 and most women over 30. It also brought in single election dates and settled on Thursday being the norm. This is a convention, not a rule. In 1918 and 1923 the school was already closed due to influenza and scarlet fever, so presumably it was opened for polling. The same Reform Act also extended the franchise to women on the same terms as men for local elections, and the school also closed for these to take place. The last time that the school was used as a polling station was in 1974.

Punishments

The first record of any punishment is in October 1878 in the Girls' log, when Harriet Dix was punished for playing truant. It is assumed that this was a caning, although it was not recorded as such. The first record of a caning in the Girls' log was in March 1879 when infant Henry Hewitt was caned by Miss Brett, Mistress of the Girls' school, for throwing stones. She caned Bessie Payne and Anne Crowe for disobedience.

Adeline Wells was caned for being late in April 1881. In June the Girls' school was amalgamated with the Boys', and Miss Brett left the school.

Punishments meted out to pupils in the Infants' and Boys' schools are not recorded until 1900, when a punishment book was started.

Punishment Book

The first punishment recorded here is on 26th July 1900, for persistent truanting by Henry Turner. Records then stopped on the 24th November 1903. Why they suddenly start being recorded and then just as suddenly stop is a mystery. The Headmaster at this time was Mr Amies, who had been in post for 22 years, and continued until 1913, a further ten years after his last entry. It is highly unlikely that he only punished pupils for that three year period. The last entry under Mr Amies was again for Henry Turner, who was bullying boys and girls outside.

The idea that a child would be caned for not begging the teacher's pardon is a difficult concept today.
Girls' log 29th June 1880

The first page of the punishment book. This was actually on page 40 of what had originally been the Girls' log book.
Henry Turner's name appears most often.
Punishment book 1900.

There is no indication of what the punishments were. The misdemeanours include laziness in class, lying, bullying, impertinence and fighting.

The entries start again in 1915, two years after Mr Jones has taken over as Headmaster. He states how many strokes or cuts of the cane are delivered.

Two entries in particular stand out:

W. Saunders is probably William; Gray Reynolds has not been identified.
Punishment book 26th July and 16th October 1902.

Reggie George seems to be the only frequent offender, being caned six times in five years for a different offence on each occasion, including setting fire to a bush on the road in 1919.
Punishment book 26th February 1919.

Are any of the miscreants in this photograph? c1923.
The Southrepps Society collection.

These entries continue for another two pages until 1932, so there were only 3–4 events a year and sometimes none at all, suggesting that those children must have really tried his patience.

Bad work and disobedience are the most frequent offences.

There is again a delay in the use of the book, this time of four years, after the appointment of a new Headmaster (Mr Dack). From 1942 to 1959 Headmasters only cane 13 children and seven of those were on one occasion, when they each got one stroke for disobedience. The rest are all for rudeness to teachers.

Mr Hare tended to give one stroke as punishment. In fact there were only two occasions when he gave two strokes, which were P Cook for continued disobedience and David Turner for insolence to a teacher.

The last entry in the book is in January 1959, when a child is caned for bullying a very timid boy.

June 7. 18   John Reynolds   2 cuts
2 cuts
Interfering with Stamp or School.

John Reynolds' transgression is more unusual. Punishment book 7th June 1918.

Mr Hare's entries in the book are far more informative about the misbehaviour than those of his predecessors. Punishment book 26th September and 22nd November 1956

Nov. 22nd   Neville Grimes (8)   1 stroke each
Peter Thurston (10)   for disobedience
in fetching apples from garden & throwing them in playground.
(Many carpentry boys and others throwing apples & acorns, two boys named above began it. Teacher responsible for playground supervision Mr Smith, handicraft instructor).

1 stroke each for riding smaller boys' bicycles and causing damage to one (E Studd's)

Vocational subjects

From the time the school opened, the children were taught the basics of reading, writing and arithmetic as well as religious observance.

Needlework and Knitting

In the early days all the children in the Infants', boys and girls, were taught basic sewing skills. They learnt techniques such as turning a hem or sewing a seam. Children as young as five were examined on their sewing as a specific part of the annual inspection, and the school had money deducted from its grant if the standards were poor.

In 1901 the syllabus for Standard I was to make dusters from pieces of calico and knit coloured reins and strips. Embroidery was also taught. By 1902 the sewing lessons were restricted to girls only.

The Girls' log also records the progress made in needlework, and the 1881 HM Inspector's report records that the work is of a good standard. In the next report the Boys' and Girls' schools had been amalgamated and the standard of needlework had deteriorated to such a degree that the school narrowly avoided having its grant reduced. Matters did improve, and there are many accounts over the next 50 years of sewing being taught in school, most often by the Headmaster's wife. From 1900–1904 Miss Gertrude Leman was employed as a sewing-mistress.

Cookery and Laundry

From 1882 grants were available for the teaching of cookery, and from 1890 also for laundry. These were subjects taught only to the older girls, but do not appear to have started at Antingham and Southrepps School until 1905. The first reference is in the Minute book from May 1905, when the possibility and location of such lessons were discussed.

Final agreement was reached on the 25th September 1905. The first lesson started on the Wednesday 3rd November, when 32 girls were taught by the appropriately named Miss Hemp. The lessons were weekly over the winter months and were also attended by girls from Roughton and Trimingham schools. That first series of lessons continued until 23rd February 1906. In 1909 the girls were taught by the brilliantly named Miss Curry. On 23rd November 1911

Needlework was an important skill. There are numerous references to sewing in the log books.
Infants' log 16th October 1882.

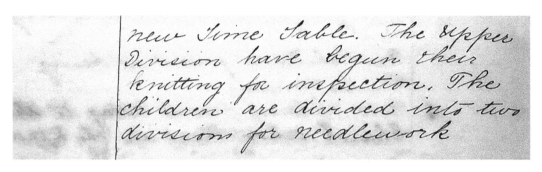

Then you have the practicalities of keeping the children's work clean.
Infants' log 25th July 1900.

The question of starting the cookery class and making Southrepps the centre was discussed and agreed to

The Rev J Sullivan kindly offered his Barn at 20/- for the Session of 20 lessons which offer was unanimously accepted and the Chairman agreed to see that Pillow the Secretary and explain fully the views of the managers upon the subject

3rd November | Cookery Class held on Wednesday in the Barn 32 girls attended in the morning.

the clerk to the managers was instructed to apply for forms for the cookery and laundry scholarships that were by then available.

Unfortunately no other details of the barn are known; it is not even clear if it was near the rectory in Upper Street or closer to the school in Lower Street.

In 1919 the managers approached Mrs Watson of Crossways in Lower Street to enquire if the school could use her barn. It was later described in a letter in the Norfolk County Archive as being 45 feet long by 18 feet wide, with a superficial area of 810 square feet, situated 500 yards from the school and half a mile from Gunton Station. It had no toilet facilities, but the committee were happy to put in two earth closets. The cookery classes would be for four weeks once a year, and the laundry for two weeks, also once a year. The barn was also to be used once a week for handicrafts. The rent was to be £12 a year. Mrs Watson agreed, as did the Education Committee.

By 1924 the Headmaster, Mr Jones, was unhappy with the arrangements and wrote to the Education Department about the unsatisfactory nature of the 'barn' with its leaky roof, ill-fitting windows and doors, and no heating.

He stated that "I consider it is at the very best an extremely poor makeshift and I have from time to time pleaded for an iron or wooden structure to be placed on school premises". He added that "even a railway coach would be better than what we have".

SOUTHREPPS SCHOOL AND COMMON.

14

LESSON XI.

Lentil or Pea Soup.

Ingredients.

Half a pound lentils or peas, one carrot, one turnip (small), one onion, one ounce of dripping, one ounce of flour for thickening, and two quarts of water.

Method. Wash the peas and soak overnight; prepare and slice the vegetables; melt the fat in a pan, add the vegetables and lentils; stir and cook in the fat for three or four minutes; add the water, bring to the boil and skim; simmer gently three hours, or until the vegetables are quite tender. Bruise the soup smooth with a spoon, or pass through a sieve or colander. Moisten the flour with a little milk or water, add to the soup gradually. Bring to the boil, cook for five minutes, season and serve.

Cost, 3*d.*: makes two quarts.

Bread, see page 9.

Dumplings, see page 12.

LESSON XII.

*Oatmeal Biscuits.

Ingredients.

Three ounces oatmeal (medium), three ounces flour, one ounce dripping, three-quarters ounce sugar, a pinch of salt, a pinch of carbonate of soda, one tablespoonful water.

Method. Mix the oatmeal and flour, rub in the fat, add the rest of the dry ingredients. Mix to a stiff paste with the water. Roll out and cut into biscuits. Bake fifteen minutes in a moderate oven. Cost, 3*d.*

LESSON XIII.

Boiled Meat (Fresh) and Broth.

Ingredients.

Two pounds neck of mutton, one carrot, one turnip, one ounce pearl barley, pepper and salt, one tablespoonful finely chopped parsley, boiling water to cover the meat.

Soup Making

soup is a liquid in which vegetables, meat, or bones have been cooked for a long time

cook very slowly for a long time

the longer and slower a soup is cooked the better it will be

cup up all the ingredients

Put in plenty of vegetables and salt to give the soup a good flavour

Keep the lid on the pan.

Use cold water when making a meat soup

A meat soup must never boil

Use boiling water when making a vegetable soup

The Norfolk Schools Cookery Book contained printed recipes and space for pupils to write their own notes, which were then marked by the teacher. Instructions in the book included advice on how to clean silver; this must surely have been to prepare them for a life in domestic service.

Norfolk Museums Service (Gressenhall Farm and Workhouse).

It is interesting to note that the girls had to attend on the 9th December, even though the school was closed for polling.

Boys' log 9th December 1910

From the turn of the century Norfolk produced a Norfolk Schools Cookery book.

These lessons continue annually over winter from 1920 to 1945, when the last reference is found. Former pupils have no recollection of cookery instruction after that date, but it is known that in the 1980s, when Mrs Anne Daniels was the school cook, she taught cookery in the kitchen of the school house.

Woodwork

The managers first wrote to the Education Committee enquiring as to their responsibilities regarding woodwork classes in 1919. The first

---

28th Nov.

14 girls are to attend a Laundry Class at the Barn' for two weeks. Teacher – Miss Irene Wilkins

9th Dec

Laundry class ended on the 9th

On Wednesday 7th the School was used as a Polling Station, but the girls attended the laundry class.

1937: The handicraft hut and the woodwork class.
The Southrepps Society, Bullimore collection.

lessons started on the 28th October 1921, and were for the older boys. They were conducted in the barn, on separate days from cookery and laundry.

A former pupil of the school remembers his woodwork classes in the 1940s in the handicraft centre. It had large windows, which folded in half across the middle, and one afternoon when kept in for detention he and another lad escaped out of these windows. Unfortunately the other pupil got his belt hooked on the window catch and was apprehended! Derek got clean away.

With the reorganisation of Norfolk schools in 1957, Antingham and Southrepps became a primary school and woodwork lessons ended. The handicraft centre stood empty, the tools were removed in 1966, and the hut was finally dismantled in 1983.

Gardening

In 1910 the managers discussed the possibility of setting up gardening classes, and the Headmaster was tasked with the job of finding a suitable plot of land as close to the school as

> The woodwork Centre is now to be open on three days a week i.e. Tuesday Thursday and Friday.
> On Tuesday (yesterday) 20 boys from Mundesley and Gimingham were here
> On Thursday there will be boys from Southrepps, Knapton and Bacton
> On Friday boys from Southrepps and Roughton.

As with the cookery and laundry, Antingham and Southrepps School was the local centre for woodwork. Boys came from Gimingham, Mundesley, Knapton, Bacton, Roughton and, in a later entry, from Ashmanhaugh as well.
School log 13th September 1950.

The logs record the fact that extra gardening lessons take place and one in particular relates the need for the lads to reach 20 hours tuition. This is believed to be so that they could get a certificate for employment purposes on leaving school.
Boys' log 23rd April 1913.

Mr Jones spent many hours of his own time preparing the allotment
for the use of the boys.
Boys' log 14th February 1917.

1926 pamphlet from Norfolk Education Committee with helpful advice on the subject of the school garden.
Norfolk Museums Service (Gressenhall Farm and Workhouse).

NORFOLK EDUCATION COMMITTEE.

County Education Office,

Shirehall, Norwich.

November, 1926.

To Head Teachers and Staffs of Elementary Schools.

SCHOOL GARDENS.

The Committee have recently received from the Board of Education their Report on School Gardens in Norfolk. In addition to a criticism of the school gardening work, it contains several useful hints upon the subject, some of which are embodied in the following:—

Time devoted to Gardening.

Two hours per week are usually allotted to practical work, but the same amount of time per week need not be taken throughout the year. Two hours per week are generally necessary in the early spring, but later in the year one hour may be sufficient. All teachers of school gardening are aware that it is not possible to carry out gardening operations strictly in accordance with a pre-arranged Time Table. When weather or soil conditions interfere with the work during the regular gardening period, the lesson should be taken at another time and a suitable entry made in the School log book.

Practical Gardening.

The Board's Report states, "A suitable range of vegetable crops is grown at nearly all the schools. At a few, such crops as tomatoes, marrows, leeks and celery are included. It is pleasing to find that many schools grow some fruit and that the number of these

possible. This was hired from Mr Temple at four shillings per annum. Unfortunately the location of the plot has not been found, but the school is surrounded by farmland.

Gardening was seen as important enough to have its own horticultural inspector. In the report for June 1913, after suggesting a small plot for the propagation of herbs, the inspector recommended that rhubarb should be established in the autumn. He also said there was no room for fruit or flower culture in the allotment. Mr Jones's response was to offer his garden for this purpose. The inspector urged the managers to accept the offer, which they did. The inspector also advised that one load of farmyard manure was needed for the winter crops.

The school received a grant, but only if enough hours of tuition were received, and the weather was not always obliging.

In 1926 the Education Board produced a four-page leaflet for schools, with advice on how the gardens and lessons should be conducted. It concluded with the need for the schools to supply felt slippers, which were to be made by the schools from the material supplied! These were to be worn in school to prevent mud being walked in.

Gardening continued but was no longer routinely recorded in the log books, apart from the occasional interesting entry such as this from 1955: "Messrs Boots invoice for 1 pkt Derris spray and 1 DDT distributor"; this was long before the insecticide DDT was banned in 1972.

Gardening was eventually taught to both the boys and the girls although it was not a risk-

The medals bought by the managers for Evening class student were inspected by the managers. A report on the work of the Class was read & Considered very satisfactory.

The managers paid for medals to be awarded for the evening classes.
Minute log 25th May 1911.

16th Sept | Miss Ayden commenced French lessons with all 8+ chn today. 9.30 am to 10.15am. Two grps first aged 9 and 10 numbering 17 Second. aged 8 numbering 20.

Miss Ayden was the peripatetic French teacher and was to remain so for many years, leaving in 1974. She was replaced by Mrs Randall.
School log 16th September 1968.

free lesson, as Marion Cooke could attest when she stuck a fork through the side of her big toe on the 21st October 1968, necessitating a trip to the doctor and a tetanus injection.

Evening classes

These were held in the winter months. In November 1899 the managers agreed to let Mr Clutterbuck of North Walsham Technical Education Committee hold a series of poultry-keeping lectures at the school, and in 1900 Mr Amies was given permission to hold evening classes. Nowhere is it made clear whether these were for adults or for existing school pupils. Subjects are known to have included music, singing and geography. The board at first accepted no responsibility for them. Perhaps the managers' attitude to evening classes changed after a positive comment by HM inspectors in 1911.

There are intermittent references to evening classes, the final one being the report of the first session of dress-making classes on the 22nd of September 1969.

The Workers Educational Association also held evening lectures weekly from October to December at the school during 1978 and 1979.

French Lessons

It is not really a vocational subject, but in 1968 French lessons started. These were taught across Norfolk.

In 1971 there was a school trip to Paris and in July 1974 a boules tournament was held at Roughton School. In 1975 17 children were taken to North Walsham cinema to see the French film 'Traffic', followed a month later by a trip to Holt Hall for a festival of spoken French. Miss Ayden returned in 1976 to teach two mornings a week.

Over the years the school also had peripatetic music teachers, teachers of country dancing, and cycling proficiency lessons from the local police constable. Similar activities continue today.

In the 2000s the pupils produced a magazine called The Ant.
courtesy of Janine and Dave Spanton.

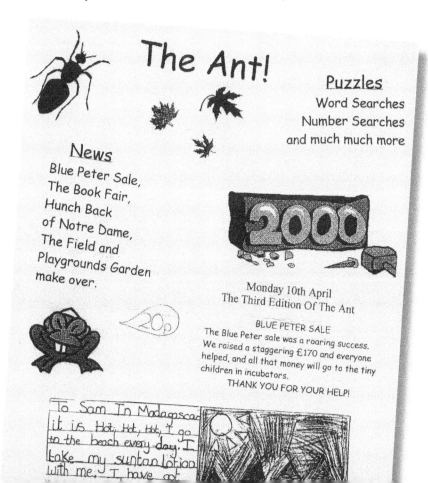

The Ant!

News
Blue Peter Sale,
The Book Fair,
Hunch Back
of Notre Dame,
The Field and
Playgrounds Garden
make over.

Puzzles
Word Searches
Number Searches
and much much more

2000

Monday 10th April
The Third Edition Of The Ant

BLUE PETER SALE
The Blue Peter sale was a roaring success. We raised a staggering £170 and everyone helped, and all that money will go to the tiny children in incubators.
THANK YOU FOR YOUR HELP!

To Sam In Madagascar
it is Hot, Hot, Hot, I go
to the beach every day. I
take my suntan lotion
with me. I have got

Recreation and sport

Playtime

The 1833 plan of the school shows one large playground to the rear. The flint wall separating the girls' playground from the Headmaster's garden was built in 1877. This was when the school was extended and it was probably then that the playgrounds were separated by gender. Plans from 1948 still show separate playgrounds for the boys and girls. It is likely that the advent of common car ownership, and the need for a staff car park, eventually saw the end of the boys' playground.

There are several interesting entries in the minute books relating to the children's playtime.

The first is from 8th November 1878 when the Board resolved that children not returning home at dinner hour were forbidden to play on the highways or the common, but were to remain in the school yard. This new rule appears in the log four days earlier, on the 4th November 1878: "that children should play on the playgrounds only at the dinner hour as the Board objected to them playing on the common". This was clearly passed by the Board

In October 1899 the Board is concerned about what the pupils do when in the playground. A Giant Stride is a maypole-like structure from which ropes or chains are hung; the hub at the top rotates and the children swing round on the ropes. There is no record of either a seesaw or Giant Stride being installed in the girls' playground; however, a Giant Stride was erected in the boys' playground on the 19th October 1900.
Boys' log 20th October 1899.

> 20th Oct. At the last Board Meeting it was thought that a Football might be obtained for the boys and a See-saw or Giant-stride for the girls.
>
> 27th Oct The football is having a good effect on the boys attendance.

The boys were clearly less than impressed with the new rules.
Boys' log 9th December 1878.

> 9th Several boys kept in on Monday afternoon for one hour for disobedience to the Board rule about playing on the common

George Gray. Two George Grays have been found to have lived in the area at this time. One went on to be a miller, the other disappeared from the records.
Boys' log 10th July 1885.

> On Thursday noontime George Gray fell from one of the trees in the playground and was severely hurt about the head. Warned all the boys that climbing trees in the playground must be stopped.

6th July.

Joan Dunham (born 15.10.44) cut her right leg below the knee-cap today in the dinner-hour. The accident occurred on the Common and not on School premises. The child apparently climbed on the step at the back of a stationary ice cream vendor's van, in spite of repeated tellings that no-child should do so. The van was stationary and the man in charge selling over the side counter. Joan stood on the back step in her eagerness to get some ice-cream, and in slipping off, her knee struck the abrupt end of the near-side rear bumper and she sustained a nasty gash immediately below the knee cap

Not only were the children allowed out on the common, but an ice-cream van would turn up at lunchtime to sell ice-creams to the children outside the school.
School log 6th July 1951.

retrospectively, so was probably decided by the chairman and then minuted.

The rules about playing on the common during dinner hour have varied over the years. Former pupils from their time at school in the 1930s and 40s recall being allowed to play on the common at the dinner hour, including climbing the trees.

The last references to the children playing on the common, and to separate playgrounds, are in 1957, although former pupils recall playing on the common in the dinner hour as late as the 1960s. They were also allowed to play on the public swings.

Physical exercise

The children's school activities included drill. This was the Victorian term for physical exercise (PE). It involved a series of formal exercises such as marching on the spot, arm swinging, trunk

Cricket team? This photograph from 1914 seems to be suggesting they may be a team, with the presence of the bats and the fact that all the boys wear ties and very similar outfits. It is totally unlike any other of the school pictures.
The Southrepps Society; Bullimore collection.

bending, skipping, etc. It was thought to help children follow instructions, improve coordination and health, and prepare them for work and military service. The lesson was led by the class teacher. After the First World War a drill instructor coordinator would visit the school to improve standards; this may have been in response to how unfit the nation had proved to be at the start of the war.

The school used the village recreation ground in Upper Street for organised sport. They would walk there up the footpath across the fields.

Former pupils also tell of using the sand pits on the common for long jump. In December 1969 the unsuitability of the sports ground in Upper Street was raised and the possibility of using part of the common was suggested; letters were sent both to the parish council and the Honourable Miss Harbord. Following a let-

ter from the chief education officer this option was not pursued. However, it was suggested that the farmer who owned the land surrounding the school should be approached, and in 1970 he agreed in principle to sell it. After delays, the sale was eventually agreed in 1972. There was then further delay following a disagreement about the height of the fence surrounding the new playing field, meaning that the school had to hold fund-raising events to pay for the extra height of fencing. It was not until May 1973 that a deposit was paid, and in July the field was ready for sowing. Finally, in July 1974, permission was given to hold sports day on the new playing field.

It is possible that the nature area and garden were also constructed at this time.

In 1972 the children started swimming lessons at Cromer Secondary Modern School. These ceased within the year, as the pool went

The Headmaster said that the County Education Authority were unable to provide goal posts for the playing field, and he had purchased timber, and was constructing them himself. It had been possible to purchase the timber with funds still available.

out of service. Lessons restarted at Mundesley School in 1975, and continue to this day.

Inter-school sports are not recorded in the log until 1984, when they played football, netball and softball.

The frequency of these matches increased when the school joined the North Norfolk Small Schools Federation. The fact that the Federation owned two mini-buses made transporting the children easier. They could also make use of the gym facilities at Gresham Village School, which was one of the schools in the federation.

The governors made an unsuccessful representation in 1986 under the 1980 Education Act for a Sports Hall to be built.

There are several references in the minute books from 1976 and again in the 1980s to children being taken on weekend camping trips to Holt Hall.

The annual school journey for year 6 pupils continues today. In 2008 the destination was Devon and the quickest and most cost-effective

way to get there was to fly to Exeter. On the return the direct flight to Norwich was cancelled and they had to return via Manchester! What would the original pupils have thought of that?

School's sports team from the c1940s.
The Southrepps Society; Bullimore collection.

Class of 2008 all set for takeoff at Norwich airport.
Thanks to Freja Duncan-Coates who is somewhere in the picture.

Diseases and health care

Communicable diseases were common: scarlet fever, measles, influenza, chicken pox/water pox, whooping cough, diphtheria, typhoid, polio, German measles and mumps all took their toll.

Scarlet fever

Scarlet fever (sometimes known as scarlatina) is a disease little heard of today, and if caught early is quickly and effectively treated with antibiotics. Its symptoms are sore throat, rash and fever, but its complications include infected sores, meningitis, pneumonia, rheumatic fever, and liver and kidney damage. For those who survived, these after-effects could have life-long implications. Its decline had begun before the 1950s and the age of the antibiotics, possibly due to mutation of the pathogen, but decreased crowding, improved hygiene and even milk pasteurization are thought to have all played a part, and this is certainly reflected in the reduction in references to it in the log books. The first reference found was on the 7th January 1880 in the Girls' log when three girls were ill with the disease.

There are sporadic references to small numbers of children being affected by the disease,

but in 1906 there was a major outbreak starting on 28th September, when two children were excluded from the school on the orders of the medical officer. By the next week three more families were excluded, the aim being to control the spread of the disease. More and more families were excluded until on the 12th October the whole school was closed for two weeks. When the school reopened in November, the attendance remained low as the children made slow recovery from the disease. The following year there was another outbreak necessitating the closure of the school. It started on the 2nd August and then continued through the harvest holiday break. The holiday was extended that year because of building work, not reopening until the 23rd October. The disease was still rife and the medical officer forced a further closure of two weeks from the 25th October.

1907/1908 was a poor year for illness, with both scarlet fever and measles being present in the community, striking again in the December, with half the infants absent. There were a few isolated cases of the disease in January 1908, and a single entry on the 22nd March 1935

Scarlet fever can have lifelong effects, as recorded here.
Infants' log 12th August 1908.

90

498

⅓th March. Nurse Chadwick called and swabbed throats of all children in Class 3, 4, 5

16th " Nurse brought results of swabbings. Gave Exclusion Orders for 5 children and issued penicillin chewing gum to 2 others.

20th " Nurse reports on swabs from 5 excluded children. They are all positive & must still be excluded.

21st " Dr. called & confirmed exclusion orders

23rd " Reported one more case of Scarletina and one contact with Scarletina. Nurse called and reported John Balkin may come back to school on Monday. Others are still showing positive swabs.

27th " Nurse called, reported that all children on whom E.Os were served, may return to School

The school nurse screens all the children for signs of disease and this time she dispenses Penicillin chewing gum to two children, but does not exclude them from school. Perhaps it was an early preventative measure.
Boys' log 13th March 1950.

recorded that the school was now closed until after Easter on account of scarlet fever.

Fortunately, scarlet fever disappears from the log books until 1946, when two children below school age were reported to have the disease. Their siblings were excluded from school by the medical officer to contain the outbreak and the whole school was screened as a preventative measure to reduce the spread of the disease. This positive response to controlling the spread of communicable disease is demonstrated again on 13th March 1950. Three cases of scarlet fever were reported to the medical officer, and the same day the school nurse came to the school to screen all the children for signs of infection.

The last reference to the occurrence of scarlet fever was in June 1957.

Measles

The infection that had the biggest impact on the school was measles, a highly infectious viral disease that can be fatal.

From 1880 to 1891 there are occasional entries recording small numbers of children absent on account of measles, at roughly two-yearly intervals. The much larger 1891 outbreak began on 16th January. On 20th February measles cases were being reported in both the Infants' and the Mixed school. Then on the 6th March the Board decided to shut the school, as from a roll of over 200 only 49 children were in attendance.

As is the nature of these diseases, all was quiet for a few years, but then in 1899 there was another severe outbreak, the first indication being on 27th February with the entry in the Infants' log of 12 children being absent. As increasing numbers of children were being infected, the managers consulted the medical authorities. As a result, the school was closed for a month on the instructions of the medical officer, Dr Richardson.

The disease continued to linger in the district for another month, with attendance being very poor.

The school reopened on the 5th April with the sad news that one of the Infant children had died as a result of complications following measles.
Boys' log 7th April 1899.

> **7th April** | The Schools re-opened on the 5th inst several children are still absent as the epidemic has not yet cleared off. V. Daniels died from an illness following measles. The school rooms have been thoroughly cleaned during the 4 weeks.

In 1911 a fresh outbreak was controlled, probably due to the prompt action of the medical officer. It was only the Infants' school that was closed.
Infants' log 28th March 1911.

> **March 28th** | Received order from the School medical officer to close the school because of the occurrence of a case of measles.
>
> **April 3rd** | School re-opened. No further cases have occurred, probably the result of such prompt measures on the part of the medical officer.

On this occasion it was the presence of both English and German measles that was reducing school numbers. German measles (Rubella) is a totally different viral disease.
School log 29th June 1956.

> **24th.** | School re-opened today. Attendance has suffered severely for the last five weeks because of an outbreak of measles, both English and German. Attendances have been:-
> Week ending June 1st.   79.8 p.c.
> "   "   "   8th   73.2 "
> "   "   "   15th   84.6 "
> "   "   "   22nd   87.7 "
> "   "   "   29th   85.6 "

In 1914 there was another epidemic of measles. Both the Infants' and Mixed schools were affected, but only the Infants' was shut. Starting on 8th June with six cases in the Infants', this then escalated so that on the 19th the Infants' school was closed for two weeks. The Infants' school was closed again on the 31st July, not opening again until after the Harvest holidays on 14th September. In the Mixed school they had cases of measles from May onwards, and on the 31st July Mr Jones contacted Dr Nash, the school medical officer, seeking to close the school as the attendance figures were very low. To his frustration, the Mixed school remained open.

The last time the school was shut due to measles and colds was for a week in 1941. Measles continued to occur, for example in 1956 when Mr Hare the Headmaster recorded the poor attendance.

Influenza

Another serious disrupter of the children's education was influenza. This is also a viral disease which can range from mild to severe, and can lead to death.

Throughout the logs there are references to the occasional case of influenza, but the enormous event that hit the school was that which affected the whole country, in fact the world, in 1918-1919.

The school was closed from 21st Nov 1918 until 9th December 1918 and promptly shut again as the attendance levels were even lower than prior to the earlier closure. It remained shut until after the Christmas holidays, reopening on the 6th January, after a break of over six weeks. Ten days after the school had reopened the attendance was still low and only 27 of the 71 children on the Infant roll were in school.

Three years later influenza was back, and in January 1922 the school was again closed, this time for ten days. It was not a good year at all for the health and education of the children; the Infants' school closed again on the 31st July until after the harvest holiday, due to whooping cough. The Mixed school suffered an unseasonal dose of influenza, causing them to shut early for the harvest holiday. The freedom for the school to choose its own holiday dates allowed Mr Jones to open the Mixed school early, on 25th August, a whole month ahead of the Infants'.

The whole school closed again because of influenza in March 1925, February 1927 and March 1932.

The first log entries for the pandemic are in November 1918, when members of staff are absent.
Boys' log 18th November 1918.

Miss Bent recorded on the return of the Infants that they appeared to have benefitted greatly from their long holiday (eight weeks) and are in good health now. This photograph was taken in the 1920s
The Southrepps Society; Bullimore collection.

Other infectious diseases

Other infectious diseases appear sporadically throughout the logs. Chicken pox was a regular occurrence. In 1902 a child is reported as suffering from typhoid, a bacterial infection spread by eating or drinking contaminated food or water. Fortunately this appears to have been the only case. Mumps, diphtheria and German measles all get an occasional mention. An episode of whooping cough in 1912 was severe enough to shut the Infants' school.

Poliomyelitis

Polio does cause a few ripples outside the school. Polio or Infantile Paralysis was a terrible disease that as the name suggests caused paralysis, not just of the limbs, but could spread to the muscles of the chest, making it impossible to breathe without mechanical assistance. There were never any cases in the school, but a mother did contract the virus and as a result her two children were excluded for a time. It took four weeks for the other villages to realise there had been a case of polio.

Fear of Polio was very real and could result in somewhat drastic if rather belated measures. There was a major outbreak in Britain during the early 1950s, so this reaction, if a little excessive, is understandable.
School log 3rd October 1952.

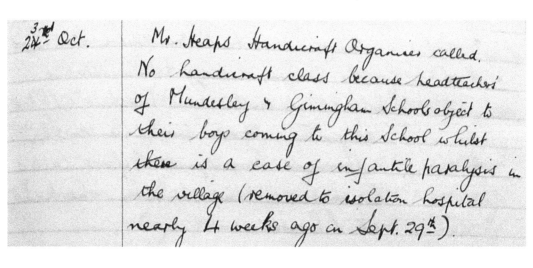

24^{3rd} Oct. Mr. Heaps Handicraft Organiser called. No handicraft class because headteachers of Mundesley & Gimingham Schools object to their boys coming to this School whilst there is a case of infantile paralysis in the village (removed to isolation hospital nearly 4 weeks ago on Sept. 29th).

School Medical Service

The School Medical Service was introduced in 1907. This was as a result of the Boer Wars when it was discovered that between 40% and 60% of army recruits were rejected on health grounds. Compulsory school medical inspections were recommended in 1903 but were not introduced until the 1907 Education Act made them compulsory, along with dental inspections and treatment. In 1913 the chief medical officer of the Board of Education estimated that of the six million children in elementary education in England and Wales:

10% suffered from a serious vision defect
5% had defective hearing
3% suffered from 'suppurating ears'
3% had adenoids or enlarged tonsils
50% had 'injurious decay of their teeth'
10% were dirty
2% had tuberculosis
1% had heart disease
1% had ringworm

Gillard D (2018) *Education in England: a history.*
www.educationengland.org.uk/history

Children's health was inspected, but before the establishment of the NHS in 1948 the implications could be serious if a problem was found.

The parents would have had to fund the treatment, and many would have been unable to do so.

Improved medical knowledge and public health interventions, combined with the arrival of vaccinations and close links with the school medical officer and school nurse, resulted in a marked decrease in childhood infectious disease. The first record for mass vaccinations being carried out in the school was in 1941, when the pupils were immunised against diphtheria.

In 1952 the board room was converted into the medical examinations room and there were then regular inspections of the children's health, both by the school doctor as well as from the school nurse. These continued well into the 1970s. A programme of Polio vaccinations was introduced in 1958.

Schools were very important in raising the health of the population in early screening. There are two references to Mr Hare taking children for X-ray screening for tuberculosis.

Dentistry

Initially the dental inspections were carried out by doctors, but after pressure from the dental profession they became the responsibility of dentists. The first reference found to the dentist visiting is not until 1914. Frequent references to

Virol was a by-product of the brewing industry, packed full of nutrients, including vitamins A, B and D, riboflavin, malt, sugar, egg, orange juice and refined fats.
Courtesy of Pauline Hull.

" 10th Dr. Douglas I.M.O. and Nurse Ives inspected about 50 older children and 50 infants on the 9th Mr. Learner called on behalf of the managers, and several parents attended.

In this extract from June 1910 it is interesting to note that Mr Learner also attended. He was one of the managers of the school.
Boys' log 10th June 1910.

20th July Nurse Flurmage (née Cole) called with Cod Liver Oil, Mallalene and Iron and Virol for six children.

Indeed, she was far from just being the nit nurse, also supplying tonics for under-nourished pupils.
School log 20th July 1953.

28th Nov. Head Teacher took two children to mass radiography unit at North Walsham.

How did he take them? Bus, train, or private car?
School log 28th November 1955.

annual inspections then appeared. There are several entries recording children being collected from school by the dentists' clerk and taken to Cromer for treatment.

With the advent of the NHS the general health of the pupils improved and the entries in the logs reduced. There is one from 1970 reporting that Dr McMurdo, the medical officer, had inspected the premises for a sanitary report.

The longest school closure for infectious disease occurred in 2020 when the school shut from March to September by order of the Government to control the pandemic of Covid 19. The school was open only for a small number of children whose parents were classified as keyworkers.

School meals

The provision of school meals became a very important way of improving children's health.

With the distances that some of the children walked to school many would have had to bring lunch with them. In 1899 the minutes record that a kettle was purchased for the use of children unable to go home on account of the distance.

The first of the school HM inspectors' reports for 1905 stated:

'As so many children stay to dinner some means should be adopted to provide a place where the food may be kept outside the rooms occupied by children during their school hours.'

A later report that year recommended fire guards; because so many children stayed for dinner the unguarded fires were dangerous. This seems to suggest that the children were unsupervised in the lunch break.

The 1903 government report found a link between lack of nutrition and poor health and estimated that about a third of children were malnourished. This resulted in the 1906 Education (Provision of Meals) Act which gave local authorities the power to provide free school meals. They were not compelled to do so, and there is no mention in the minute book or the log books that any were supplied at Antingham and Southrepps School.

The 1914 Education (Provision of Meals) Act extended local authorities' powers to provide school meals, but again this was not compulsory, nor were they free. There is some oral evidence that basic hot meals were supplied to the pupils in the 1930s and 40s.

As noted elsewhere the school did not acquire canteen facilities until 1946, although oral history again records that basic hot meals

It must have been a chilling sight for the children to see the arrival of the dentist's travelling van. It took several days to inspect and treat the children's teeth
Boys' log 15th April 1948.

This is a slightly alarming entry. Sadly, it probably refers to the children now identified as having additional needs. We have come a long way since then.
School log 21st July 1971.

The 100 children who remain in school for the mid-day meal are, at a small cost, provided with a nourishing hot drink.

In 1929 the school did provide a hot nourishing drink for the pupils. This is acknowledged in the HM inspector's report for that year.
Boys' log March 1929.

89

1956

3rd May '56   A child (Sally Ann Reynolds) aged 8) found splinters of glass floating in her milk (on the cream of course) this morning. The class teacher Miss Allen, showed them to the Head teacher who took them out and mounted them with cellotape on black paper. He also informed the School Medical Officer through the Local Health Office by telephone. The mounted splinters will be retained.

School milk does carry its dangers. There is no record of the outcome of the complaints or what happened to the splinters.
School log 3rd May 1956.

were cooked in the medical room. Indeed, there is a reference to the cook being absent in 1942.

The canteen cooked meals for the children and possibly for Northrepps School as well. In the 1970s the meals-on-wheels for Southrepps were also prepared there. The school kitchen was threatened with closure in 1981, as the number of children having cooked meals fluctuated, making it uneconomic to continue. The kitchen finally closed in 1985 when Mrs Fousler the cook left, although the canteen continued to be used by the children to eat their lunches. For those who were still having cooked meals, these were supplied by Overstrand School. The kitchen was renovated in 2014, when free school meals for early years pupils came into law.

School milk

Both the 1906 and the later 1921 Education Acts gave and extended the power of local authorities to supply free milk, but it was not until 1946 that provision of free school milk was made compulsory to the age of 18. This provision has gradually reduced over the years to it now only being supplied free to under-fives.

The school and agriculture

Agriculture played a very important role in the life of the school. Of the 177 families named in the log books from the period 1878–1917, census returns show that 101 were directly dependent on agriculture. 69 fathers were listed as either agricultural labourers or farm labourers, and there were 12 horsemen, teamsters or grooms, four farmers, four gamekeepers, three blacksmiths, two wagoners, two farm bailiffs, one farm steward, one dairyman, one market gardener, one maltster and one corn merchant. In some cases occupations changed between censuses.

Whilst it is difficult to draw a direct correlation between the data for fathers and their sons, what is very clear is that low paid agricultural work and associated trades remained the mainstay of the community up to at least 1914 and beyond. There were some emigrations to Canada and Australia, but nonetheless the vast majority of families stayed in the villages where they were born.

Where a woman's job is recorded she is usually single, and she is either a teacher or in domestic service. There is one record of a single mother being listed as an agricultural worker. That was Jane Pardon, born in Southrepps in 1837. The fact that no occupation was recorded did not mean that they were not an essential part of the agricultural work force, helping in the fields and with the harvest, in addition to running the home. The children would of course have helped in the home, in the fields and on the domestic plot.

The first mention of the part played by agriculture is the closing of the school on the 17th June 1878 for a half day for the Agricultural Show in North Walsham.

Trips to the Agricultural Show carried on intermittently throughout the life of the school,

16th School closed on 16th on account of two Club Feasts, and to allow teachers to see the Agricultural Show at Norwich

July 11th Rain and haymaking lowered the attendance Moved the classes to different groups of desks for convenience in using the classrooms. Oral Lessons. Sect.1. Paper making – Sect.II. Pins

" 18th Attendance lower – haymaking and club feast. Oral Lessons Sect.1. a Lead Pencil II. The Whale.

" 25th Attendance low – haymaking – Received permission to order reading books, maps &c.

with decades when there were none at all, and other times when the school closed for two days. In 1987 the school actually closed for three whole days, and then the trips came to a complete stop, to be reinstated county-wide at some point in the 2000s.

The needs of local agriculture dictated the start date and duration of the harvest holidays, and the school managers were responsible for these decisions. These tended to be for four weeks, the start dates ranging from as early as 31st July in 1896 to as late as 31st August in 1888. It was not unusual for an extra week to be added if the harvest was late or unfinished. Even when it became a council school this practice continued. In 1917, for example, the Headmaster consulted Mr Owles and Mr Learner, both managers and local farmers.

The absence of children during June for haymaking was an annual problem. Children over the age of 12 could apply for extra holiday to allow them to pick blackcurrants or lift potatoes, but they were limited to an extra two weeks.

As a result of wartime shortages, in 1918 the Government introduced an autumn blackberry-picking scheme, where in school hours the children would go out and pick the fruit, which was then sent to the 'Government jam-

making scheme'; pots of blackberry and apple jam were made to send to the serving soldiers. Other reports say that it was the juice that was sent to them, as it was high in vitamins and fibre.

With the mechanisation of agriculture and the changing attitudes to education, the influence the land has over school life has diminished, although farming is still an essential element of the working life of the villages.

Hay making in Southrepps.
The Southrepps Society; Tyler collection.

Sep. 24th During the blackberry season the following arrangements are made for each Tuesday and Thursday —
Commence secular instruction 9-10 am — recreation 10-15 to 10-35 close morning session 11-30 am. Commence afternoon work 12-40, recreation 1-40 to 1-55 — close 2-30 p.m. The schoolmaster will collect all the blackberries gathered and pay 3 per lb. for them.

The children were paid for the work, with the school receiving a cheque for the weight of fruit picked; that money was then divided up amongst the pupils.
Infants' log 24th September 1918.

The school and the two World Wars

There are surprisingly few entries about life in the school during the two wars, but they are poignant and interesting.

World War One

The outbreak of war does not warrant a mention in either of the log books or the managers' minute book. The first entry is however rather surprising, as it records that the army had commandeered the whole of the Infants' school without any prior warning. The reading room to which the pupils had been decanted was on the corner of Chapel Road and Pit Street, a quarter of a mile from the school. The soldiers were probably from the Norfolk Regiment, as villagers tell of them being billeted around the village.

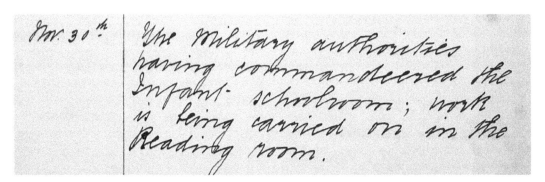

The army commandeers the Infants' school
Infants' log 30th November 1914.

Nov. 30th The Military authorities having commandeered the Infant schoolroom; work is being carried on in the Reading room.

The infant boys displaced by the army in 1914.
The Southrepps Society; Bird collection.

The Headmaster Mr Jones went to the education offices in Norwich the same day to discuss the billeting.

Within days, the Infants' school was relocated to Mrs Watson's barn on the corner of Chapel Road and Pit Street. This was the same barn that was later used by the school for cookery, laundry and handicraft lessons. The Mixed school continued to function as normal. However, did the girls continue to play on the girls' playground and use the toilet block in the corner? That wing of the school had only one exit directly onto the playground itself. The other doorway was into the Mixed school. It must have made the everyday running of the main school very difficult, not to mention the task of trying to teach 71 infants in a barn in winter! There was absolutely no reference to the impact on the children. Fortunately, it was not for too long, as Miss Bent reported that the infants had returned to the school on the 11th January 1915.

That was not to be the end of the matter; the school was considerably out of pocket due to the adaptations to the barn and then they received a demand to pay for the straw used by the soldiers! This was too much to be borne and the demand was referred back to the military authorities.

On the 7th March 1915 the Infants' log records the death in action of the husband of one of the teachers, Liena Montesole, née Roche.

On the 21st May 1915, the infant children gave forty-eight pennies to the Overseas Club towards comfort for the soldiers. This was a large sum of money from a poor rural school.

On the 10th September, the managers received a letter from Colonel Harrison of the Royal Army Medical Corps requesting to use two rooms of the school as a temporary military hospital. He had inspected the school with the chairman of the managers, and they felt that the school would be able to carry on without these two rooms, one large and one small. The managers sent the request to the Board of Education in Whitehall saying that in the very exceptional circumstances they intended to give

What makes this entry particularly sad is that they had only been married in September 1914. Second Lieutenant Eric Alfred Montesole of the Royal Sussex regiment was killed on 3rd March 1915. He is commemorated on the Loos memorial in Belgium.
Infants' log 7th March 1915.

There were lighting restrictions to prevent Zeppelin attacks, and also perhaps to conserve fuel. In 1916 the Summertime Act was passed, and the first day of British Summer Time (BST) was 21st May 1916. The original hours that the children attended cannot be found.
Minute book 7th October 1915.

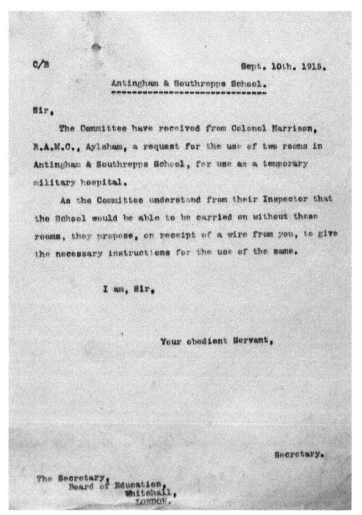

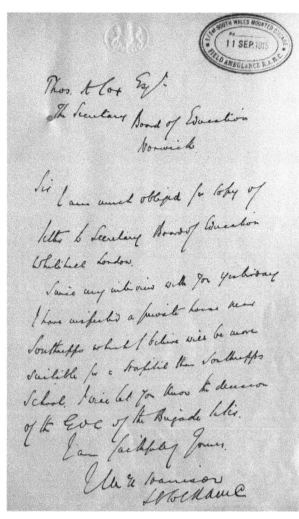

permission, if the Department of Education agreed. It is not clear which two rooms they had in mind; a guess would be the infant classroom and the babies' room, but this would require the children passing through these rooms to reach the playground and toilets. Would they have constructed a separate set of toilets for the injured soldiers? It seems very impractical.

On 28th September 1915, the Head-master informed the managers that he was considering joining the St. John's Ambulance Brigade as a result of the War Office appeal for 10,000 men. He asked them if they would keep his job open for him. The St. John's Ambulance Brigade had offered to make good the drop in salary that would occur. With great reluctance the managers agreed to his request, but only on condition that he thoroughly examined the pros and cons of such an action. As is evident from the school log books, he did not volunteer and, as entries elsewhere show, the children's educa-

tion would have been significantly poorer if he had gone to war.

Miss Bent records in the Infants' log the actions and death of several of her former pupils. Albert Hurn was born in Southrepps in 1895, the son of Leonard and Ann, and was an estate labourer before departing for war; he served in the Norfolk Regiment. He was discharged in 1917 following gunshot wounds to both legs. He died in Norwich in 1967.

Two former pupils are awarded medals. Arthur Hurn, who was born in Thorpe Market in 1899 to Walter and Hannah, received the Distinguished Conduct Medal. He also served in the Norfolk Regiment.

Sidney Greenfield was an 11 year-old lodger at Rectory Farm in Antingham in 1911. Details of his parents are unknown. This is the same address where Miss Bent herself lived. Sidney served in the Northumberland Fusiliers and was awarded the Military Cross.

Above left: Letter from the Board of Education agreeing to the army request that two school rooms could be used as a military hospital. Norfolk Record Office. GTN C/ED 68/12. 3/

Above: Fortunately, there was another letter from the Colonel thanking them for their assistance, and that he had since inspected a private house near Southrepps that he believed would be more suitable than the school. Overstrand Hall opened its doors as an Auxiliary Hospital in August 1916, so this may well have been the private house mentioned in the letter. Norfolk Record Office. GTN C/ED 68/12. 3/3.

The Military Medal was
instituted in March 1916
and awarded to non-
commissioned soldiers for
bravery on land.
Infant log 11th July 1916.

> June 19th
> July 11th | Re-Opened school.
> Albert Hurn son of Leonard
> Hurn has received the
> Military Medal for saving
> the life of an officer. Albert
> was a pupil in this
> school.

Two more former pupils
were awarded medals.
Infants' log 23rd May 1917.

> " 23 | Arthur Hurn an old
> scholar of this school has
> been awarded the D.C.M.
> Sidney Greenfield another
> old scholar has been
> awarded the M.C.

Sadly, this entry records the
death in action of a former
pupil.
Infants' log 25th May 1917.

> Timothy Gibbons an old scholar
> was awarded the military medal
> after his death in battle.

The final old boy to be
mentioned was Reggie
Drury, who was awarded
the Military Medal.
Infants' log 9th July 1917.

> July 9th | Reggie Drury has been awarded
> the Military Medal.

Timothy Gibbons was born on 4th May 1884 to William and Elizabeth in Thorpe Market. He served in the 8th Battalion Norfolk Regiment and died on the 19th July 1916. He is commemorated on the Thiepval memorial in France and the Thorpe Market memorial. His is the only death of a former pupil recorded in the log books, though not the only one that occurred.

Reggie Drury was born in Southrepps in 1898 to William and Ellen, the oldest of six children. He served in the Machine Gun Corps. He was listed as missing in 1918, but was then captured and made a prisoner of war. He transferred to the RAF and served in the Second World War as a regional flying officer. He died in Southrepps in 1973.

The school supported the war effort, even closing for half a day to allow the building to be used as a location for a sale of work for the War Workers' Association on Friday 23rd February 1917.

The war impacted on everyday school life in other ways. One huge issue was the warmth in the school.

The coldest temperature on the chart is 38° Fahrenheit (3° Centigrade) and the warmest 56° Fahrenheit (13° Centigrade). The children are unlikely to have had thick winter coats.

An oil-fired stove was supplied for that winter and the next. In 1912 Miss Bent pointed out that the open fire only heated one end of a very large room. The HM Inspector's report of 1912 commented on low winter temperatures, and by September 1913 hot water pipes had been installed in the main infants' room. How the water was heated is unclear.

Thermometer readings.

Date	nine o'clock	twelve o'clock
Nov. 27th	43°	52°
" 28th	44°	52°
" 29th	50°	56°
" 30th	46°	53°
Dec. 1st	46°	52°
" 4th	48°	52°
" 5th	48°	52°
" 6th	46°	54°
" 7th	46°	52°
" 8	42°	50°
Jan. 8th	38°	46°
" 17th	48°	48°
" 18	41°	46°
Feb. 2nd	40°	46°
" 5th	38°	46°

Feb 7th A large oil stove received for use during winter. By means of this stove the heat can be so regulated that the room can be kept at a reasonable warmth

Heating Apparatus   The Managers expressed regret at the action taken by the Education Committee in charging the parish with the whole cost of the new heating apparatus installed in the School. The Head Master was asked to furnish the Chairman with particulars as to the saving in cost of coal likely to be made as the result of the new system of heating

Miss Bent in particular was very concerned about the room temperature in the Infants' school, and back in the winter of 1911-1912 had recorded the weekly temperatures in the Infants' classroom.

It conjures the image of little children clustered round the open fire, which had only recently been protected by fire guards.
Infants' log winter 1911-12.

Fortunately for the pupils and staff of the school the managers were more concerned about their health than the Education Committee was. It had only taken Miss Bent seven years to get half-decent heating.
Minute book 7th February 1918.

*Back row L to R:
Albert Hurn, Cyril Gotts,
Ernest Bane, Charles
Hewitt, Robert Gotts,
Wilfred Hewitt*.*

*Middle row: John Hewitt,
Sam Burton-Pye, Sidney
Hewitt, William Burton-
Pye, Mr Pearson, Jack
Whitwood*, William
Rogers.*

Front row: Ernest Smith,
Major Burton–Pye*,
William Moy*, Herbert
Pitcher*.*

** denotes those later
killed in action.*

*Some of those named
appear in the log books
and some in the table in
the appendix to this book.
It is very likely that they all
attended the school.*
*The Southrepps Society
collection.*

*After the start of the war
the images on the
attendance certificates
changed from those of the
royal family to include Lord
Kitchener and, in 1917,
John Travers Cornwell, a
16 year-old posthumously
awarded the Victoria Cross
at the Battle of Jutland.*
*Norfolk Museums Service
(Gressenhall Farm and
Workhouse).*

*This moving entry recorded
that the whole school
observed the first Armistice
silence.*
Infants' log 11th November 1919.

In March 1917 she again complained to the managers that the rooms were insufficiently warm and her temperature charts were forwarded to the Education Committee with a recommendation that something needed to be done to remedy the situation. The Education Committee's response was that it was not a priority and could wait until the end of the war. The managers decided that this was not good enough: new heating was installed in October 1917, but the Education Committee refused to meet the cost.

The last reference to the war whilst the conflict continued was a Red Cross sale in February 1918.

World War Two

The first reference that occurs in the logs is the declaration of war and the immediate arrival of evacuees. This arrangement, though pre-planned, must have come as a shock. At least the winter term did not start until the 11th September, which gave the school a little time to work out how best to tackle the huge influx of 223 additional children.

From the reminiscences of some of the evacuees it is clear that they had no more warning than the receiving school. They had arrived at Dagenham County High School on the 2nd September, from where the children and their teachers were driven by lorry to Dagenham Dock. There they boarded the Golden Eagle and the Royal Daffodil, both paddle steamers, which took them to Great Yarmouth and Lowestoft. Here they were fed and each given a straw palliasse for the night, before being sent on by bus to the village hall at Southrepps.

The villagers came to choose which children they were happy to give homes to, the strongest looking boys being the first to be snapped up by the farmers. One evacuee recounts that he and his friend had been the last two children chosen by the Southrepps families. "When we first arrived we all stood in the school and the villagers came in to choose the children. After all the other youngsters had gone we realised no-one wanted us, so we had to be taken round the village to find a home to stay!"

One pupil of the time does not recall being taught with the London children so perhaps the

Mr Dack the Headmaster was very clear about what the war was about. War was actually declared on Sunday 3rd September. This enormous upheaval will surely excuse Mr Dack's confusion over the dates.
Boys' log 4th September 1939.

107

classes were separated during the morning session, with the older London children being taught in the afternoon. The numbers work out at 241 children being in school in the morning and 129 in the afternoon. The school roll had tripled overnight.

The large numbers of children attending the school would appear to have been a consider-able strain on all concerned, and in December a solution was found for the High School pupils to be taught elsewhere in the village.

Despite the older children now being taught at Hill House, 51 elementary children brought the number at the school to 185.

One of the evacuees remembers the lessons in the big house, and evenings being spent in

There were two groups of pupils working on a shift system. Mr Frost lodged with Mr and Mrs Dack in the school house. The other evacuee teachers must have lodged elsewhere.
Boys log 11th September 1939.

1939.   *426*

Monday 11th Sept. — School re-opened after Summer Holiday working on a Shift System. Southrepps children (137) plus 94 Elementary Evacuees attending in the morning & Dagenham County High School (Hd. Master. Mr. E. Frost.) attending in the afternoon. Staff. Existing Staff + 6 Evacuee Teachers.

Reference has been found to air raid precautions but unfortunately there are no further details of these initial plans.
Minute log 7th November.

Correspondence relating to A.R.P. & Evacuees was read & commented upon.

The elementary school children and the high school pupils were separated as the older pupils' education continued at Hill House in Pit Street.
Boys' log 4th December 1939.

4th Dec — Dagenham County High School has now removed to Hill House. & today normal morning and afternoon sessions were commenced. Staff now reduced to seven. Three evacuated teachers have returned to Dagenham and are engaged in house-to-house teaching. no. on Bks. 185.

427

1939.
Friday
22nd Dec.

School closed at noon today for Xmas Holidays. On Monday, Tuesday, Wednesday & Thursday of this week parties were arranged for the children of this school together with all elementary & secondary evacuees living in & around Southrepps.

Four Christmas parties were arranged for all the school pupils.
Boys' log 22nd December 1939.

With regard to A.R.P. Mr. Dennis proposed & Mr. Grimes seconded that if time permitted the older children should shelter in the natural trenches on the common in the event of serious bombing.

Following on from the earlier ARP report this raises an interesting question; where were the younger children to shelter?
Minute book 10th May 1940.

Southrepps Home Guard
Back row L to R: David Lawrence, Walter Hurn, George Punchard, Ted Burton, Herbert Hurn, Reggie Hurn, John Gotts, Sid Hardingham
Seated: Sam Burton, Ernie Plummer, Sid Hewitt.

the village hall, supervised by a teacher. Another recalled that "our speech and backgrounds were totally different. My council house had electricity, gas, running water and a bathroom". The semi-detached cottage in Lower Street where she was billeted had "oil lamps, kitchen range, a pump in the back yard and outside lavatory".

Fortunately, no bombs fell on Southrepps. There were some zig-zag trenches dug on School Common for training the Home Guard; these are still visible today.

Dispensation was given to children to help with harvest and they were actively encouraged to assist. For example, there was a two-week

After nine months the last of the evacuees returned home.
Boys log 3rd June 1940.

Victory in Europe day.
Boys log 8th May 1945.

Victory in Japan day.
Boys' log 12th October 1945.

currant-picking holiday in July 1943, and on 21st Sept, 16 children started lifting potatoes. Apart from these two entries about the end of hostilities, the logs make no other reference to the war.

A group of former evacuees returned to the village in September 1989 on the 50th anniversary of their evacuation. The plaque that was presented to the village can be seen in the village hall.

In the index pages of the boys' log book, this entry was found. There follow the names and addresses of 28 evacuees and one teacher, Mr Mackenzie the woodwork master, who had been sent to Southrepps.
Boys' log page J in the index.

16 - 9 - 89. The evacuees from Dagenham visited the school today in view of the 50th anniversary of the outbreak of the war this year.

Names & Addresses of those visiting Southrepps.

8th June, 1946

TO-DAY, AS WE CELEBRATE VICTORY, I send this personal message to you and all other boys and girls at school. For you have shared in the hardships and dangers of a total war and you have shared no less in the triumph of the Allied Nations.

I know you will always feel proud to belong to a country which was capable of such supreme effort; proud, too, of parents and elder brothers and sisters who by their courage, endurance and enterprise brought victory. May these qualities be yours as you grow up and join in the common effort to establish among the nations of the world unity and peace.

George R.I.

All school children throughout the country were given a copy of this letter from the King.
Southrepps Society collection.

150th Anniversary

The school marked the 150th anniversary of its founding in July 1976. The original doorway to the former managers' room at the front of the school had been bricked up in a rather unsightly manner and so for the anniversary it was decided to face it with knapped flint and inset the dates of the school in the space above. It was built by Mr Collier of Warren Road, Southrepps. The dates are still visible, but the flints have been replaced with a doorway, which was made to access the new oil boiler in 1977.

Letters were written from the governors asking for donations of £5 and a coffee evening was held at Antingham Village Hall, as well as a Jumble sale at the school, to pay for the alterations. The Parish Councils of Thorpe Market and Southrepps are known to have made donations. The owner of Templewood at the time, who was a Fellow of Royal Institute of British Architects, wrote congratulating them on the flint infill, and how it was refreshing when trouble was taken to preserve the character of a building he had long admired. His family had always known it as "the college".

Parents, governors and former staff members were invited to the celebrations of singing,

L to R: John Grey (Wellington), Joanne Bowles, Jennifer, William Almey (Eamonn Andrews), Robert Pike, Nikki Klokskov (Napoleon), Mark Williams, Robert Eastern (Nelson).

112

The Infants also performed for the guests.

Judging by this letter the Infants' performance must have been about Noah, and truly memorable.

sports and gymnastic display as well as a 'This Is Your Life' performance starring Napoleon Bonaparte. This was later repeated at an inter-school drama competition. Teas were also served, as at any good school celebration. The dedication of the panel was carried out by Mr David Coatesworth MBE, M.Sc (tech), C.Eng., F.I E. E., M.B.I.M., County Education Officer, as carefully recorded in the log book.

One of the thank-you letters received by the school congratulated the school cook on her beautiful floral arrangements.

The children were all presented with commemorative mugs and at least one is still being used today.

THE PASTON SCHOOL,
NORTH WALSHAM,
NORFOLK.

5 July 76

Dear Headmaster,

Thank you for inviting me to your celebrations last Friday afternoon. I enjoyed coming and seeing and hearing everybody; I felt the singing of Mr. Noah and his Helpers was especially interesting.

Yours sincerely,

Michael Hare

Appendix

This section contains the following tables:

His and Her Majesty's Inspectors' reports: These are the transcribed Inspectors' reports that appear in the log books from 1878 to 1961. They give a fascinating insight into the life of the school and what was deemed important by the Inspectors. Some of them give a glowing account of the education available; others worry about the ventilation.

Date Table: A list of events that have occurred in the life of the school from the log and minute books. Some are mentioned in the text, but for others this is the only reference.

Staff: This lists all the staff who have worked at the school from the first Headmaster until the 1980s. It gives their post and duration as well as any additional information that has been discovered about them.

Ida Watts, known affectionately by the pupils as Ida Spider Dirt Track Rider. She was a teacher at the school from 1927 until 1941.

Southrepps Society; Reading collection.

Pupils: This extensive table is a record of the children who attended the school. The school registers did not survive, so these are the names that appear in the log books from 1878 until 1918. The information regarding the individual families comes from public records available on the internet and may not be completely accurate. Nor is it complete, as there are a small number of pupils who could not be traced at all. It is probably safe to assume that all the siblings also attended the school, and in some cases the family line can be followed down through a generation. There may well be errors when it is a common local name. The language used in the school logs is of its time, and in the case of children who struggled with their education, the terms used may be unacceptable today. Although the majority were born locally there is an interesting geographical spread across the country. The families were much bigger than now, the majority living to adulthood, but there was still a high number of maternal deaths and those of children dying in childhood. After 1911 it is very difficult to trace people, as census records are not yet available. From that time the number of individuals actually named in the log books diminishes considerably. There are a few duplicated entries when it is unclear which child is being referred to.

Whole school photograph from the 1900s.
Southrepps Society collection.

Appendix: HMI School reports transcribed

Date	His/Her Majesty's Inspectors Report

1878

Boys' School

The school is orderly, and classification careful, and a good beginning of work has been made. The weights of the ventilators are dangerous and should be altered. The windows open inconveniently for ventilation. The supply of reading-books will be insufficient for the coming year. General improvement will be expected in all Departments next year if a deduction is to be avoided under article 32(b).

Girls' School

School visited by me Francis Synge. Some efficient help is much needed without delay. I do not see how it can be managed under present circumstances except by an assistant teacher qualified under Art 79. More bks needed.

Infants' School

School visited by me Francis Synge. 65 children present. Only 51 marked on registers. Time table should be drawn up without delay and section seven of the Education Act hung up. Door should not be bolted.

Neither discipline nor instruction in this school are as yet satisfactory. A gentler manner and the help of at least some efficient monitors are needed.
Blinds are wanted. The weights of the ventilators are dangerous and should be altered. A urinal should be provided for the boys.

1879

Boys' School

The boys are as yet in low standards but have done their work well. Arithmetic is intelligently taught and the boys knew their geography well.
Staff: W. E. Amies, Second Class; F. Richardson, Assistant

Girls' School

The School is orderly, the classification careful, and a good beginning of work has been made. The help of an assistant teacher is needed for the present and monitors who will ultimately be apprenticed are needed also for a future staff. The supply of reading books will be insufficient for the coming year.
The windows open inconveniently and the weights on the ventilators are dangerous and should be altered.
I am to request your attention to Article 32(c) in the case of the Girls' school. The staff is at present insufficient. General improvement will be expected in all Departments next year if a deduction is to be avoided under Article 32(c).

1880

Boys' School

The teaching continues to be intelligent and the boys have done their work well. A good deal of the building work seems to have been badly done and to be in a dangerous condition. The Registers should be checked at least once a quarter by managers in accordance with the Regulations of circular 65.
Staff: Will. E. Amies Head teacher; Fred. Richardson assistant teacher.

Girls' School

The school is being conducted in a quiet and orderly manner and the children have passed a very fair examination, though as yet low in Standards. The supply of reading books is insufficient. The windows noticed last year have not been altered and should be without delay.

Infants' school

The school has been little more than a month under the present teacher. The children are very backward and the order is not yet as good as it ought to be. The help of efficient monitors is much needed. Blinds have not yet been provided and will be much needed when the hot weather comes.

1881

Boys' School

The teaching continues intelligent and the boys have done their work well, and answered well in geography.

Girls' school

The school has passed a fairly good examination. The buildings are in an unsatisfactory condition. The geography is passed with hesitation.

The school is doing good work, it is quietly conducted and the children do their work very creditably as to style, accuracy and intelligence. Both needlework and geography were good also the singing.

The Girls' school is amalgamated with the Boys' school

Infants' school

This little school has improved during the year, but there is still room for improvement both in order and instruction. The registers should be checked by managers in accordance with the regulation of circular 65.

The attendance has been even more irregular than in previous years, but the school is fairly conducted and taught. The children should be taught to work without copying or counting their fingers. A clock that will go is needed.

1882   Mixed school

The year has been a difficult one owing to the change of organisation, but the children have done their work very fairly, and the teaching has been intelligent. The needlework grant is recommended with hesitation as much of the work was poor and the girls were presented in low stages.
Staff: Will. E. Amies C. M.; Fredk. W. Richardson, assist. Master; Annie Chapple, assist. Mistress

Infants' school

The year has been a difficult one owing to the introduction of first standard into the infant room. The school is on the whole tolerable, but in several points needs improvement.

1883   Mixed school

The children have passed a fair examination on the whole. Though most of the teaching appears to have been intelligent, there are a considerable number who have failed or barely passed, especially in arithmetic. The buildings are in a dangerous condition and need immediate attention.
Staff: W. E. Amies C. M.;F. W. Richardson A. M.; Charlotte Watson A.M.

1884   Mixed school

The order is very fair and the children have passed a fair examination on the whole, but the work of the second standard is poor, and the arithmetic of the fourth standard. Recitation was very fair, but grammar was too poor for the grant to be recommended. The boys answered well on the whole in geography and the needlework is very fair. Most of the locks are out of order.
Staff: W. E. Amies C.M.; F. W. Richardson A.M.; Char. Watson A.M.

Infants' school

The school has changed teachers during the year; both discipline and attainment are very poor. The school should be conducted with much less noise. The children should be taught to add up without counting on their fingers.

1885   Mixed school

The work done in this big school is barely fair, and the discipline is not good. The grammar is so weak in the third and fourth standards that the grant cannot be recommended as the recitation is also poor. The list of representation is very large, but it does not appear the children are fit for higher work. The merit grant is recommended with some hesitation.
E.M. Amies has passed fairly.

Infants' school

Discipline and attainment are still poor in this school. The work of the first standard was especially poor. The pupil teacher has yet everything to learn as to the teaching and management of her class. E.M. Amies has passed fairly but should attend to teaching. The issue of a certificate to Miss Trollope is deferred for a more favourable report.
Amount of grant £140 13s.

1886   Mixed school

The condition of the school is only just fair. The long illness of the master has been a great disadvantage: owing, no doubt, a good deal to this, the order in the upper half of the school is still unsatisfactory. There was again a very long list of children represented in the same standard. The first standard did poorly in all their work: the other standards fairly except in arithmetic, which was below fair in the third, fourth and sixth standards. English was just good enough for the lower grant, but the third and fourth standards did badly in grammar: Geography was quite below the mark, except in the top class. Needlework and singing by note were well done.
E.M. Amies has passed fairly. She should be informed that she is now qualified under article 50, but not under article 52.
G. Amies' attainments do not qualify him for a shortened term of apprenticeship.

Infants' school

The number of children in this school is much too great for a single teacher, and the standard of discipline and instruction in all subjects is still low. Some efficient help should be given to the mistress without delay. The issue of a certificate to Miss Trollope is deferred for a more favourable report.

The mistress of the Infants' department is still without efficient help. The attendance is very unsatisfactory, only 46 children in average attendance out of 80 on the books. The elementary work and object lessons were fairly done; Singing by note good. On the whole there is a distinct improvement.

1887 **Mixed school**

The school seems to have suffered much from the change of teachers during the year. It seems to need some drill and better discipline and to be conducted with more energy. The merit grant and the grant for geography are recommended after a good deal of hesitation. Needlework seems to need more time. The exception schedule should have more careful attention from the managers.

Staff: W. E. Amies H. M.; Hector E. Suffling asst. M.; Lizzie Craig asst. Mist.; George Amies P. T.

Infants' school

There are a great many children over seven in this school who are not up to the work of the first standard. This is partly due to their late admission and partly to the want of efficient help. If the children really were Infants then the work might be considered very fair. As it is, the merit grant is recommended with a good deal of hesitation, and only because the mistress has done her work satisfactorily. Children over eight should not be retained in the Infants' school.

1888 **Mixed school**

The order is only fair and the children have passed a fair examination. The third standard should write without double lines, and writing altogether should be better. The room should be coloured not whitewashed.

G. Amies has passed fairly, but should attend to teaching.

Staff: W. E. Amies Hd. M; H. E. Suffling A. Master; L. S. Craig A. Mistress; G. Amies P. T.

Infants' school

The children still enter very late into this school and the mistress having only a monitor to help her cannot properly teach all that attend in the summer. She has done her work fairly under the circumstances, and the object lessons and singing by note were good. The merit grant is again recommended with much hesitation as the children are backward for their age.

1889 **Mixed school**

The children have passed a fair examination in the elementary subjects, and the results differ little from those obtained last year. Arithmetic, both oral and written, is weak, and there is much counting instead of adding. Reading needs more expression, and the second standard is backward in all subjects. Copybooks need more supervision. English and geography are both fair, and needlework is very fair. I am glad that the managers propose to improve the appearance of the school by colouring the walls, as recommended in the last report.

Infants' school

Though the children over seven in the first class are very backward owing to the late age at which they were admitted the other children have been fairly taught and the school is improving.

1890 **Mixed school**

The school shows improvement. The order is fairly good, and the children have passed a fairly good examination on the whole. But the reading is poor in the lower standards and also the arithmetic, and the children in the second standard should be taught to add without counting. Grammar is week in the fourth standard. The registers especially the admission register, should be completely kept. The classroom is mostly overcrowded and should be better ventilated.

G. Amies Teaching. He should be informed that he is now qualified under art.50, but not under article 52.

Staff: W. E. Amies Head Master; H. E. Suffling Asst Master; E. Alcock Asst Mistress; E. W. Watson P.T.

Infants' school

Writing and object lessons have been well taught, but reading should be better and number is only fair. The late age at which most of the children begin to attend is still a drawback to this school. The children's names should not be removed from the registers on account of absence unless the managers have ascertained that the children have left the school or neighbourhood.

J.H. Amies has passed fairly but should attend to spelling and geography.

1891 **Mixed school**

The order is fairly good on the whole. The work generally both in the elementary and class subjects is good, but the reading and recitation are wanting in style and expression. Sewing is good on the whole but in the first standard, hemming and knitting need attention, and in the third standard, group A, the tape should be placed at one end and not at the top of the band.

E. W. Watson has passed well, and H.J. Amies fairly.

Mr Suffling will receive his certificate in due course.

Staff: W. E. Amies Headmaster; H. E. Suffling Asst master; R. Alcock Asst mistress; E. W. Watson P.T. 2nd Year.

Infants' school

The Infants' school is in good order. The classification is somewhat low for the ages, but the children have long distances to come to school. The elementary subjects are on the whole fairly taught, handwriting is well taught. Object lessons and varied occupations are carefully taught. Sewing is good.

J.H. Amies has passed fairly.

1892 Mixed school

Order is fairly good. Writing is well taught, and copy-books are satisfactory, but paper work in examination might with advantage be neater. More expression and intelligence should be shewn in reading and recitation. With the exception of the points noticed above, the work in elementary subjects is satisfactory. English, geography, and needlework are successfully taught.

E. W. Watson has passed fairly

Staff: W. E. Amies Head Master; H. E. Suffling asst Master; R. Alcock asst Mistress; E. W. Watson P.T.; M. Atkins monitoress.

Infants' school

The order is good and the instruction is very fair on the whole. Needlework and varied occupations are very praiseworthy. Reading and arithmetic need attention, but writing is good.

Staff: E. C. Soames Headmistress; J. H. Amies P.T.; R. E. Thain P.T.

1893 Mixed school

The school is in good order and the children have passed a very fair examination in the elementary and class subjects. Reading and recitation are still lacking in expression. Spelling is weak in the fourth standard and arithmetic in the V and VI standards. English is weak in the fourth and fifth standards, and must improve if the grant at the higher rate is to be recommended in the future.

The roof at the junction of the main room and the classroom shows signs of settlement: it should be seen to. The boys' offices are dark. The girls' cloakroom should have more pegs, and the classroom should not any longer be used as a cloakroom. The ventilation in the two classrooms is too low: some of the higher windows should be made to open as ventilators. The indentures of the pupil teachers were not at school. The registers should be tested at least once in each quarter.

In a special report on the premises, H.M. Inspector states that the ceiling should be removed in the boys' offices, which for light and ventilation should be made open to the roof. The classrooms he points out are inconveniently shaped (rule 7(a) of schedule VII of the code) and he adds that the roof at the joining of the classroom and the main room shows signs of settlement. My Lords particularly request the attention of the managers to these defects and I am to refer them to the enclosed form 69. E. W. Watson Mathematics.

Staff: W. E. Amies Headmaster; H. E. Suffling asst master; R. Alcock Asst mistress; E. W. Watson P.T. 4th yr; M. Atkins P.T. 1st yr

Infants' school

The order is good and the instruction generally satisfactory. Ethel Thain has passed fairly.

Staff: E. C. Soames Headmistress; R. E. Thain P.T.

1894 Mixed school

The discipline on the whole is kindly, though somewhat wanting in precision. In the first standard the order is rather weak, and (probably in consequence of the lack of adult assistants) the attention of the children is hardly so well sustained as it might be. The character of the instruction generally is creditable in the circumstances, though some weakness appears in the arithmetic of the fifth standard. In English, though the third standard did well, the answering should be more general and more intelligent. Geography and needlework are both satisfactory: a compass should be obtained.

Infants' school

The discipline is very fair, and the instruction generally fairly satisfactory, though improvement may with advantage be effected in the methods of teaching reading and arithmetic. The full educational value of the kindergarten employments seems scarcely to be realised.

R.E. Thain has passed fairly but must attend to geography and history.

Staff: H. L. Tilney Mistress; R. E. Thain P.T.; B. Watson (Art 33).

1895 Mixed school

The order and instruction are, on the whole, satisfactory, the weakest part of the instruction being in the 1st standard which has been taught to a great extent by a young candidate. This is a defect in the organisation which should be remedied in the future. English is fair and geog. satisfactory. The schedules should be completely prepared.

Infants' school

Both discipline and instruction have improved. The children are fairly bright and attentive, and the varied occupation and object lessons are given with a creditable degree of intelligence and success.

R.E. Thain has passed fairly but must attend to music theory and arithmetic.

Miss Tilney will receive her certificate in due course.

My Lords have sanctioned on the special recommendation of Her Majesty's Inspector the omission of the annual inspection of the Infant department of your school, due in June 1896.

Staff: H. L. Tilney Mistress; R. E. Thain 4th yr P.T.; B. Watson 1st yr P.T.

1895 **Report of Diocesan Inspector**
The order, discipline and general tone of the school are excellent. Throughout the several standards there is evidence of honest and careful instruction on the part of the Head Teacher and his staff. The children by their intelligent and ready answers in the portions of the Old and New Testament presented for examination show an interest in their work, and that labour has not been misspent on them. The scripture repetition was given with care and accuracy, as were also the Lord's prayer the apostles' creed and the 10 commandments. The satisfactory attendance on the day of the religious examination deserves to be specially mentioned.

1896 **Mixed school**
The discipline is satisfactory, but the organisation of the school is not good as the teacher in charge of the first and second standards has too many children under her. The instruction has improved in many respects though spelling in second standards is weak.
M. Atkins has passed well.
Staff: W. E. Amies Head Master; E. Hammond Asst Mistress; J. H. Amies Asst Mistress; M. Atkins P.T 4th yr; K. Amies P.T. 1st yr

Infants' school
Good methods are employed, the children are interested and the instruction continues to improve. The order is satisfactory. Additional pegs are wanted in the cloakroom for the infants. R.E. Thain is recognised under article 50 of the code
B. Watson – Spelling*
Staff: H. S. Tilney Mistress; Bessie Watson pupil teacher 2nd year.

1897 **Mixed school**
The school is in an orderly state and instruction is given in a satisfactory manner. The syllabus and records should be fuller. Care must be taken not to allow the classes for collective lessons to be too large. The school requires more frequent sweeping.
G. Amies is recognised under article 50 of the code. Katie Amies 'Below fair'. Geog. & Hist.
The annual inspection due in June 1898 is omitted.

Infants' school
The infants are nicely taught.
Present staff: J. H. Amies Temporary mistress; Bessie Watson P.T. 3rd yr.; Bessie Watson. Passed fairly (Handwriting).

1898 **Mixed school**
The children are quiet and attentive, and have been taught with creditable success. In class subjects there is improvement. The rooms are swept only twice a week and owing to the general untidy and dirty state of the premises mentioned in last year's report, it is impossible to recommend the higher grant for discipline (art 101b of the code). The walls should be coloured and the lower parts wainscoted.
The necessary improvements in the cleanliness of the premises of the Mixed school should be made without any further delay.
L.M. Clements is recognised under article 68 of the code subject to furnishing a satisfactory medical certificate on the enclosed form.
Staff: W. E. Amies Hd Master; E. M. Bolton Asst Mistress; M. Atkins Asst Mistress; K. Amies P.T. 3rd yr; A. Kimm P.T. 1st yr
L. M. Clemments art 68

Infants' school
Order and instruction are, on the whole fairly good, but simultaneous answering must be discouraged. The registers should be tested at least once in each quarter by the managers.
Staff
Naomi Bent C.M.
Bessie Watson P.T. 4th yr.

Scripture report
Old Testament – very good
New Testament – very good
Repetition – very good
General Remarks
Having examined this school on Thursday 16th day of June I beg to report that the religious instruction in this school is of a very satisfactory kind, and that it fully maintains its high standards of excellence both as regards efficiency and discipline. The children answered readily, and gave with accuracy portions of the scripture prepared for repetition. The V. VI. & VII standard written papers were very creditable. The moral tone of the school is good.

1899 Mixed school

The condition of the premises has been greatly improved during the past year, and the general neatness and order justify the recommendation of the higher discipline grant. The instruction on the whole is very creditable; English, however, should be taught more intelligently especially in the upper standards and the children encouraged to apply the knowledge they acquire for themselves, or the higher grant for this subject can hardly be recommended another year.

L. M. Clements is recognised under art 68 of the code, subject to her furnishing a satisfactory medical certificate on the enclosed form.

Staff: Head Master W. E. Amies; Assist. Mistress M. Bolton; Assist. Mistress M. Atkins; Art 68 L. Clements P.T.; 4th year K. Amies; P.T. 2nd year A. Kimm.

Diocesan Inspection

Old Testament – very good

New Testament – very good

General remarks

The teaching throughout the school is painstaking and thorough. The children have shown an intelligent knowledge of the holy scriptures, and their answers both in the Old and New testament portions of the syllabus were very good. The scripture repetition deserves special recommendation. The order and discipline are very good and the general tone of the school excellent.

Infants' school

Discipline is good and instruction on the whole very creditable, but care must be taken that it does not become mechanical. More music and brightness in the conduct of this department would be an advantage. Space for marching etc is limited, and the gallery disproportionately large. If part of it were removed more space would be gained and the disadvantage of two large and somewhat noisy classes being conducted in too close proximity considerably obviated.

Staff: Naomi Bent C.T.; Bessie Watson ex P.T.; Madge Amies monitoress.

1900 Mixed school

Discipline at the second inspection was fairly satisfactory, and the children appeared less inattentive. The instruction on the whole is fair, but the supervision of the school is unmethodical and reports on examinations are not duly made. The children do not read or speak with sufficient distinctness, and English should improve to deserve the higher grant.

L. Clements is continued under art 68 of the code. E.M. Betts is recognised under that article, subject to her furnishing a satisfactory medical certificate on the enclosed form.

Staff: W. E. Amies Head Master; A. M. Hall Assistant Mistress (50); L. Clements Assistant mistress (68); E. M. Betts Assistant Mistress (68); K. Amies Assistant Mistress (68).

Infants' school

The infants are under good discipline, and instruction is creditable.

Staff: Naomi Bent C.T; Bessie Watson ex P.T.; Madge Amies Monitoress.

1901 Mixed school

The children are orderly. They are taught in a painstaking manner and creditable results are obtained.

Staff: W. E. Amies C.M. Headmaster V, VI, VII; A. M. Hall art 50 Assistant IV & drawing; E. M. Betts art 60 III; L. Clements art 60 I, II.

Infants' school

Discipline is satisfactory, though somewhat lacking in smartness. Instruction is fairly successful, but is given in a mechanical and uninteresting manner.

Staff: Naomi Bent C.T.; Bessie Watson P.T.; Madge Amies. Candidate.

1902 Mixed school

The school is in a satisfactory state of efficiency: and with the present staff should do well in the future. Insufficient time is devoted to physical training.

Staff: W. E. Amies C.M. Section I; Dennis Burton C.M. Section II; Lily Clements art 68 Section III.

Infants' school

The assistant under article 68 teaches the needlework of the older girls and by this work is taken away from the infants several times during the week. At the latter part of the school year when the school is full, this arrangement is unsatisfactory as the discipline suffers owing to want of sufficient staff. Probably the adoption of an educational year ending March 31st would remedy this difficulty. The infants are fairly well taught on the whole, but the discipline (owing to the reasons above stated) was not satisfactory.

| 1903 | **Becomes a board school under control of the local authority.** |

| 1903 | **Mixed school** |

The discipline is good and work carried on steadily and effectively.
Separate cloakroom accommodation is required for the girls.
Staff: W. E. Amies Headmaster; D. W. Burton Cert. Asst; Lily Clements art 68;
Gertrude Leman Art 68 sewing mistress.

Infants' school

The school makes satisfactory progress. Better accommodation for babies would be of much advantage, and the provision of some new furniture should be considered.
Staff: Naomi Bent C.T.; Gertrude Leman art 68; Margaret Amies P.T.

| 1904 | **Mixed school** |

The children attend regularly and they are neat in person and orderly in manner. Their attainments are fairly satisfactory, but much of the instruction might be more practically treated. Slates should be more sparingly used for written work, especially in the upper portion of the school.

Infants' school

The room now used by the babies should be properly furnished and equipped, or a new one provided.
The Head teacher is industrious and zealous, but her efforts are not ably seconded by the subordinate members of the staff. There is too much simultaneous answering, causing unnecessary noise and confusion. Fair progress is being made on the whole.
Staff: Naomi Bent C.T; Frances Atkins Art 68; Margaret Amies P.T.

| 1905 | **Mixed school** |

Nothing has been yet done to improve the cloakroom accommodation, which was asked for and for which plans have been approved. As so many children stay to dinner some means should be adopted to provide a place where the food may be kept outside the rooms occupied by the children during their school hours.
The instruction of the lower standards might be advantageously of a more interesting character; and lessons are somewhat long. A desk (or low table) is wanted in the baby room, as one of the desks is badly broken.

Mixed school

I am to call attention to article 23 of the code, which must in future be strictly observed. H.M. Inspector further reports that proposals for cloakroom accommodation and removal of galleries were sanctioned by him as minor alterations in Dec 1904. I am therefore to remind your authority that a fulfilment of art 18 of the code is one of the requirements of the Board of Education if an undiminished grant is to be paid in future years. I am further to enquire what steps will be taken to remedy the various defects noted by H.M.I.
Copy of report after visit of 22nd Nov '05. Nothing has yet been done to enlarge the cloakrooms; or to provide space for the children's dinners. The office accommodation is scarcely sufficient for such a large school. Fireguards should be provided throughout without delay. With so many children staying to dinner unguarded fires are a great danger. While alterations are being carried out, the two galleries might be removed with advantage: and efficient washing apparatus arranged. The staff in both departments needs strengthening. At present the school is suffering from insufficient staff. The last report must be copied into the Log Book and signed by the Correspondent.

| 1906 | **Infants' school** |

Nothing has yet been done to enlarge the cloak rooms or to provide space for the children's dinners. The office accommodation is scarcely sufficient for such a large school. Fireguards should be provided throughout without delay. With so many children staying to dinner unguarded fires are a great danger. While alterations are being carried out the two galleries might be removed with advantage and efficient washing apparatus arranged. The staff in both dpts. needs strengthening. At present the school is suffering from insufficient staff.
Staff: Naomi Bent C.T.; Frances Atkins S.T.; Elsie Evison Mon.

Mixed school

Discipline is imperfect, and insufficiency of staff has so far prevented proper organisation. Article 14 of the code is broken in the case of the recently appointed supplementary teacher. Many of the books and slates in use are in a dilapidated condition. Due care does not seem to have been taken of the former.
The staff should be strengthened without delay, and attention is drawn to art 20 of the code. The board trust that your authority's proposals for the improvement of the offices, lavatories and cloakroom accommodation will be carried out during the forthcoming summer vacation.

1911   **Infants' school**
Owing to the great happiness of the children, their ready response, and interest in their work, a visit to this school is an unmixed pleasure. The head mistress directs her assistants, wisely, and her own work is invaluable. I saw nothing but genuinely good work either at this visit or at the visit I paid a year ago.
Staff: Naomi Bent C.T.; Elizabeth Wright S.

1912   **Infants' school**
The heating of the main room is insufficient owing to the fire place being at one end. On January 8th at 12.noon the thermometer registered only 46 degrees.
Staff: N. Bent; Amy Roberts C.T.; Elizabeth Wright S.

1915   **Mixed school**
Since the present Master took charge of this School nearly two years ago considerable improvement has taken place especially in the junior division. Discipline is as a rule good but in the senior division the children should be more alert and self-reliant.
The course of instruction has been carefully planned and the headmaster carefully supervises the work of his subordinates. A fairly liberal curriculum is provided and it is wisely intended to develop more definitively the practical side of the work. There are a few matters connected with the organisation which would well repay some consideration. The methods of teaching and the routine of the lowest classes have been brought more closely into touch with those followed in the Infants' school. It would be well to extend these modifications to other sections of the junior division. A more elastic system of promotion should be introduced in order to allow the more advanced scholars to pass more rapidly to the highest classes. The arrangement whereby the whole of the girls numbering 86 at present are taught needlework by only two teachers is open to objection as progress is thereby hampered. The attainments of the scholars in reading, recitation, composition, handwriting and spelling are creditable. Practical arithmetic and speech training should receive increased attention.

1920   **Infants' school**
The small size of the school permits of more individual treatment than is possible in many cases and the mistress takes full advantage of the opportunities offered. By the adoption of varied and original methods highly creditable results are obtained.

Mixed school.
General:
There are many praiseworthy features about this school. It is exceptionally well taught and conducted, as a whole, but the following points merit special mention.
The intelligent and wide knowledge of the older scholars, their industry and legitimate pride in their work, have had their due influence with the parents who take a keen interest in their children's progress and in the school generally.
Map reading and construction and the principles of geography are thoroughly well taught and much in advance of anything usually attempted in a village school.
The use of the sliding scale in connection with the teaching of arithmetic is also unique; hence the boys take a keener and more intelligent interest in this subject, and are able to solve more advanced problems expeditiously and correctly than in most schools.

1923   **Mixed school**
The high level of efficiency referred to in the last report is fully maintained. The Headmaster's aim has been to make the children intelligent and to induce them to rely mainly on their own efforts. In this he has been very successful. The scholars work steadily and shew a keenness when questioned orally whilst the written exercises in their books reach a very satisfactory level of neatness and accuracy. Special mention must be made of the very efficient teaching of arithmetic and geography in the senior division. In the latter subject the home-made maps and diagrams and the survey of the district have largely contributed to the success achieved.
The very creditable proportion of scholars who reach the first class is evidence of the sound work done in the lower part of the school.
Although the teaching of English throughout meets with a fair measure of success, progress is retarded by the inadequate supply of story books, and by the practice followed in some classes of grouping pupils of widely differing capacity for instruction in the subject.
The training the children receive in games and physical exercises, and the teaching of music deserve special praise.

1924   **Infants' school**
The Head Mistress who has been in charge of this school for nearly thirty years continues to carry out her duties with care and thought. The children are kindly managed and receive a careful training on individual lines: they have made good progress in reading and number but in oral expression there is room for improvement.

1924	Infants' school amalgamated into Mixed school.

1926 School report

This is in many ways a rural school of outstanding merit. The distinction is due in a special degree to the admirable leadership and keen professional spirit of the head master who has imbued his staff and pupils with his own earnestness of purpose and cheerfulness.

In the senior class the plan of instruction affords ample scope for training the scholars to think and act for themselves. The methods adopted have been attended with very gratifying results: the children apply themselves to their tasks with zest and make most praiseworthy progress, whilst the standard reached by the older members of the class is unusually high especially as regards arithmetic and geography.

The general condition of the other classes continues to be highly satisfactory. The minor weaknesses which exist are fully recognised by the Head Master and they are receiving careful attention. Among other points which were discussed at the visit was the advisability of co-ordinating the work of standard I more closely with that of the Infants division. The teacher of the older infants is painstaking and has spent a considerable amount of time in the study of progressive methods and in the preparation of apparatus for the individual use of children but, in ways which were indicated, some of her teaching is not fully effective.

The recently purchased gramophone has already proved a valuable acquisition: it has increased the children's interest in good music and has facilitated the teaching out-of-doors of the folk dances so heartily enjoyed by the boys and girls.

1929 School report

This school continues to reach a highly creditable level of efficiency.

In attainment and intelligence the senior children of the upper two classes show to advantage when compared with many others taught in similar surroundings. This result is due in a large measure to the skilful teaching which recognises the value of close correlation of the work of the school with the natural and social environment of the child. The teaching of geography, history and elementary mathematics may be specially mentioned as being exceptionally successful.

The Junior classes (4 and 5) are in the hands of young teachers possessing natural aptitude for teaching. The children are industrious and happy and are making good all-round progress.

The older Infants (class 6) are most sympathetically managed and taught. The atmosphere of the class is cheerful and homelike. Work and play appear to be synonymous terms in the minds of the children; the lessons in the three R's are just as welcome and attractive as the lighter activities.

The Head Master has carefully studied the trend of recent developments concerning the education of both seniors and juniors. He has planned modifications in the curriculum and changes in the organisation for the coming educational year. These were constructively criticised especially on points bearing on

    (a) The position of handiwork in the junior classes.

    (b) The widening of the treatment of the elementary mathematics.

    (c) The training of the older backward children who are at present more or less "shelved" in the third class.

The loudspeaker and the gramophone are effectively used as adjuncts to the teaching.

The 100 children who remain in school for the mid-day meal are, at a small cost provided with a nourishing hot drink.

1932 School report

This well conducted school fully maintains its reputation for good work. The earnestness of the Head Master and all members of the staff has a most helpful and healthy influence on the scholars, whose industry – thoughtfully guided and supervised – leads to excellent results.

The teaching throughout is skilful and is directed towards enlisting the children's interest and to the formation of habits of self-reliance. The older scholars are trained to use books intelligently in the study of several subjects and it is clear from the tests which were given at the inspection that most of the seniors are able to profit by private study methods.

While the pupils' attainments in general continue to reach a high standard, the subjects that are taught with outstanding success are English, elementary mathematics and arithmetic, and geography. The methods employed in nature study are stimulating. Singing and drawing also deserve mention.

In the two classes of Infants good judgement is shown in the planning of a well-balanced scheme of training and in the selection of teaching methods. Both of the teachers are doing successful work. The children are natural and well behaved and by means of the good start they receive in reading, writing and number and by the interesting and varied lighter activities, they gradually learn to rely upon themselves and to show consideration to each other.

The intelligent management of the sixth division during the long illness of the class teacher deserves commendation.

1936 School report

The 156 children in attendance at this unreorganised village school are organised into Infant, Junior and Senior Divisions; of the five classes two comprise the junior and two the senior divisions. The premises include three large classrooms, two of which are partitioned. The playground is of adequate size and a suitable field is available for games.

The Headmaster, who has held his present appointment for twenty–three years, is approaching the end of his teaching career. Under his direction the school has earned a reputation for sound work in essential directions and this is fully maintained. He will retire with the satisfaction of knowing that his efforts on behalf of the children have been greatly appreciated.

The Infant division comprising 40 children is in the charge of an experienced certificated mistress. The primary subjects of the curriculum receive due attention; the pupils are carefully grouped according to their age and attainments, and on the whole they make useful progress. More opportunities for practising speech might be given. The class is accommodated in a spacious room and the possibility of developing the training on even more active lines might be considered.

The two junior classes share an unpartitioned room and in consequence, their activities are somewhat restricted. The teachers apply themselves to their duties in an earnest manner and their pupils make steady progress.

The Headmaster and an energetic assistant mistress are responsible for the instruction of the senior classes. The results of the tests that were given show that a satisfactory standard of attainment is reached in arithmetic and English; the former subject includes some effective practical work and the latter the study of literature. The written exercises of the top class are above the average in quality. The practical work in geography, which is carried out under the direction of the Head Teacher, is deserving of special mention; the school is reasonably well equipped with instruments and the pupils find much interest in the course.

The older scholars receive instruction in woodwork and housecraft at the centre which stands in the playground. Elementary book craft and needlecraft are included in the work done in the classrooms.

1961   School report

This three-class school of 73 children, between the ages of 5 and 11, occupies an imposing building constructed of dressed flint with turrets and buttresses, and large windows looking out over the rolling countryside of North Norfolk. It was built by Lord Suffield in 1826 to serve the needs of his estate tenants. There are five good rooms, providing ample space for the school's activities. Electric light, mains water and a modern sanitation system have been installed and with its spacious paved playgrounds, the school is well equipped. There is a detached kitchen dining room.

The mistress in charge of the Infants has given 35 years of devoted service to the school. Two adjacent classrooms are available for this class and there is a reasonable supply of apparatus and teaching material. More books are essential, however, particularly those of an attractive character. A fair measure of success is achieved in the basic subjects but more careful organisation is necessary to ensure that children of varying ability are given suitable work.

The middle class has had a succession of teachers. The graduate master now in charge of it joined the staff at the beginning of this term. He has yet to make really effective contact with the children in his class. Much of what they do is not clearly related to their capacities and their written exercises are frequently lacking in care.

The Head master takes the top class, most of whom read fluently enough. One or two of them read quite widely and are interested in books. The County Library provides a very useful service but the school needs a better supply of books of its own, well displayed. The amount and quality of written English is somewhat limited and relatively few of the older boys and girls can express themselves with any degree of fluency in speech or in writing. A good deal of time is spent in working at unrelated English exercises. Geography, history and nature study could provide many opportunities for written work of a more useful kind than the present copied notes. A reasonable standard of accuracy is obtained in arithmetical exercises, and especially in mental work. The girls do some quite attractive needlework and the older boys carry out experimental work in the garden in addition to the routine operations.

During its long history the school has accumulated many books and a great deal of material, much of which is distributed about the rooms, in corners and under tables. A good clean out would be beneficial.

A good deal of hard work goes on but the abler children in the school are not yet stretched as far as their ability warrants and they would benefit from more stimulating and vigorous teaching.

Appendix: Timeline

Date	Event
1826	School built by Lord Suffield for the children of Lower Street, Antingham, Bradfield, Gunton and Thorpe Market. Edward Harbord 3rd Lord Suffield active campaigner to abolish the slave trade. Mr Birt Headmaster.
1829	Mr Wortley Headmaster.
1830	William IV becomes King.
1833	"One Daily School contains 62 males and 58 females and is supported principally by Lord Suffield; who allows a salary of £50 per annum to the School Master and his wife together with the occupation of 6 acres of land rent free and four chaldron of coals annually, and partly by small payments from the parents of children varying from 1d to 6d per week per child according to the rent paid by the parents but a less sum where two are sent; and nothing extra for all of the same family above two. Those who are tenants of Lord Suffield pay less than those who are not; this school was instituted for the instruction of the poor of the parishes of Thorpe-Market, Antingham, Bradfield and the Lower Street Southrepps; But the children of the poor inhabitants of the Upper street will be admitted until the numbers from the other places shall be considered by Lord Suffield to be sufficient". *House of Commons Education Enquiry 1833.*
1837	Victoria becomes Queen.
1854	Mr Elden Headmaster.
1870	Forster Education Act requiring the setting up of board schools if education in the area deemed inadequate.
1875	A School Board established. Mrs Earl schoolmistress. Miss Pilcher to assist Mrs Earl. Miss Pilcher later warned against 'hardness to the children'.
1854	Advert for couple to work at Lord Suffield's school.
1876	Lord Suffield gifts the school to the parishes of Southrepps, Antingham, Thorpe Market, Gunton and Bradfield.
1877	School bulding extended one extra bay at each end and one class extension to the side. Intake to be 260 children. School Board borrows £1356 to pay for the building works. 13th July Mr Amies appointed Headmaster £130 per annum + house. Miss Allan mistress of the Girls' school £70 per annum, own lodgings. The board members wanted stabling for their horses and carriages during meetings, the loan would not cover this. Mr Matthew Welden builder of Swanton Abbot given job of alterations, tendered £1,145.
1878	28th January Mr Amies opened the Antingham and Southrepps United District Board School Boys' department. 59 boys over 7 admitted, by July this had increased to 96 and divided into 3 classes. The Girls' school was opened on the same day by Miss Allan; 40 girls, 29th January 20 more admitted, 4th February admitted 30 more. School fees of 2d a head not exceeding 6d per family. 8th April Infants' school opened as a separate department first entry in the school log 46 children and the Headmistress was Miss Maguir £45 per annum. Miss Maguir removed from post, not a certified teacher. School roll 350 children.
1879	Miss Allan resigned as Head of Girls' school; Miss Brett appointed £70 per annum. Alteration to the windows to allow proper ventilation. Miss Balle appointed Headmistress of Infants' school. Received grant for Boys' and Girls' schools, grant for Infants' school reduced. Several children left to attend private school in Upper Street. Girls stopped from taking books home as they were becoming dirty and spoiled. Alteration to pump and well carried out by Mr Starling £2 14s 0d.

1880	Education compulsory from the age of five years to ten years. 109 boys on the school register. Mr Robert Woods cautioned about continued employment of Robert Moy aged ten. Building works substandard and dangerous requiring immediate repair.
1881	Head of the Girls' school left on the 14th June. 24th June Boys' and Girls' schools combined.
1882	Miss Trollope Headmistress Infants' school. Circular to be sent to parents re fees.
1883	Buildings deemed to be in a dangerous condition requiring immediate attention.
1884	16th May part of the ceiling in the Infants' school collapsed. Infants taught in Mixed school whilst repairs carried out to ceiling and gallery. The Inspectors' report judged the standard of grammar taught too low for the grant to be recommended.
1885	17th April Lady Suffield visited the school. 10th July George Gray severely hurt about the head following a fall from the trees in the playground. All boys warned that climbing trees must be stopped. Miss Soames appointed Headmistress Infant's school. 4th December school closed this week; elections.
1886	28th May school report the number of children in the Infants' school is too great for one teacher. 9th July 1886 school closed for half day to prepare for elections the next day (Saturday).
1887	21st June the school was closed for Queen Victoria's Golden Jubilee. Again, standards questioned, and the grant only reluctantly paid. Children over eight should not be kept in the Infant dept. 199 children on the books of the mixed school. Mixed school standards also deemed poor some grant withheld. 21st October walls and chimneys repaired. Parents dissatisfied that their children are expected to clean the school. Two local ladies Mrs Hewitt and Mrs Burton employed offered one shilling between them. Refused. Paid one shilling each. Death of Sydney Drury one of the 1st class boys.
1888	Walls to be coloured not whitewashed. Standards remain an issue. Several children examined for the exemption list and found to be 'dull and backward'.
1889	The school found to be improving. Six parents prosecuted and convicted of non or poor attendance of children. Hon. Harbord Harbord re-elected to board. Mr Amies granted use of house and garden free of charge whilst in post.
1890	R. Rogers and G. Gray punished for gross insubordination. The report for this year states that the classroom is mostly over crowded.
1891	Free education in board schools. School received last fees on 28th August. This year's report is that the Infants' school is in good order. 6th March school closed for four weeks due to measles. This year's report found the knitting needed attention.
1892	7th and 8th October the school was closed so that a bazaar could be held on behalf of the Lower Street Coffee Rooms. £60 was raised. Three parents fined at Cromer for irregular attendance. Friday 15th July rooms prepared for elections on Saturday.
1893	School closed Thursday 6th July for Royal wedding of the Duke of York to Mary of Teck (Later George V and Queen Mary). The boys' outside toilets were found to be lacking in light and ventilation and there was settlement of roof of the adjoining

classroom to the main school.

24th November school closed in the afternoon as HRH Edward Prince of Wales was shooting at Thorpe Market.

School compulsory to 11 years.

1895	Monday 26th July school closed for general election.
1896	January outbreak of scarlet fever.
1897	22nd and 23rd June school closed for Diamond Jubilee. School closed again on July 13th and 14th on account of Jubilee fetes at Gunton, Antingham, Suffield and Thorpe Market. 5th November three boys punished for attempting to light fires on the common.
1898	4th February children marched around the room from 9-9.15 because the weather was so cold. During August one of the scholars Walter Dyball was accidentally killed. The school was found to be untidy and dirty and in need of painting the lower parts to be wainscoted.
1899	6th March school closed for four weeks on advice of doctor due to measles epidemic causing the death of one child. 20th October the board thought a football might be obtained for the boys and a seesaw for the girls. The football was found to have had a good effect on the boys' attendance. School compulsory to 12 years.
1900	Monday 8th October school closed for general election.
1901	Edward VII becomes King.
1902	4th June holiday given for Southrepps fair and proclamation of peace. 26th and 27th June school closed for coronation festivities.
1903	The school becomes the responsibility of the Local Authority. Separate Babies' room established in the Mixed school. 9th December only 21 children in the Infants' school out of 89 on the register.
1904	During the summer months a class of infants will occasionally spend half hour playing in the sand pit on the common The school well once empty was to be deepened by three feet, the cost was £3 2s 6d. Alterations to the Infants' department and extra cloakroom space were requested. New bye-laws issued requiring children to remain at school until 14.
1905	Temperature recorded as 40°F (5°C) 16th Jan. Dispute with the Briggs family using the school well. 28th September it was agreed to start cookery lessons and make Southrepps the centre for other schools. Giant Stride erected in the boys' playground suggested and paid for by the board. 4th December Inspectors' report was unhappy with the cloakrooms, the classrooms and the number of staff.
1906	April closure of the small private school in Upper Street. A galvanized tin with drinking cups was fixed in each playground for the use of the children. 12th October School closed for two weeks due to scarlet fever. Free school meals provided to needy children. 26th January election held in the school.
1907	During this year major holiday alterations were made to the school with the Babies' room becoming the new cloakroom. The external door being moved into the cloakroom area and the door being changed to a window, fireplaces and doorways moved. Galleries removed from the Infants' schoolroom and the Boys' schoolroom and a glass partition erected in the Infants' schoolroom. New toilets built, walls and partitions added or removed. School closed for 15 weeks 2nd August until November.
1908	Ventilation of the classrooms seen to by the addition of Boyles ventilators.
1909	Another bad outbreak of measles causing the closure of the school. So many children were missing before Christmas that they did not receive their Christmas gifts, so the tree had been kept until 15th January. Toys, sweets and oranges were distributed. 30th July two watches given as prizes for attendance.

1910   George V becomes King.

28th January Tuesday election polling station.

Gardening classes to start, a piece of land was hired from Mr Temple to be fenced and gated at the school's expense.

Laundry classes also to start.

26th October some boys were reprimanded for noisy behaviour outside the school buildings during evening class hours.

9th December Wednesday election polling station.

1911   25th May Charles Whitwood was recommended for special reward as having seven years perfect attendance.

30th June school closed for the coronation of George V; coronation mugs given to all Southrepps scholars.

23rd November a letter from the Headmaster to the managers about the need for more heating apparatus in the Infants' department. The managers agreed to the fire being lit at 7.30 instead of 8am.

An unpleasantness had occurred between Mr Gainsbury (teacher) and Mr Thurston (parent) resulting in Mr Gainsbury being moved to another school.

1912   February Inspectors' report highlighting the inadequate heating in the Infant Department.

A large oil stove was received on the 7th February for use during the winter months.

25th November building inspector came to see if hot water pipes could be put into the Infant dept.

1913   31st Jan retirement of Mr Amies after 35 years as Headmaster.

Mr Jones appointed Headmaster.

11th July half day granted on account of school treat in Upper Street.

22nd July a half day holiday was granted this afternoon on account of another school treat in Upper Street.

1914   30th November the military commandeered the Infants' schoolroom. Scholars taught in the reading room. Infants' lessons then taken in Mrs Watson's barn.

1915   1st February dentist visited the school.

The clerk was requested to see the office scavenger with reference to the complaint that the offices were never cleaned out more than once a fortnight and to inform him that under his contract he is required to empty them twice weekly.

1916   24th and 25th February snowstorm, school closed.

29th March blizzards.

1917   10th August closed pm for harvest vacation for five weeks; would have closed last evening but the wet weather allowed the school to continue one more day.

18th October it was decided to undertake the organised gathering of horse chestnuts as suggested by the Education Committee circular.

1918   14th February the managers expressed regret at the action taken by the Education Committee in charging the parish with the whole cost of the heating apparatus installed in the school. The Headmaster was asked to furnish the chairman with particulars as to the savings in cost of coal likely to be made as a result of the new system of heating.

24th September during the blackberry season the following arrangements are made for each Tuesday and Thursday. Commence secular instruction 9.10am recreation, 10.15–10.35am close morning session, 11.30am commence afternoon session 12.40pm recreation, 1.40–1.55pm, close 2.30pm.

The schoolmaster will collect all the blackberries gathered and pay 3d per pound for them.

21st November school closed due to influenza.

1919   11th March for two days there has been no coal in the school.

13th March Headmaster given permission to close the school if coal could not be obtained and the weather very cold.

1920   30th April number of children on books 141.

1921   School leaving age raised to 14.

Woodwork lessons start.

1922   15th November holiday given as election to be held at school.

1923   1st December school closed until Christmas, scarlet fever.

6th December general election.

1924	29th February there are sixty-seven children on the register.
	29th October general election.
1925	25th March Miss Bent left the Infants' school.
	1st April from this date the Infant and Mixed schools are amalgamated.
1927	11th July replacing of the concrete floors of the school with wood blocks.
1929	30th June general election.
1936	Accession and Abdication of Edward VIII.
	Accession of George VI
	156 children on roll
1938	31st October Mr Jones retired.
	1st November Mr Dack takes up post of Headmaster.
1939	School trip to London Zoo.
	5th September Monday 123 children and 14 teachers and helpers arrived today from Dagenham.
	4th December Dagenham High school children removed to Hill House.
	Number on books 185.
1940	Mon 8th January number on books 195, 144 Southrepps, 51 evacuees.
	3rd June evacuees left. 148 children on books.
1943	2nd July currant picking holiday.
	21st September sixteen children started picking potatoes on the blue card system.
1944	Education Act, raising the school leaving age to 15. Provision of school meals.
1945	Tuesday 8th May VE day school closed for two day national holiday.
	29th June Mr Dack leaves school.
	9th July Mr Crane takes temporary charge of the school.
	12th October Half term and VJ holiday 3 days.
	1st November Mr Hare takes up post of Headmaster.
1946	Delivery of light bulbs and shades.
	Erection of HORSA in Headmaster's garden.
	Fruit picking a fortnight in July.
1947	Heavy snow school closed for one week then very low attendance.
	Decomposed mouse found in drinking water tank.
	20th November marriage of Princess Elizabeth school closed.
1948	Mrs Hare starts as clerical assistant three hours for three days a week.
1949	9ft high metal fencing erected around playgrounds.
	Discussion of electricity for school.
1950	Mr Clarke suffering from snake bite.
	Refusal of education authority to install electricity to the school.
	School to take senior students from Roughton.
	Clerical assistance increased to half time.
	Woodwork centre to be open three days a week.
	Employment officer interviewed leavers.
1951	Electricity installed.
	Case of polio in the village.
1952	Accession of Elizabeth II.
	Whole school listened to funeral of George VI.
	Medical room built in old boardroom.

Whole school watched film with the County Bee Organiser.

County Projectionist and Film strip project. The school borrowed many films.

Children taken by a teacher to North Walsham for X-ray.

1953	First mention of acquiring a school playing field.
	152 pupils and all staff went to Cromer cinema to see a film 'Elizabeth is Queen'.
	Discussions as to whether to make school an emergency rest and feeding station.
1954	Windows lowered in infant school and fire door added through to Headmaster's garden.
	Partial eclipse of the sun on 30th June, lunch brought forward so children could watch it.
1955	Chimney sweeping to be arranged by Headmaster.
	Drinking water tanks to be emptied and cleaned.
	BBC programmes for country schools available.
1956	Ash pit to be emptied and repaired.
	PC Moore spoke to children about road safety and inspected bicycles.
1957	Reorganisation of schools to Primary and Secondary.
	Children from Ashmanhaugh at the handicraft centre.
	Cellar discovered under the bedroom floor during repairs.
	School now a primary school, handicrafts discontinued. Gardening will continue partly mixed, partly boys only.
1958	British Railways projection team in school.
	Heavy snow.
	30 children on school trip to London. School closed.
	9th September re-opened with three classes.
1959	Heavy snow.
	26th May temperature below 52° Fahrenheit, fires lit.
1960	Scavenger contract terminated; septic tanks had been installed.
1962	Needlework organiser visited.
1964	School closed general election.
1966	Removal of tools from the handicraft hut.
	Telephone installed phone number Southrepps 282.
1968	School hours to change in winter to 9.30–12.30, 1 hour break then 1.30–3.45.
	French lessons start.
	Gardening lessons continue.
1969	11th February heavy snow school closed at lunch time.
	Mr Hare retires 28th February.
	Mr Gladwin takes up appointment as Headmaster.
	Mrs Nouse appointed clerical assistant.
	First evening class in dressmaking.
1970	First correspondence about sale of land to the West as a playing field.
1971	Mr Gladwin leaves the school house. He had been complaining for over a year about the heating.
	School trip to Paris.
	School house let to tenant Mr MacDonald.
1972	Power cuts due to miners' strike.
	Swimming lessons start in Cromer with transport laid on; December swimming lessons suspended.
1973	Farmland was purchased for the school field. There were prolonged difficulties over planning permission and then about the height of the fence.

1974	The field was cut for the first time and hoped to be in use by end of the summer term. The Education Authority unable to pay for goal posts. Mr Gladwin purchased timber and made the goal posts himself.
1975	Swimming lessons move to Mundesley. Eleven-plus exams cease. A boules tournament held with teams from Northrepps, Roughton, Gresham, Aylmerton, Gimingham and Overstrand.
1976	Decision by Education Authority that Antingham and Southrepps would become a first school. This did not happen 150-year commemoration. Bricked-up front of porch faced with knapped flints and date in pebbles put above. New oil boiler fitted to replace the anthracite one.
1977	28th February two ponies from the school house found in the playground. 1st March large horse on school premises.
1979	School closed due to snow.
1980	Accepted offer by Education Authority for three toilets for pupils, one for staff inside. Also, a staffroom and school office Mr Gladwin retires. Miss Wallace acting Headmistress.
1981	Miss Speed acting Headmistress. Indoor toilets finally installed at both ends of the building. Mrs Marett appointed as Head teacher. Colour Television bought by PTA.
1982	School house becomes vacant. New roof. Ceilings in classrooms lowered.
1983	The school house is handed over to the school for their use. A doorway was to be knocked through and central heating installed. The PTA was to fund the doorway and heating. The school hut was removed and the wall behind repaired. Playgroup given permission to use the school house. Two rooms two days a week. School house kitchen used as cookery room.
1984	School bus to replace all taxis that had previously brought children to school. School's first computer collected. School library fitted out and ready for use.
1985	Very poor weather conditions. Mrs Marrett seconded to UEA for two terms. A lot of industrial action by staff this year. Small Schools Federation set up.
1987	Blizzards. First 'Baker Day', teacher training days introduced by Kenneth Baker then Secretary of State for Education. Mr Barrett appointed Head teacher. The log records now move into the old Infants' log book end of Log and Minute books.
1990s	Mobile classrooms erected .
2003	Mrs Day appointed Head teacher.
2007	Teachers begin training for Forest School qualification.
2011	Mrs Kingman appointed Head teacher new Infant's block opened.
2013	Miss Howse appointed Head teacher.
2014	Became part of the North Norfolk Academy Trust.

Appendix: Staff of the school

	Position	Dates	Biography if known
Original School			
Mr Joseph Birt	Headmaster	1826–1829	Born 1797 Gloucester.
Mr John Wortley	Headmaster	1829–1854	Born 1795 Ludham.
Mr John Elden	Headmaster	1854–1877	Born 1836 Aylsham.
Mrs Earl	Mistress	?–1877	Born 1826 Eckington, Derbyshire.
Ann Pilcher	Mistress	1875–1876	
Girls' School			
Miss Louisa Allen	Mistress	1878–1879	
Miss Lydia Rix	Assistant mistress	1878	Resigned on account of ill health after a month.
Miss Mary Butler	Assistant mistress	1878–1881	Born 1858 Ryde, Isle of Wight, one of ten children. She lodged at Laburnum Cottage, Southrepps.
Miss Emily Brett	Mistress	1879–1881	Born 1859 Downham. Lodged at Laburnum Cottage, Southrepps.
Infants' School			
Miss Rebekah Jane Maguir	Mistress	1878–1878	Removed from position after four months as she was not a certified teacher.
Miss Mary Balle	Mistress	1879–1882	Born 1860 Montacute, Somerset. Living with her widowed mother in 1881 in Lower Street. In the 1891 census she is teaching in Snowhill, Gloucestershire. She married David Hart in 1892 and emigrated to Canada in 1894, taking her mother with her.
Miss Elizabeth Martha Amies	Pupil teacher	1881–1887	Transferred to Mixed school 21st July 1884, she passed as a pupil teacher 1885 and transferred back from Mixed school 3rd August 1886. Most of October 1886 was spent in the Mixed school. She married Herbert Farrow in 1902.
Miss Inez Trollope	Mistress	1882–1885	Born 1861. In 1892 she is teaching in Heigham, living with her parents. 1901 she is Headmistress in Syderstone. In 1911 she is a foster mother governess at an institution in Norwich.
Miss Jessie Amies	Pupil teacher	1892–1892	Daughter of the Headmaster. On the 8th July 1892 attended a scholarship exam. She left the school on 14th September 1892, 31st March 1897 returned having taught at St James Infant School, Colchester.
Miss Ethel Thain	Pupil teacher	1892–1896	She had a four-year contract £7 for the 1st year, £10 for the 2nd, £13 for the 3rd and £16 for the final year. On the 26th October 1895 she sat the Queen's Scholarship exam.
Miss Bessie Watson	Monitoress/ pupil teacher	1894–1901	Born 1880 Antingham, Bessie lived at Rectory Farm where Naomi Bent lodged. On the 12th December 1898 she attended her scholarship exam at Norwich training school. She left to go to Lincoln Training College. In the course of her training she came back to take lessons in the school. In the 1911 census she is a certified teacher in Kingston upon Thames.
Miss Eleanor Soames	Mistress	1885–1893	
Miss Harriet Louisa Tilney	Mistress	1894–1897	
Miss Naomi Bent	Mistress	1897–1925	Born 1865 Leicestershire, in 1881 she is a pupil teacher living at home. Lodged at Rectory Farm, Antingham with the Watsons.
Miss Madge Amies	Pupil teacher	1901–1905	Daughter of Headmaster.

Boys' School

Mr William Amies	Headmaster	1877–1913	Born 1848 Bacton.
Mr Nursey	Assistant master	1878	For five months.
Mr Fred Richardson	Assistant master	1879–1886	Left to take up post with the Erpingham Union as relieving officer for the Holt District.
Miss Youngman	Assistant mistress	1881	Left after a week as she wanted to teach infants.
Miss Emma Ballard	Assistant mistress	1881	
Miss Annie Chappelle	Assistant mistress	1881–1882	
Miss Charlotte Watson	Assistant mistress	1883–1885	Left to take charge of Knapton School.
Miss Jane Roberts	Assistant teacher	1885	Taught for two months.
Miss Martha Barker	Assistant teacher	1885–1886	
Miss Elizabeth Peeke	Probationary teacher	1885	Left after a month.
Mr A. Farrington	Temporary Headmaster	1885–1886	Acting head whilst Mr Amies was ill.
Mr George Amies	Monitor/pupil teacher	1886–1897	Son of Headmaster.
Mr Hector Suffling	Assistant master	1886–1893	Born 1866 Hanworth. Left for an assistant master's post at the Brompton Higher Grade School in London.
Miss Ada Ridley	Assistant mistress	1886–1887	
Miss Lizzie Spence Craig	Assistant mistress	1887	Left after six months.
Miss Jane Forden	Assistant master	1888–1889	
Miss Rosetta Alcock	Assistant master	1889–1894	
Mr Ernest Watson	Pupil teacher	1890–1895	Born 1876 Worstead, he lived at Rectory Farm Antingham and was the brother of Bessie Watson. He left to train at St Mark's College. He married Gertrude Nicholson and remained a school teacher all his working life.
Miss Marion Atkins	Monitoress/ pupil teacher/ assistant teacher	1892–1899	Born 1879 Durston, daughter of the station master at Gunton. Left to a post at East Finchley Church School.
Miss Edith Hammond	Assistant mistress	1894–1897	
Mr George Samuel Ducker	Assistant master	1894	Left after two months. Former pupil teacher at Hempnall Board School.
Miss Harriet E. Fuller	Assistant mistress	1894	Left after two months.
Miss Maud E Bolton	Assistant mistress	1897–1890	Formerly of Swainsthorpe and Bury St Edmunds. She left to take up a business opportunity in Norwich.
Miss Lily M. Clements	Article 68 teacher	1889	Born 1880 in Northrepps. Previously taught at Swafield School. Married George Bruce.
Miss Ethel Madeline Betts	Article 68 teacher	1899–1901	Formerly a pupil teacher in the Girls' department at Wells school.
Miss A. M. Hall	Assistant mistress	1899–1901	Formerly of Elm Road Board School (Girls) Wisbech.
Miss Mabel Harriet Dack	Assistant mistress	1901	Born 1883 Holt, formerly of Holt Board School.
Miss Gertrude Leman	Sewing mistress	1901–1904	
Mr Dennis Burton	Assistant master	1902–1907	Formerly of Holt Church School.
Miss Frances Atkins	Temporary mistress	1903–1904	Born 1885 Burnham, daughter of the station master at Gunton.
Miss Elsie Andrews	Monitoress/ pupil teacher	1905–1909	Trained for a term at pupil teacher centre in Norwich 1907.
Miss Ethel Katie Points	Sewing mistress	1906–1919	

Miss Agnes Lawson Venters	Assistant mistress	1907	From Horden College School, Durham.
Miss Guyton	Assistant mistress	1907–1908	
Miss Gibbons	Assistant mistress	1909–1910	From Keswick.
Mr Leonard Burrough Gainsbury	Assistant master	1908–1912	Born 1879 Wisbech Cambridge, he was then a pupil teacher in New Walsoken for four years. He married Hephizabah Hopkin and had two sons. Following a disagreement with a parent he went to a post in Downham Market where he died in October 1912.
Mr Hector Percy Jones	Headmaster	1913–1938	Born 1878 Aberdare, Glamorgan.
Mr Frederick Charles Crane	Uncertificated assistant master	1913–1946	Born 1885 Norwich. Acting Headmaster on the departure of Mr Dack and the arrival of Mr Hare.
Miss MacArthur	Assistant mistress	1913–17	Left to be married.
Miss London	Assistant mistress	1914–1916	Transferred to another school.
Miss Hilda Gibbons	Pupil teacher	1916	
Miss Florrie Gray	Pupil teacher	1917–1922	Passed Cambridge Senior exam becoming an uncertificated teacher.
Mrs Ramm	Assistant mistress	1919–1920	
Miss Christabel Drury	Probationary teacher	1920	
Mrs Burton	Assistant mistress	1920–1928	
Miss G.E. Reynolds	Uncertificated mistress	1922–1927	

Mixed School

Miss Mabel Agnes Stone	Head of Infants	1925–1965	Born 1902 Norwich. She left after 40 years working in the school. She carried on working as a supply teacher in the school for many years.
Mr Frank Golden	Student teacher	1925–1926	
Miss Burdett	Student teacher	1927–1928	
Miss Ida Watts	Uncertificated teacher	1927–1941	Born 1908 Worstead, known by the pupils as *Ida Spider Dirt Track Rider*. She left the school in 1941 to go to College, her leaving gift was a gold wrist watch. She returned in 1943 for four months before being appointed Headmistress at Smallburgh. She died in 2004 in North Walsham.
Mrs Chasteney	Uncertificated teacher	1928	
Miss Ruth Tomason	Uncertificated teacher	1928–1933	
Mr George Marling	Student teacher	1929	
Miss Joyce Marling	Student teacher	1931–1932	
Mr Thomas Dack	Head teacher	1938–1945	Born 1908 Walsingham.
Miss Whitear	Teacher	1941–1947	Left to get married.
Mrs Evans	Temporary teacher	1944–1946	Transferred to Worstead.
Mr John Hare	Head teacher	1945–1969	Born 1904 Shardlow, Derbyshire.
Mr Catling	Temporary teacher	1946–1947	He was an ex-service trainee. He left to go to college.
Mr Edward Meatyard	Probationary teacher	1947–1951	He had had one year's training under ex-services emergency training. He successfully passed his probation in 1949 and left to teach at Sprowston as it was nearer his home.
Miss Vilma Patricia Allen	Teacher	1948–1958	Left due to reduction in school size.
Mr N. A. Clarke	Teacher	1949–1953	He was bitten by a snake and brought the snake into school in a bottle of methylated spirits (as recalled by a former pupil).
Mr George B. Amis	Teacher	1952–1955	Emergency trained teacher on probation until Dec 1952. The 1939 England and Wales register records his occupation at the start of the war as a bricklayer. He had previously taught at Old Buckenham. He was

clearly not a well man; there is a series of entries about his ill health and sadly he was admitted to Cromer Hospital where he died in 1955.

Mr Victor Allen Grace	Teacher	1954–1961	
Mr R.W. Edmondson	Temporary teacher	1955–1956	
Mr Green	Teacher	1957–1958	Contract not renewed due to reduction in number of pupils.
Mr M. Hyslop	Teacher	1961–1970	
Mrs Elizabeth Wallace	Infant teacher	1965–1982	1980 acting Headmistress for one term. She left after 17 years at the school.
Mr Harold Gladwin	Head teacher	1969–1980	Born 1920 Stockport, Cheshire.
Mr R. H. Pope	Teacher	1970–1974	
Miss R. Judd	Teacher	1974–1975	
Mr Robert J. W. Bone	Teacher	1975–	Previously taught in Matlock.
Miss Trott	Teacher	1976	For one term covering for Mr Bone who was on a one term French course at Norwich College.
Mrs B. Hendon	Probationary teacher	1977–1980	Part–time, until 1978. Maternity leave in 1979, left to take a post at Cawston College.
Mrs Dye	Teacher	1978– 1988?	
Miss Lee	Teacher	1979–1980	Maternity cover then full–time post from 1980.
Mrs M. Freston	Teacher	1980–1982	
Miss Speed	Acting Headteacher	1981	County unattached Head.
Mrs Veronica Marett	Head teacher	1981–1987	
Mrs Wright	Teacher	1982–1985	
Mrs Moir	Teacher	1985	One term contract.
Mr Scargill	Teacher	1983–1986	Acting head for one term, in 1985 left to become head of Aldborough School.
Mr Baldwin	Deputy head	1986–?	
Mrs Elizabeth Player	Teacher	1986–1999	
Mr Ron Barrett	Head teacher	1987–2003	Very musical, used to play the guitar.
Miss Linda Hodgkinson	Teacher		
Miss Sue Augood (Love)	Teacher		
Mrs Lucy Care	Teacher		Very musical, she was responsible for getting the grant from the Judith Bartram Trust to convert the carriage shed to a music room.
Mr Stephen Maunder	Teacher	1999–2003	
Mrs Sara Wilkinson	Teacher	1999–2019	Level 3 Forest School.
Mrs Sue Day	Head teacher	2003–2011	
Miss Sophie Robinson (Cairns)	Teacher	2003–2013	Level 3 Forest School.
Ms Emma Harwood	Teacher	2003–2012	Level 3 Forest School.
Mr John Paul Ringer	Teacher	2003–2013	Level 3 Forest School.
Mr Nick Morrow	Teacher	2010–2011	
Mrs Janice Kingman	Head teacher	2011–2013	
Miss Julia Howse	Head teacher	2013–2014	

Appendix: Pupils

Where there is uncertainty about the individual referred to in the log book, the entry had been recorded against both names.

Name and where living	Log book entry giving date and reason (if any)	Parents' date and place of birth Occupation (if known)	Date and place of birth of all children in family Outcome eg. occupation (if known)
ALLARD **Stephen** **Emma** Gimingham	**1883** Admitted to school **1895** Emma too backward to work with III will have hard work to do II standard	**William** 1848 Gimingham Carpenter **Elizabeth Colman** 1847 Gimingham	**Stephen** 1871 Gimingham docker on Tyneside **Mary** 1875 Gimingham m. Alfred Payne **Charlotte** 1877 Gimingham housemaid **Albert** 1879 Gimingham farm labourer m. Marian Mosedale **Maria Hannah** 1882 Gimingham m. Robert Dix **Emma** 1884 Gimingham **Francis** 1889 Gimingham fish hawker m. Emily Loads
AMIES **Edith** Antingham	**1879** Edith absented herself from school for three weeks to pick turnips	**Unknown** **Unknown**	**Arthur** 1866 Trunch cabinet maker **Edith** 1869 Antingham Both living with their grandparents James and Elizabeth Thurston
AMIS **Rosa** Church Cottages Antingham	**1892** Has left the school having removed to another parish	**Robert** 1856 Suffield Agricultural Labourer **Eliza Osborne** 1856 North Walsham	**Charles** 1880 Bradfield forester in Derbyshire m. Mary Turner **Florence** 1882 Bradfield m. Samuel Grand **Elizabeth** 1884 Bradfield servant **Rosa** 1886 Antingham m. Bruce Wilkins **George** 1887 Antingham farm carter **Marion** 1890 Antingham **John** 1892 Antingham farm carter **Daisy** 1894 Hanworth m. Percy Youngs
ATKINS **Marian** The Station House Gunton	**1892** Readmitted with a view of testing her fitness as a monitoress and give her an opportunity of passing 7th standard	**James** 1840 Thetford Stationmaster **Mary Ann** 1843 Eccles	**Ellen** 1865 Brantham, Suffolk m. John Evison **Eliza** 1869 Ipswich died 1888 aged 19 **Sidney** 1873 Felstead, Essex maltster's clerk m. Anna Hall **William** 1875 Durston **Marian** 1879 Durston teacher taught at the School leaving on the 15th Sept 1899 m. James Mott **Mabel** 1882 Durston died 1904 **Frances** 1885 Burnham teacher at the School in 1903
ATTEW **Laura** **Alberta** Lower Street	**1879** Laura should be taken on as monitoress for this dept each to teach one week in turn and to receive one shilling in payment for the week they are in school **1880** Children sent home due to outbreak of measles **1880** Laura at home with the measles on that account obliged to send home Alberta **1886** Alberta monitoress	**James** 1839 Southrepps Agricultural labourer died 1875 **Caroline Gibbons**	**Ralph** 1863 Trunch gamekeeper m. Emily Howes **Laura Elizabeth** 1866 Colby m. George Cooper **Charles** 1869 Colby policeman m. Annie Gardiner **Walter** 1870 Colby gamekeeper m. Emily Hannant **Selina Alberta** 1872 Thorpe Market m. John Howlett **Albert** 1873 Southrepps Albert served with the Norfolk Regiment
BACON **Benjamin** **Tabitha** **Absalom** **Medonia** Thorpe Market	**1883** School fees owing were remitted. Medonia moved up from infants due to age, only fit to work with second class infants	**Alfred** 1836 Thorpe Market Agricultural labourer **Charlotte Sarah Reynolds** 1840 Northrepps	**Adolphus** 1861 Northrepps died 1881 aged 21 **Kerenhappuck** 1863 Thorpe Market **Alfred** 1864 Thorpe Market m. Mary Brigham **John** 1867 Thorpe Market m. Lily Scott **Malaha** 1869 Thorpe Market m. Giovanni Marcontonio **Benjamin** 1871 Thorpe Market **Tabitha** 1873 Thorpe Market died 1897 aged 25 **Absolum** 1876 Thorpe Market cowman in Yorkshire m. Sarah Overfield **Medonia** 1881 Thorpe Market m. Thomas Hand in Surrey
BAKER **Mary Ann** Southrepps	**1879** Should be taken on as monitoress for this dept each to teach one week in turn and to receive one shilling in payment for the week they are in school	**Unknown** **Charlotte Baker** 1845 Southrepps	**George** 1864 Southrepps farm labourer m. Anna Maria Bright **Mary Ann** 1867 Southrepps m. Robert Moore

BAKER George Southrepps	**1879** Admitted George William Baker from Trimingham School	**James** 1831 Southrepps Agricultural labourer **Ann Doe** 1837 Southrepps	**Emily** 1862 Southrepps lived in Southrepps **George** 1867 Southrepps lived with his sister, became a merchant carter
BAKER Sarah Ann Southrepps	**1879** Should be taken on as monitoress for this dept each to teach one week in turn and to receive one shilling in payment for the week they are in school	**George** 1842 Southrepps Agricultural labourer **Maria (Dixon)?** 1849 Trunch **Harriet Buck** 1847 Buxton	**Sarah Ann** 1868 Southrepps m. Fred Mann **Ann Maria** 1870 Southrepps m. Arthur Dye **Charlotte** 1871 Southrepps m. Cecil Cubitt **Louisa** 1873 Southrepps m. Charles Hamling **Alice** 1874 Southrepps m. James Amis **Walter** 1876 Southrepps gardener **Hannah** 1877 Southrepps m. James Gunning **Edith** 1881 Southrepps housekeeper **Rosa Mary** 1885 Southrepps housemaid
BAKER Harriet Lower Street	**1880** Harriet transferred from Infant room	**Moore** **Dix**	**Harriet** 1874 Southrepps m. George Reeves Living with her grandparents Charles and Mary Dix
BAKER Henry (Harry) Barn Row Upper Street	**1903** Sullen disobedience Ill behaviour in class Idleness	**Henry** 1860 Southrepps Agricultural labourer **Matilda Copeman** 1863 Wreningham	**Laura** 1886 Southrepps housemaid **Ellen** 1889 Southrepps **Harry** 1892 Southrepps farm labourer **Edward** 1898 Southrepps
BAKER Ella Upper Street	**1910** Received a watch	**Arthur** 1869 Southrepps Farm labourer **Keyoma Gotts** 1872 Southrepps	**Ernest** 1895 Southrepps farm labourer served with the Coldstream Guards WWI **Ella** 1897 Southrepps **Hilda** 1900 Southrepps **Keyoma** 1901 Southrepps m. Frank Fairhead **Gladys** 1904 Southrepps m. Thomas West **Mabel** 1906 Southrepps **Phyllis** 1908 Southrepps **Basil** 1910 Southrepps
BANE Robert Herbert Church Street Upper Street	**1879** Both boys admitted to school **1888** Robert backward and slow fit for the exemption schedule	**Henry** 1861 Southrepps Agricultural labourer **Georgina Bullimore** 1862 Gimingham	**Robert** 1880 Southrepps stoker stationary engine served with the Royal Navy in WWI m. Charlotte Beck **Herbert** 1882 Southrepps gardener served with the Royal Engineers m. Isabel Lawes **John** 1885 Southrepps served with the Black Watch died at sea following submarine attack on HMT Aragon 1917 Commemorated on Chatby Memorial, Alexandria
BANE (BEAN) William John T Bradfield	**1888** William dull and backward **1895** John weak health and intellect	**William** 1861 Southrepps Agricultural labourer **Elizabeth Bond** 1853 North Walsham	**William** 1881 Southrepps lived in Bradfield **John** 1884 Southrepps **Arthur** 1886 Antingham farm labourer **Mary** 1889 Antingham **Laura** 1891 Bradfield **George** 1896 Bradfield served with the Royal Navy and died in 1918 from influenza
BANE Ernest Warren Lane Lower Street	**1902** Continued idleness	**William** 1839 Southrepps Farm labourer **Mary Larke** 1849 Southrepps	**Susan** 1871 Southrepps **William** 1874 Southrepps farm labourer m. Judith Dunning **John** 1877 Southrepps farm labourer m. Ellen Bullimore **Lucy** 1880 Southrepps m. Joseph Grout **Robert** 1882 Southrepps labourer **James** 1885 farm labourer m. Ethel Burton-Pye **Ernest** 1892 Southrepps labourer m. Martha Whitwood
BEANE (BANE) Laura James May Blanche Lodge Cottages Upper Street	**1888** Laura absent sickness being still in the family **1902** James wilful mischief **1905** Measles	**John** 1855 Southrepps Horseman on farm **Susannah Neave** 1857 Southrepps	**Laura** 1882 Southrepps m. George Allard **Anna** 1883 Southrepps died 1903 aged 20 **George** 1884 Southrepps bricklayer **Frederick** 1886 Southrepps hock feeder on farm **Harriet** 1887 Southrepps m. Donald Peggs **John** 1889 Southrepps died 1894 aged 5 **James** 1891 Southrepps farm labourer m. Margaret Clark 1916, served with the Norfolk Regiment died Oct 1916, buried Grove Town Cemetery, Meaulte, Somme **Edith** 1892 Southrepps m. Ernest Plummer **May** 1894 Southrepps **Blanche** 1896 Southrepps m. John Dix 15 children 8 survived

BEANE (BANE) **Florence** **Rose** **Lily** Upper Street	**1901** Florence was 5 years and 5 months when admitted **1902** R Bane idleness in class **1905** Rose measles **1911** Lily Bane visited by the attendance officer	**Charles** 1875 Southrepps Platelayer on railway **Louisa Reynolds** 1875 Cromer	**Florence** 1896 Northrepps lived in Upper Street **Rose** 1898 Southrepps m. Walter Francis **Dorothy** 1902 Southrepps m. Frederick Chapman **Lily** 1905 Southrepps moved to London
BELL **Lucy** Antingham	**1884** Lucy has been monitoress this week	**Thomas** 1825 Antingham Maltster **Tamitha Gee** 1831 North Walsham	**Harriet** 1853 Antingham m. James Willlis **Thomas** 1854 Antingham maltster m. Maria Gee **Alice** 1856 Antingham m. Walter Sparrow **Ann** 1858 Antingham cook **Eliza** 1860 Antingham m. Henry Hewitt **Daniel** 1862 Antingham drayman m. Rosetta Smith **Rosa** 1864 Antingham m. Joseph Hammond **John** 1866 Antingham died 1876 aged 11 **Elizabeth** 1869 Antingham lady's maid **Lucy** 1872 Antingham housekeeper m James Kirk **Durrant** 1876 Antingham farmer m. Gertrude Dunning
BIRD **Kate** Upper Street	**c1900** Juvenile Grammar book 1886	**Thomas** 1855 Cromer Butcher **Susannah Edwards** 1857 Northrepps died 1882 **Mary Hewitt** 1856 Swafield	**Thomas** W 1878 Southrepps butcher m. Blanche Kirchen **Thomas** E 1884 Southrepps butcher m. Mabel Miller **Kate** 1886 Southrepps lived at home
BLOOM **James** Trunch	**1888** Obviously dull **1888** Weak intellect	**Antony** 1811 Trunch Agricultural labourer **Sophia Bond** 1837 Swafield	**Walter** 1859 Southrepps teamster on farm served with the Royal Horse Artillery m. Elizabeth Frary **Henry** 1861 Southend, Essex agricultural labourer lived with his parents **Alfred** 1864 Sorn, Suffolk agricultural labourer m. Sarah Oakley **George** 1865 Sorn, Suffolk agricultural labourer m. Harriet Wiseman **Edward** 1867 Southrepps agricultural labourer m. Elizabeth Whitwood **Harriet** 1868 Southrepps m. George Morter **Herbert** 1872 Southrepps agricultural labourer m. Eliza **Robert** 1874 Trimingham agricultural labourer m. Alice Rosebrow **Frederick** 1875 Trimingham agricultural labourer **James** 1878 Trimingham agricultural labourer m. Annie Bullimore **Elizabeth** 1879 Trunch died 1898 **Jane** 1881 Trunch m. William Spalding
BRADFIELD **Phillip** **Eva** Lower Street with their mother and grandparents	**1901** Philip 3rd prize for attendance Attendance prize 398 out of 408 sessions **1902** Eva 392 out of 408 sessions	**Charles** 1856 North Elmham Bus man **Harriet Saunders** 1872 Southrepps	**Philip** 1896 Cromer bullock feeder m. Dorothy Reynolds **Charles** 1897 Cromer died 1897 **Eva** 1897 Cromer **Bertie** 1904 labourer m. Margaret Dennis By 1911 the surviving three had been adopted by the Massingham family
BRIGGS **Walter** **Herb** Lower Street	**1910** Walter and Herb awarded white medals	**Earnest** 1868 Tasburgh Horseman on farm **Mary Ann Hawes** 1868 Dickleburgh	**Herbert** 1899 Southrepps engine driver m. Elsie Childs served with the Royal Navy in WWI **Walter** 1901 Southrepps **Bertie** 1902 Southrepps general labourer m. Ethnie Wright **Violet** 1904 Southrepps
BULLIMORE **Frederick** **Mary** Heath Lane Gimingham	**1884** Rev Dolphin promised to pay their fees from this week	**William** 1850 Gimingham Agricultural labourer **Ann Oakley** 1851 Brundall	**Frederick (John)** 1873 Gimingham farm labourer m. Laura Powles **Mary** 1875 Gimingham m. Charles Dix **Matilda** 1880 Gimingham m. Clifford Allen **Ann** 1882 Gimingham m. Henry Wayte **William** 1884 Gimingham general labourer **Sarah** 1886 Gimingham m. Albert High **Cubitt** 1888 Gimingham farm labourer served with the Norfolk Regiment WWI m. Esther Garrod

BULLIMORE **Walter** **James** Thorpe Market	**1910** Walter awarded white medal **1910** Attendance certificate **1911** James visited by the attendance officer	**James** 1875 Gimingham General labourer **Susan Thurston** 1881 Antingham	**Alice** 1900 Southrepps **Mary** 1901 Southrepps m. Harold Webster **Walter** 1903 Southrepps general labourer m. Ellen Nicholls **Frank** 1903 Southrepps market gardener m. Deborah West **James** 1906 Southrepps m. Theresa Storey **Susan** 1908 Southrepps **Noel** 1911 Thorpe Market died 1926 aged 15
BUMFREY **Muriel** Thorpe Market	**1911** Kept back in Infant department because she is an epileptic and also cannot learn anything	**George** 1876 Gimingham Teamster on farm **Mary Shaw** 1874 Field Dalling	**Muriel** 1904 Metton died 1921 aged 17
BURRELL **Betty (Elizabeth)** Southrepps	**1878** Admitted to school 25th February **1879** Readmitted 21st April	**James** 1843 Ingworth, Norfolk Mole destroyer **Hannah Balls** Field Dalling died 1874	**Laura** 1865 Gimingham m. Horace Stevenson **Elizabeth** 1868 Thorpe Market in 1881 she is living with her grandparents the rest of the family is at the Crown Upper Street **Robert** 1870 Thorpe Market m. Emma Jacob father re married and became the publican at the Crown
BURRIDGE **Joseph** Upper Street	**1911** Admitted Joseph Burridge the parents of this child claim exemption from religious instruction	**Charles** 1862 Stratford, Essex Policeman **Kate Amelia Towerzey** 1874 Blandford, Dorset	**Winifred** 1892 Deptford, London **Bernard** 1896 Paddington London served with the Royal Lancaster's killed in action Salonika, Greece **Cicily** 1900 Paddington **Joseph** 1905 Kensal Green
BURTON **Edward** **William** Lower Street	**1900** Edward continued Idleness and talking William received a book prize for best marks earned in each standard in late examinations standard VI	**William** 1866 Southrepps Bricklayer **Mary Bullimore** 1868 Gimingham	**Herbert** 1887 Southrepps police officer Norwich m. Maria Alice Moy **Edward** 1889 Southrepps served with the Coldstream Guards died of Wounds France and Flanders 1914 buried Ypres Stedelijke Begraafplaats **Maud** 1891 Southrepps m. Frederick Hurn **William** 1893 Southrepps
BURTON (PYE) **Arthur** **Samuel** **Gertrude** Lower Street	**1900** Samuel obtained a special prize for making 100% attendances **1900** Arthur disobedience **1904** Gertrude received a book prize for best marks earned in each standard in late examinations standard III	**Frank** 1861 Southrepps Bricklayer **Edith Woodhouse** 1864 Southrepps died 1901	**Ethel** 1886 Southrepps m. James Bane **Laura** 1888 Southrepps m. Charles Neave **Arthur** 1890 Southrepps horticultural labourer m. Edith Craske **Samuel** 1895 Southrepps granary man m. Winifred Briggs, served with the Norfolk Regiment, prisoner of war in Bulgaria Dec 1915 to Nov 1918 **Gertrude** 1896 Southrepps m. Robert Gotts **Ernest** 1897 Southrepps served with the Norfolk Regiment killed in action 1916 no known grave, commemorated at Thiepval Memorial **Hilda** 1900 Southrepps
BURTON-PYE **John** Lower Street	**1880** Fees remitted 2s 2d	**Henry** 1846 Southrepps Bricklayer **Eleanor Earl** 1843 Northrepps	**Lucy Earl** 1864 Northrepps **Susannah** 1862 Northrepps m. Robert Burton Pye **John** 1870 Southrepps bricklayer m. Frances Mabel Dunning 1891 served with the Royal Engineers, died Aug 1916 no known grave, commemorated on Somme, Thiepval Memorial **Mary** 1872 Southrepps m. Edwin Roper **Martha** 1874 Southrepps m. Edwin Roper **Margaret** 1877 Southrepps m. James Stone **Henry** 1880 Southrepps bricklayer m. Alice Amis **Edward** 1882 Southrepps farm labourer m. Caroline Culley
CHADWICK **Sidney** Pond Street Northrepps	**1879** Admitted to school	**Elijah** 1839 Overstrand Agricultural labourer **Mary Matthews** 1839 Northrepps	**George** 1866 Overstrand groom in livery stables m. Frances Grout **Frederick** 1868 Overstrand tin plate workers store keeper London m. Eliza Watkins **James** W 1871 Overstrand gas works labourer m. Alice Jacob **Sidney** 1873 Overstrand agricultural labourer **John H** 1875 Northrepps contractors foreman Essex m. Emily Skerrit **Sarah** 1878 Northrepps m. Samuel Skerritt **Harriet** 1880 Northrepps cook

CHADWICK **Kenneth** Lower Street	**1908** 6 years and 10 months when admitted	**Arthur** 1872 Southrepps Carpenter **Annie** 1879 Normanton, Leicestershire	**Kenneth** 1901 Southrepps road labourer m. Lily Flaxman
CHILDS **Francis** Lower Street	**1886** Returned to school after several weeks' illness	**Charles** 1845 Antingham Plate layer **Matilda Mayes** 1847 Southrepps	**Hetty** 1874 Southrepps m. James Abbs **Francis** 1876 Southrepps cabinet maker m. Lucy Irwin **Lillian** 1880 Southrepps m. Hedley Browning **Florence** 1883 Southrepps m. Jedidah Johnson **Maud** 1886 Southrepps m. Jessie Browning moved to Kendal
CLABBURN **James** Upper Street	**1907** Absent on account of scarletina/measles	**Unknown** **Edith Clabburn** 1877 Coltishall	**James** 1897 Southrepps **Ernest** 1900 Southrepps served with the East Surrey Regiment WWI
CODLING **Anna** **Florence** **Alice** Bradfield	**1879** 3rd February admitted Florence 4th February admitted Anna Florence cautioned for being late. All three girls absented themselves from school this week to pick turnips	**Robert** 1841 Bradfield Agricultural labourer **Charlotte Suffolk** 1841 Bradfield	**Robert** 1862 Bradfield agricultural labourer brewer's drayman London m. Helena Yaxley **Anna (Julianna)** 1867 Bradfield m. William Hurn **Florence** 1871 Bradfield **Alice** 1873 Bradfield died 1886 aged 13 **Herbert** 1878 Bradfield
CODLING **George** Rose Cottage Bradfield	**1907** Absent on account of scarletina/measles	**Elija** 1865 Bradfield Farm labourer **Alice Bullimore** 1866 North Walsham	**George** 1897 Bradfield farm labourer m. Emily Cooper
CODLING **Amelia** **Jack (John)** Southrepps	**1913** Amelia Codling was specially examined by the doctor to find if she was fit to attend school **1914** Dr visited, Amelia suffering from chest weakness **1917** John is a consumptive and quite unable to attend regularly	**John** 1865 Bradfield Roadman **Julia Craske** née **Gray** 1872 Southrepps	Edie, Edward, Frederick, and Rex are listed under Craske **Amelia** 1908 Southrepps lady's maid **Jack (John)** 1910 Southrepps horticulturist m. Eva Goodchild
COLK **Anna** Lower Street	**1878** Admitted to school	**Unknown** **Unknown**	**Anna** 1868 Southrepps lived with her grandparents Charles and Mary Colk m. William Porter
COLMAN **Violet** Upper Street	**1903** Talking in class	**Frederick** 1869 Kettlestone Sub-postmaster **Agnes Palmer** 1868 Barton Bendish	**Daisy** 1891 Norwich nursery governess **Violet** 1894 Southrepps m. Bunnell Burton **May** 1895 Roughton m. Frank Stevenson **Lily** 1896 Southrepps m. Edgar Thomas **Frederick** 1899 Southrepps emigrated to Australia
COOKE **Roland**	**1907** Little Roland Cooke a scholar in the babyroom died	**Unknown** **Unknown**	**Roland** 1902 died 1907
COSSEY **Charles** **Samuel** Lower Street	**1910** Charles received a watch Samuel gilt medal **1911** Samuel received a watch Mary received a white medal	**William** 1873 Hempnall Engine driver **Sarah** 1874 Hartlepool	**William** 1895 Hanworth farm labourer m. Bessie Goulding **James** 1897 Hanworth farm labourer served with the army WWI **Charles** 1899 Hanworth m. Lena Lawrence served with the Training Reserve Battalion WWI **Mary** 1900 Hanworth died 1923 aged 23 **Samuel** 1902 Hanworth farm labourer m. Clara Goulding **Amelia** 1909 Southrepps m. Albert Craske
CRASKE **Edith** Sandy Lane Upper Street	**1902** 5 years and 7 months when admitted	**Robert** 1868 Roughton Shoemaker died 1903 **Julia Gray** 1872 Southrepps	**Edith** 1896 Sustead m. Arthur Burton-Pye **Edward** 1898 Sustead carter served with the Machine Gun Corps in WWI m. Annie Arnold **Frederick** 1900 Southrepps agricultural worker m. Miriam Chapman **Rex** 1903 Southrepps

CROWE **Ann** Railway Gate House Antingham	**1879** Caned Ann Crowe for disobedience Ann transferred from the Infant room	**William** 1829 Antingham Plate layer **Elizabeth Knights** 1835 Southrepps	**William** 1857 Antingham platelayer m. Susannah Betts **Eliza** 1858 Antingham cook in Paddington **Benjamin** 1860 Bradfield coal hawker m. Blanche Myhill **Caroline** 1862 Antingham dressmaker **John** 1869 Antingham police sergeant Essex m. Elizabeth Gladden **Richard** 1870 Antingham footman m. Elvere Green **Ann** 1873 Antingham m. Charles Saxby **George** 1877 Antingham platelayer **Walter** 1880 Antingham railway porter Four other children who died
CUBITT **George** **John** The Crown and Anchor Trimingham	**1881** Boys admitted to school **1883** Boys left the school	**George** 1846 Trimingham licensed victualler and carpenter **Emma Senter** 1853 Hunstanton	**William** 1868 Southrepps single. "Imbecile from childhood" **George** 1869 Southrepps farmer m. Annie Futter **John** 1871 Southrepps farm steward m. Edith Dawes **Mabel** 1885 Trimingham m. Robert Bartram
CUSHION **Emily** Thorpe Market	**1888** Backward and slow fit for the exemption schedule	**Stephen** 1845 Thorpe Market Farm labourer died 1888 **Emily Cork** 1854	**Amelia** 1875 Southrepps m. Ernest Hurn **Susannah** 1877 Southrepps m. Frederick Pardon **George** 1879 Southrepps horseman on farm m. Alice Waller **Emily** 1880 Southrepps died 1897 aged 17 **Robert** 1886 Southrepps agricultural labourer m. Helena Baxter
DANIELS **Reggie** **Edgar** Poplar House Antingham	**1908** Reggie 5 years and 7 months when admitted **1911** Edgar two, three months over age but very slow to learn and could not possibly do Standard I work	**James** 1879 Gimingham Horseman on farm **Eliza Sharrod** 1880 West Walton	**Reggie** 1903 Antingham died 1929 aged 26 **Edgar** 1904 Antingham engineer m. Winifred Davies
DIX **Harriet** Church Street Upper Street	**1878** Punished Harriet Dix for playing the truant	**Thomas** 1813 Bradfield Agricultural labourer **Sarah Ward** 1825 Aylmerton	**John Ward** 1849 Gimingham agricultural labourer m. Ann Secker **William** 1852 Southrepps agricultural labourer m. Rosa Jarvis **James** 1853 Beckham agricultural labourer m. Emma Wilson **Simon** 1857 Southrepps **Rebecca** 1862 Southrepps chambermaid London **Reuben** 1864 Southrepps agricultural labourer m. Honor Hicks **Lucy** 1865 Southrepps m. Joseph Reynolds **Eliza** 1867 Southrepps died 1883 aged 17 **Harriet** 1868 Southrepps m. William Chadwick
DIX **Mary Ann** Gimingham	**1879** Admitted to school 24th March	**James** 1839 Southrepps Agricultural labourer **Sarah Hardingham** 1841 Southrepps	**James** 1866 Southrepps shepherd m. Hannah Bullimore **Charles** 1867 Southrepps agricultural labourer m. Mary Bullimore **Mary Ann** 1872 Southrepps m. Thomas Sexton **Robert** 1875 Southrepps horseman on farm m. Hannah Allard **William** 1877 Gimingham horseman on farm **Albert** 18789 Gimingham farm labourer m. Susannah Weston **Harriet** 1886 Gimingham m. William Chadwick
DIX **Robert** Lower Street	**1888** Backward and slow fit for the exemption schedule	**James** 1854 Antingham Agricultural labourer **Julia Pardon** 1857 Trimingham	**Florence** 1877 Shotten Colliery, Durham m. James Palmer **Robert** 1879 Shotten Colliery, Durham blacksmith m. Mary Sutton **Violet** 1885 Southrepps died 1909 aged 24
DIX **Robert** Upper Street	**1888** Backward and slow fit for the exemption schedule	**James** 1853 Beckham Agent for Prudential died 1890 **Emma Wilson** 1858 Knapton	**Robert** 1881 Beckham bricklayer **Eliza** 1884 Southrepps m. Ernest Reynolds **Walter (James)** 1889 Southrepps police constable m. Annie Holburn

Name / Address	School records	Parents	Siblings / Children
DIX Robert Reuben Church Street Upper Street	**1905** Measles	**Reuben** 1864 Southrepps Reserve solider **Honor Hicks** 1869 Felmingham	**Robert** 1897 Southrepps farm labourer served with the Norfolk Regiment killed in action Palestine 1917 buried Gaza War Cemetery **Reuben** 1899 Southrepps baker **Frederick** 1906 Southrepps chauffeur m Dorothy Bullimore **Muriel** 1907 Southrepps Two other non-surviving children
DOVE Charlotte Alfred	**1888** Have left the district	**Martin** 1839 Suffield Agricultural labourer **Mary Harmer** 1843 Coltishall	Family moved about a lot 8 children
DRURY John Upper Street	**1880** Admitted to school	**Chapman** 1845 Skeyton Baker **Eliza Nobbs** 1848 Asmanhaugh	**Alice** 1873 Southrepps m. Arthur Tuthill **John** 1874 Southrepps master baker m. Edith **William** 1876 Southrepps journeyman baker m. Tabitha Wallage **Ellen** 1887 Southrepps m. Frederick Wallage **Robert** 1879 Southrepps journeyman baker m. Alice Knights **Ernest** 1883 Southrepps joiner enlisted RFC 1917 m. Edith Ellis **Elsie** 1888 Southrepps Elsie died 1907 aged 19
DRURY Reggie Church Street Southrepps	**1910** Reggie won a book prize **1917** Reggie Drury has been awarded the Military Medal	**William** 1876 Southrepps Shopkeeper **Tabitha (Ellen) Wallage** 1875 North Walsham	**Reginald** 1898 Southrepps journeyman baker served with the Machine Gun Corps WWI served with RAF in WWII **Nellie** 1900 Southrepps m. Clifford Clarke **Bernard** 1903 Southrepps painter m. Charlotte Maria Marling served with the Labour Corps in WWI **Cristobel** 1906 Southrepps m. Herbert Morris **Frederick** 1907 Southrepps lorry driver **May** 1909 Southrepps m John Howes
DUNNING Ann Herbert Lower Street	**1880** Sent home Ann with the measles **1891** Too backward to work with standard I	**Edward** 1847 North Walsham Assistant labourer died 1886 **Hannah Harmer** 1849 Southrepps	**Ann** 1869 Southrepps m. Cornelius Culley **Emma** 1870 Southrepps m. John Bickel **Susan** 1871 Southrepps **William** 1873 Southrepps agricultural labourer m. Edith Bailey **Edward** 1876 Southrepps farm labourer m. Julia Rivett **Robert** 1877 Southrepps horseman on farm m. Rosa Harvey **Judith** 1880 Southrepps m. William Bane **Charles** 1882 Southrepps farm labourer m. Lucy Whitby **Herbert** 1885 Southrepps labourer on farm **Gertrude** 1887 Southrepps m. Durrant Bell
DUNNING Nelson Norman Lower Street	**1903** Inattention at drill	**Unknown** **Susan Dunning** 1871 Southrepps	**Nelson** 1891 Durham parents unknown his mother might have been Susan **Norman** 1894 Southrepps farm labourer served with Argyll and Sutherland Highlanders and Norfolk Boys Both boys living with maternal grandmother Hannah Dunning
DYBALL Maud	**1888** Weak health	**William** 1856 Hackford Horse trainer **Louisa Yaxley** 1859 Scotton	**Maud** 1882 Southrepps barmaid in London hotel
EARL Anna Church Street Southrepps	**1880** Anna Earl has been monitoress for this past week	**John** 1836 Southrepps Agricultural labourer **Maryann Gray** 1831 Trimingham	**Ann** 1869 Southrepps m. William Wiltshire Living with her grandmother
EARL Edith Upper Street	**1880** Obliged to cane Edith Earl for disobedience and refusing to beg her teacher's pardon	**William** 1838 Southrepps Agricultural labourer **Lydia Basey** 1839 East Tudenham	**William** 1864 Southrepps agricultural labourer, brewer's labourer London m. Ellen Phelan **Walter** 1866 Southrepps policeman London m. Frances Yaxley **Edith** 1869 Southrepps parlour maid London died 1901 aged 32 **Mildred** 1871 Southrepps housemaid London **Elizabeth** 1875 Southrepps kitchen maid London m. Henry Ingle **Rosanna** 1878 Southrepps m. John Lawrence

EMPSOM Rhoda Southrepps	**1881** Caned **1883** Left the school	**Unknown** **Emily Empsom** 1848 Southrepps	**Elizabeth** 1867 Southrepps **Rhoda** 1870 Southrepps m. Herbert Surridge in London Mother married Richard Grey and they then took his name
EMPSOM Lily Bradfield	**1908** Admitted to school 6 years 7 months	**Charles** 1860 Southrepps Farm labourer **Malaha Newstead** 1861 Calthorpe	**Horace** 1882 Aylsham shop keeper m. Carrie Barker served with the Royal Navy in WWI **George** 1885 Aylsham farm labourer m. Mabel Hart **Alfred** 1889 Bradfield farm labourer m. Florence Moore **Rose** 1891 Bradfield m. Harry Brown **Frederick** 1895 Bradfield farm labourer m. Beryl Murray **Reginald** 1899 Bradfield m. Mary Folkes **Lily** 1901 Bradfield m. Arthur Bloom
EVISON Elsie Gunton Station Living with grandparents	**1904** Received a book prize for best marks in each standard in late examinations standard VII **1905** Left school as failed to pass the necessary exam for pupil teacher post. Had previously been a monitoress	**John** 1854 Hogsthorpe, Lincolnshire Insurance agent **Ellen Atkins** 1865 Cathawade, Essex	**Florence** 1886 Norwich elementary teacher **Elsie** 1890 Norwich nurse domestic **Grace** 1901 Earlstown, Lancashire
FRAREY John Antingham	**1888** John Frarey a first-class boy has been absent having broken his collarbone	**Elijah** 1856 Antingham Agricultural labourer **Annie Swallow** 1861 Gresham	**John** 1882 Antingham
FUTTER John North Walsham Rd Bradfield	**1901** 5 years and 9 months when admitted	**John** 1860 Hainford **Eliza Mary York** 1862 Ashmanhaugh Agricultural worker	**William** 1886 Trimingham blacksmith served with the Army Service Corps in WWI **Richard** 1890 Bradfield lorry driver served with the Labour Corps in WWI m. Alice Chapman **Ellen** 1893 Bradfield m. Edward Mileham **Robert** 1895 Bradfield farm labourer signaller in Essex Regiment killed in action France 1915 buried Corbie Communal Cemetery, France **John** 1896 Bradfield gardener killed in action Flanders 1917 8th Battalion buried Tyne Cot, Belgium **Irene (Elsie)** 1898 Bradfield m. Richard Harris **Mary** 1900 Bradfield **Emmeline** 1902 Bradfield m. Ernest Hardingham **Hetty** 1904 Bradfield m. William Douglas in Croydon
GAZE Marjorie Thorpe Lodge on the Gunton Estate	**1902** 6 years and 9 months when admitted	**George** 1860 Colby Estate carpenter **Ann Payne** 1863 Bodham	**Marjorie** 1895 Thorpe Market dressmaker
GIBBONS Amelia Thorpe Market	**1879** Amelia passed Standard I	**Robert** 1834 Trunch Waggoner **Elizabeth** 1829 Roughton Shopkeeper	**Gertrude** 1861 Roughton dressmaker m. John Hewitt **Albert** 1863 Thorpe Market waggoner m. Rachel Baker **Laura** 1868 Thorpe Market m. Robert Fox **Amelia** 1869 Thorpe Market m. James Dowling
GIBBONS Hilda Gunton park	**1915** Hilda appointed monitoress Commenced work as Pupil teacher in the mixed department	**George** 1877 Thorpe Market Estate bricklayer **Mary Booth** 1875 Alby	**Hilda** 1901 Thorpe Market m. Leonard Mitchel **Frederick** 1903 Thorpe Market emigrated to Canada m. Elsie Smith
GIBBONS Timothy Thorpe Lodge Thorpe Market	**1917** Timothy Gibbons an old scholar was awarded the Military Medal after his death in battle	**William** 1853 Trunch Gamekeeper **Elizabeth Barber** 1851 Southrepps	**Alfred** 1876 Thorpe Market gamekeeper m. Maud Riddell **George** 1877 Thorpe Market estate bricklayer m. Mary Booth **Lily** 1879 Thorpe Market m. William Barlee **Emma** 1880 Thorpe Market m. Robert Earle **Frederick** 1883 Thorpe Market gamekeeper m. Ruby Copeman served with the Norfolk Regiment **Timothy** 1884 Thorpe Market gamekeeper Sergeant Norfolk Regiment killed in action France 1916 posthumous award of Military Medal buried Thiepval Memorial **Julia** 1886 Thorpe Market m. Albert Carr **Violet** 1890 Thorpe market dressmaker

GLISTER William Gimingham	**1881** Admitted to school	**Unknown** **Unknown**	**William** 1874 Gimingham Boarder with Robert and Elizabeth Glister no further records
GOLDEN Blanche Pig and Whistle	**1879** Blanche admitted to school 27th October **1880** Blanche monitoress for past three weeks	**James** 1845 Southrepps Head groom died 1879 **Sarah Atlew** 1844 Gunton Publican	**Elisa** 1865 Gunton housekeeper **James** 1867 London agricultural labourer **Blanche** 1869 Thorpe Market m. Alfred Gee **Benjamin** 1870 Thorpe Market blind **Cecilia** 1872 m. Andrew Clarke **John** 1876 North Walsham agricultural labourer m. Rachel Gray **Herbert** 1877 North Walsham bricklayer **Violet** 1882 Southrepps m. Ernest Griffin
GOTTS Eliza Stephen Lower Street	**1878** Eliza Transferred from the Infant department **1902** Stephen playing in class	**John** 1850 Horning Norfolk Farm labourer **Priscilla Hardingham** 1852 Southrepps	**Eliza** 1871 W, Hartlepool, Durham m. Charles Hurn **Keyoma** 1873 Southrepps m. Arthur Baker **Ellen** 1876 Southrepps m. Edward Rix **Alice** 1877 Southrepps m. Walter Scott **Charles** 1879 Southrepps farm labourer m. Maria Rix **John** 1881 Southrepps farm labourer m. Nessie Neave **William** 1883 Southrepps farm labourer m. Gertrude Wilby served with Norfolk Regiment in WWI **Ida** 1886 Southrepps m. Edward Slaughter **Stephen** 1891 Southrepps farm labourer m. Alice Clements **Lillian** 1894 Southrepps m. Alfred Wright
GOTTS Cyril Bertie Mary Lower Street	**1902** Attendance prize full attendance 408 sessions **1904** Received a book prize for best marks earned in each standard late examinations Mary, Cyril, and Bertie absent due to scarletina and measles	**Matthew** 1862 Southrepps Farmer **Mary Brooks** 1864 Swafield	**Matthew** 1886 Southrepps gardener m. Elizabeth Myhill served with the Suffolk Regiment and Queens Regiment, PoW in Germany May 1918–January 1919 **Lily** 1888 Southrepps m. Herbert Thompson **Ellen** 1889 Southrepps servant **Samuel** 1890 Suffield m. Mary Jane Buckner 1910 solider with the Royal Garrison Artillery **Archie** 1892 Southrepps gardener served with the Royal Garrison Artillery in WWI m. Maud Towler **Mary** 1896 Southrepps servant **Cyril** 1898 Southrepps farm labourer served with the Norfolk Regiment and Tank Corps in WWI m. Ivy Hicks 1925 believed to have joined Metropolitan Police **Bertie** 1899 Southrepps Master builder served with the Northamptonshire Regiment in WWI m. Lily Walker **Philip** 1901 Southrepps chauffeur in Finchley m. Ada Matthews **Daisy** 1904 Southrepps went to London **Catherine** 1908 Southrepps m. Percy Brown
GRAY Caroline Upper Street	**1878** Admitted to school 11th February	**Robert** 1842 Northrepps Farm labourer **Eleanor Grout** 1842 Southrepps	**George** 1863 Southrepps farm labourer m. Harriet Rudrum **Charles** 1865 Southrepps farm labourer m. Maria (Clara) Grey **Caroline** 1868 Southrepps m. James Gray **Robert** 1876 Southrepps gardener m. Frances Richardson **Eleanor** 1880 Southrepps m. Clement Mothersole **Frederick** 1882 Southrepps gardener m. Maria Richardson
GRAY George Ellen Hannah Upper Street	**1879** Hannah admitted to Girls' school from Infants' **1879** Ellen moved up from infants due to age, only fit to work **1885** George fell from the trees in the playground and was severely hurt about the head* **1890** George punished for gross insubordination* * or boy in next entry	**Richard** 1845 Southrepps Farm Labourer **Emily Empson** 1847 Southrepps	**Hannah** 1872 Southrepps m. Charles Ryan in London **George** 1874 Southrepps butler m. Clara **Emily** 1876 Southrepps m. George Reynolds **Charles** 1878 Southrepps bricklayer m. Alice Kerry m. Alice Mabel Cole 1899 Northrepps, served with the Norfolk Regiment and Bedfordshire Regiment in WWI **Ellen** 1881 Southrepps **Julia** 1884 Southrepps **Edith** 1886 Southrepps (Elizabeth and Rhoda Empsom)

GRAY George The Mill Lower Street ~~boy~~	**1885** George fell from the trees in the playground and was severely hurt about the head* **1890** Punished for gross insubordination* * or boy in previous entry	**George** 1845 Northrepps Miller **Hannah Dennis** 1849 Overstrand Dressmaker	**Henry H** 1866 Northrepps saddle and harness maker **Edith E** 1872 Northrepps dressmaker m. Solomon Hicks **George** 1877 Southrepps miller at Ingworth m. Caroline Fairbairn **Charles R** 1881 Southrepps miller emigrated to Canada m. Gertrude Lovelock
GRAY Emma Upper Street	**1891** Too backward to work with standard I	**George** 1862 Shouldham Farm labourer died 1899 **Elizabeth Fuller** 1863 Trunch	**Emma** 1884 Southrepps domestic servant **Ann** 1886 Southrepps **Daisy** 1888 Southrepps **Ethel** 1892 Southrepps m. George Collins **Katie** 1897 Southrepps m. Frank Day
GRAY Ivy Theophilus Long Lane Southrepps	**1901** Admitted Ivy Gray aged 6 years and three months, she has not been to school before this **1908** Theophilus 5 years and 9 months when admitted Herman admitted at 6 years and 9 months	**Herbert** 1876 Northrepps Gardener **Barbara Cutting** 1871 North Walsham Dressmaker	**Ivy** 1895 North Walsham m. John Ward **Theophilus** 1897 Northrepps farm labourer served with the Essex Regiment killed in action 1916, buried Auchonvillers Military Cemetery, France **Herman** 1902 Southrepps stock feeder m. Rachel Connolly **Mildred** 1905 Southrepps
GRAY Elsie Herbert Marjorie Kathleen Lodge Cottage Southrepps	**1905** Measles **1901** Kathleen was 5 years and 9 months when admitted **1907** Kenneth was 6 years and 6 months when admitted 1906, 101 attendances 1907, 344 not transferred to Upper school	**George** 1863 Southrepps Farm labourer **Harriet Rudrum** 1864 Mundesley	**Ruth** 1885 Southrepps m. George Graver **Alice** 1887 Gimingham m. Charles Barrett **Cyril** 1889 Trimingham farm labourer m. Ivy Rudd **Kathleen** 1891 Trimingham m. Walter Seago **Elsie** 1895 Trimingham m. George Reynolds **Herbert** 1897 Trimingham farm labourer served with the Machine Gun Corps died from wounds France 1918 buried Klein-Vierstraat British Cemetery, Belgium **Marjorie** 1893 Gimingham m. Frederick Laws **Kenneth** 1901 Southrepps tractor driver m. Florence Barnes
GRAY Frederick Mary Rectory Road Southrepps	**1907** Frederick 6 years and 8 months when admitted 1906, 112 attendances 1907, 267 not transferred to Upper school **1907** Mary absent on account of scarletina and measles	**Charles** 1866 Southrepps Market gardener **Clara Grey** 1858 Fulmodeston	**Caroline** 1888 Southrepps m. George Wilkinson Hampstead **Albert** 1891 Southrepps market gardener m. Ann Elizabeth Gotts then Sarah Sutherland, served in Norfolk Yeomanry before and during WWI **Ernest** 1893 Southrepps carpenter m. Alice Larke served with the Labour Corps WWI **Mary** 1896 Southrepps m. Albert Copeman **Nelly** 1899 Southrepps **Frederick** 1901 Southrepps gamekeeper m. Lottie Rogers **Florence** 1903 Southrepps m. Albert Hammond
GRAY Margaret Southrepps	**1908** 6 years and 10 months when admitted	**Robert** 1877 Southrepps Gardener **Frances Richardson** 1877 North Runcton	**Margaret** 1901 Southrepps **Alfred** 1903 Southrepps gardener m. Doris Smith **Edith** 1905 Southrepps **John** 1907 Southrepps **Sidney** 1916 Southrepps
GREENFIELD Sidney Antingham	**1917** Sidney Greenfield another old scholar has been awarded the Military Cross	**Sidney** 1875 Leicester Tailor's cutter **Clara Bent** 1875 Leicester	**Sidney** 1897 Leicester general manager m. Irene Hardman served with the Northumberland Fusiliers **George** 1899 Leicester **Gladys** 1901 Leicester m. Herbert Morris
GROUT Lillian White Gate Road Upper Street	**1878** Lillian admitted 11th March **1891** Family absent on account of the measles	**Ephraim** 1841 Southrepps Farm labourer **Rebecca Blogg** 1842 Southrepps	**Lillian** 1870 Southrepps m. James Cutler **Joseph** 1873 Southrepps groom, gardener servant m. Lucy Bane **Rosanna** 1875 Southrepps cook in London **William** 1877 Southrepps gardener **Edgar** 1879 Southrepps cowman m. Emma Gould **Henry** 1881 Southrepps m. Harriet Debdage **Arthur** 1885 Southrepps died 1894 aged 10 **James** 1889 Southrepps farm labourer m. Mary Butcher served with Royal West Surrey Regiment and Labour Corps in WWI

GUIVER **Maude** **Mabel** Thorpe Market	**1881** Maude and Mabel admitted to school 7th February	**Charles** 1845 Chelmsford, Essex Butler **Emma Neal** 1848 Banbury, Oxfordshire	**Maude** 1870 Chelmsford m. Edwin Grafton **Mabel** 1872 Chelmsford died 1883 Fulham aged 11 **John** 1874 Chelmsford cycle maker m. Lucy Chamberlin **Violet** 1879 Chelmsford m. Raymond Burr **Lillie** 1882 London m. Thomas James emigrated to America **Edwin** 1886 Kensington, London emigrated to America
HALL **Agnes** Lower Street	**1878** Agnes admitted 16th July **1879** Cautioned for being late **1880** Agnes monitoress	**Unknown** Butcher **Elizabeth** 1842 Antingham	**Agnes** 1872 Thurlby, Lincolnshire **Alice** 1874 Thurlby, Lincolnshire **Judith** 1877 Thurlby, Lincolnshire **Olivia** 1878 Thurlby, Lincolnshire
HALL **Arthur** The Common Bradfield	**1907** Papers given to see how many of those below standard were improved sufficiently to take their places in higher standard. Arthur to stay with his class in arithmetic	**Christopher** 1859 Aylsham Agricultural labourer **Sally Yaxley** 1861 Scottow	**Ethel** 1887 Bradfield cook **Jane** 1890 Bradfield servant **Arthur** 1896 Bradfield farm labourer
HAMILTON **Maud** Lower Street	**1908** 6 years and 9 months when admitted	**Unknown** **Unknown**	**Maud** 1902 Norwich Boarder in the 1911 census with Hannah Hurn no further information found
HARDINGHAM **William** **Robert** Bradfield	**1881** Readmitted William and Robert Hardingham	**William** 1844 Southrepps Agricultural Labourer **Mary Ann Silver** 1845 Bradfield	**John (Silver)** 1866 Bradfield stepson deaf and dumb from childhood **Edith** 1868 Smallburgh **William** 1871 Southrepps gardener ostler at Royal Hotel Mundesley m. Ellen Buller **Blanche** 1874 Southrepps m. Benjamin Hall **Robert** 1875 Bradfield farm labourer **Catherine** 1876 Bradfield **Lucy** 1877 Bradfield nurse **Georgina** 1879 Bradfield m. Horace Watts **Jonas** 1883 Bradfield served with the Army Service Corps m. Hettie Amies **Sidney** 1887 Bradfield general labourer m. Lily Bullimore In the 1881 census Robert, William and Catherine are all at the Smallburgh Workhouse.
HARDINGHAM **May** **Robert** **Ernest** **Sidney** Railway crossing Antingham	**1902** May Hardingham is reported by the attendance officer as suffering from typhoid fever **1905** Robert and Ernest, measles **1911** Sidney, two, three months over age but very slow to learn and could not possibly do Standard I work	**Robert** 1873 Southrepps Agricultural labourer **Edith Amies** 1878 North Walsham	**May** 1896 North Walsham housemaid **Robert** 1898 North Walsham **Ernest** 1900 Antingham labourer m. Catherine Staples **Sidney** 1904 Antingham horseman on farm m. Helen Bird **Harry** 1908 Antingham agricultural labourer **Frederick** 1911 Antingham agricultural labourer
HARDINGHAM **Blanche** Lower Street with her grandparents William and Mary Hardingham	**1901** Prize for full attendance	**Unknown** **Georgina Hardingham** 1880 Bradfield 1903 m. Horace Watts 1876 Mundesley farm labourer	**Blanche** 1895 Mundesley m. Tom Hicks **William** 1900 Southrepps **Horace Watts** 1904 North Walsham land worker m. Elsie Wall **Charles Watts** 1906 North Walsham **John Watts** 1907 North Walsham lorry driver m. Violet Saunders
HARDINGHAM **Henrietta** The Hill Antingham	**1914** Dr visited, Hettie suffering from chest weakness	**Jonah** 1885 Bradfield Farm Labourer **Hettie Ethel Amies** 1885 North Walsham	**Henrietta** 1908 North Walsham m. Wilfred Ellis **Thomas** 1910 Antingham
HARMER **Ernest** **Edgar** Bradfield	**1888** Ernest, moved up from infants due to age, only fit to work with second class infants dull and backward **1895** Edgar weak health and long continued absence	**Jonathan** 1852 Kings Lynn Agricultural labourer **Sarah Nicholls** 1854 Matlaske	**Ernest** 1881 Matlaske died 1902 aged 21 **Edgar** 1883 Bradfield served with the Royal Flying Corps became a grocery dealer in Devon m. Marion Playford **Kathleen** 1899 Kings Lynn

HARVEY Eliza Thorpe Market	**1878** Admitted to school 25th February	**Robert** **Ann**	**Eliza** 1868 Thorpe Market baptismal record no other information
HARVEY Herbert Upper Street	**1880** Admitted to school	**John** 1845 Southrepps Agricultural labourer **Amelia Pitt** 1851 Trunch	**Herbert** 1874 Trunch jobbing gardener m. Anna Clements **Walter** 1875 Southrepps died 1882 aged 7 **Eleanor** 1880 Southrepps m. Ralph Taylor a school master and moved to Twickenham
HARRIS Charles	**1889** Left school having removed to North Walsham	**George** 1856 Stratford, Essex Groom **Elizabeth Jane** 1862 Shepreth, Cambridgeshire	**Charles** 1885 Southrepps ostler served in the Rifle Brigade in WWI m. Annie Bullimore
HEMSWORTH Church Street	**1902** Hemsworth continued playing in class	**Edward** 1864 Gainsborough Lincolnshire Bricklayer **Mary Todd** 1864 Southrepps	**William** 1889 Hull carpenter m. Minnie Gray served with the Royal Garrison in WWI **Herbert** 1893 Southrepps gardener m. Doris Booker
HEWITT (BANE) Henry Lodge Cottage Upper Street	**1879** Caned Henry Hewitt for throwing stones	**John** 1846 Southrepps Agricultural labourer **Sarah Ann Neave** 1847 Overstrand	**Charlotte** 1867 Southrepps **Caroline** 1868 Southrepps **Henry** 1873 Southrepps agricultural labourer m. Annie Beck **Harriet** 1876 Southrepps **Albert** 1880 Southrepps **Lillian** 1882 Southrepps
HEWITT Walter The Dams Southrepps	**1880** At board meeting fees were remitted 3s 10d	**John** 1850 Southrepps Gamekeeper **Martha Scottow** Overstrand	**Walter** 1875 Trimingham blacksmith m. Mary Long **Emma** 1876 Trimingham parlour maid **Rosie** 1879 Southrepps cook and housekeeper
HEWITT Elizabeth Lower Street	**1881** Admitted from infant school	**John** 1835 Southrepps Farm labourer **Charlotte Turner** 1839 Trunch	**Ann** 1864 Southrepps m. James Burton-Pye **Charlotte** 1869 Southrepps m. John Goodwin **Arthur** 1872 Knapton farm labourer m. Ellen Glister **Elizabeth** 1874 Southrepps **Eliza May** 1879 Southrepps m. Frederick Hunt
HEWITT John (Herbert) George Frederick Church Street Southrepps	**1884** Herbert. Absent through illness **1891** George. Too backward to work with standard I **1891** Frederick. in hospital with bad eyes* * or boy in next entry	**Isaac** 1853 Southrepps Farm labourer **Harriet Larke** 1854 Southrepps	**Robert** 1876 Southrepps shop fitter labourer Portsmouth m. Sarah Townsend **John** 1877 Southrepps m. Janie Elizabeth Payne 1911 served with the Royal Fusiliers killed in action France 1917 no known grave, commemorated on Arras Memorial **Ellen** 1879 Southrepps m. Charles Hedge **Frederick** 1882 Southrepps gardener m. Rebecca Temple **George** 1884 Southrepps gardener m. Clara Hurn, served in Labour Corps in WWI **James** 1887 Southrepps died 1919 aged 32 **Arthur** 1890 Southrepps general labourer **Charles** 1891 Southrepps served with the Norfolk Regiment and Suffolk Regiment during WWI and RAF after war m. Alice Edith Clarke 1914
HEWITT Charles Frederick Lower Street	**1888** Charles backward and slow fit for the exemption schedule **1888** Frederick moved up from infants due to age, only fit to work with second class infants **1888** Frederick dull and backward **1891** Frederick in hospital with bad eyes* * or boy in previous entry	**Charles** 1849 Southrepps Farm labourer **Elizabeth Frary** 1850 Southrepps	**Walter** 1870 Southrepps jobbing gardener m. Mary Burton-Pye **Ann** 1871 Southrepps **Sarah** 1874 Cawston **George** 1875 Cawston worked for Urban District Council **Mary** 1878 Southrepps m. George Allen **Charles** 1879 Southrepps farm labourer served with the Royal Dublin Fusiliers m. Ellen May Burton-Pye 1911 **Frances** 1881 Southrepps m. John Grimes **Robert** 1884 Southrepps general labourer **Frederick** 1886 Southrepps, m. Rose Elizabeth Hicks 1920 served with the Norfolk Regiment and London Regiment in WWI **Sidney** 1889 Southrepps farm labourer **Ethel** 1893 Southrepps m. Leslie Harrison

HEWITT **Florence** **John** **Ellen** **Walter** Lower Street	**1902** John attendance prize 407 out of 408 sessions **1905** Walter attendance prize 403 out of 408 sessions Measles	**Walter** 1870 Southrepps Bricklayer's labourer **Mary Ann Burton-Pye** 1876 Southrepps Died 1907	**Florence** 1895 Southrepps looked after the household on the death of her mother **John** 1897 Southrepps farm labourer m. Ethel Rosa Turner 1930 served with the Essex Regiment, Royal Welsh Fusiliers and Labour Corps in WWI **Walter** 1898 Southrepps farm labourer **Ellen** 1899 Southrepps served as a Red Cross VAD in WWI **Robert** 1900 Southrepps **Arthur** 1902 Southrepps **Caroline** 1903 Southrepps died 1904 **Harry** 1905 Southrepps **Alice** 1907 Southrepps died 1907
HEWITT **Dorothy** **Marjorie** Church Street Southrepps.	**1902** Dorothy was 5 years and 9 months when admitted **1905** Measles	**Henry** 1857 Southrepps General carter **Caroline Jarvis** 1864 Sidestrand	**Alice** 1887 Southrepps servant **Gerard** 1888 Southrepps painter m. Mabel Chadwick then Winifred Grimwood served with the Norfolk Garrison Battalion in WWI **Glynn** 1890 Southrepps gardener m. Sarah Bayes served with Norfolk Regiment mentioned in Despatches for retrieving a wounded man from no-man's land **Gladys** 1891 Southrepps m. Percy Hawkins. **Wilfred** 1894 Southrepps gardener served with the Norfolk Regiment killed in action France 1917 buried Monchy British Cemetery **Dorothy** 1896 Southrepps domestic in 1939 living with her sister Gladys **Marjorie** 1897 Southrepps m. John Mitchel **Donald** 1899 Southrepps seaman served with the Royal Navy m. Eva Aplin **Madge** 1901 Southrepps died 1925 aged 24 **Kenneth** 1902 Southrepps general labourer m. Ella Florey
HEWITT **Robert** Lower Street	**1911** Visited by the attendance officer	**Henry 1874** Southrepps teamman **Annie Beck** 1876 Limphoe	**Ethel** 1898 Southrepps m. Robert Rasberry **Albert** 1999 Southrepps served in the Royal Navy, died 1917 HMS Vanguard body not recovered, commemorated Chatham **William** 1901 Southrepps served in the Royal Navy died 1918 HMS Powerful buried Southrepps **Robert** 1906 Southrepps labourer m. Rose Cook **Frederick** 1908 Southrepps fruit grower m. Grace Edgoose **Herbert** 1905 1911 Southrepps
HEWITT **Elima (Ilma)** Southrepps	**1913** Elima 6 years and 11 months will not be transferred to the mixed department she has only made 272 attendances and is very slow to learn	**Louis** 1875 Trimingham Cattle grazier **Ruth Bright** 1874 Gimingham	**Elima** 1906 Southrepps m. Norman Dunning
HOWES **Emily** **Susannah** Gunton	**1880** Emily monitoress **1880** Susannah transferred from Infant room Admitted Emily	**Henry** 1838 Aylmerton Gashouse labourer **Elizabeth Small** 1837 Cowes Isle of Wight	**Emily** 1867 Great Ayton, Yorkshire m. Charles Pollard **Benjamin** 1869 South Stockton, Yorkshire died 1876 aged 8 Middlesborough **George** 1870 South Stockton, Yorkshire agricultural labourer m. Annie Reynolds **Susannah** 1873 Wath, Yorkshire domestic servant **Robert** 1874 Scotton, Yorkshire blacksmith m. Elizabeth Newstead **John** 1875 Scotton, Yorkshire blacksmith and Wesleyan minister **Elizabeth** 1881 Gunton

HURN **Eleanor** **Charlotte** **Lucy** **Keziah** **Alice** Thorpe Market	**1878** Lucy admitted 25th March Rev Dolphin promised to pay fees for Ellen, Lucy, and Charlotte **1879** Charlotte passed Standard I Rev Dolphin paid fees 5s 2d for Eleanor, Charlotte, and Lucy **1879** Rev Dolphin paid 5s 10d for 12 weeks fees for Eleanor, Charlotte, and Lucy Eleanor left school being thirteen years old **1888** Rev Dolphin paid 6s 6d for 13 weeks schooling for Charlotte, Lucy, and Keziah Keziah Hurn is monitoress this week left 1886 **1888** Alice moved up from infants due to age, only fit to work with second class infants	**George** 1835 Thorpe Market Agricultural worker **Harriet Moy** 1839 Thorpe Market	**Eleanor** 1866 Thorpe Market servant Swafield **Charlotte** 1867 Thorpe Market parlour maid in London m. Robert Eflett **Lucy** 1869 Thorpe Market m. James Warner **Keziah** 1872 Thorpe Market **Harold** 1874 Thorpe Market horseman on farm Durham m. **Violet Doy** died 1901 **Martin** 1876 Thorpe Market gardener m. Amelia Claxton **Robert** 1878 Thorpe Market died 1878 **Alice** 1880 Thorpe Market m. Ernest Attew
HURN **Anna Maria** Thorpe Market	**1879** Absent ill with scarletina	**William** 1837 Thorpe Market Agricultural labourer **Martha Hurn** 1838 Thorpe Market	**Walter** 1863 Thorpe Market agricultural labourer m. Hannah Sadler **Edith** 1866 Thorpe Market blind **Anna Maria** 1869 Thorpe Market m. Ashton Moy **Percy** 1871 Thorpe Market died 1871 **William** 1877 Thorpe Market rubber roller Cheshire m. Beatrice Ravenscroft
HURN **Ernest** **Arthur** Thorpe Market	**1902** 6 years and 2 months when admitted **1917** Arthur Hurn an old scholar of this school has been awarded the D.C.M.	**Walter** 1863 Thorpe Market Teamster on horse **Hannah Sadler** 1862 Honing	**Percy** 1892 Thorpe Market labourer on farm m. Maggie Jarvis **Arthur** 1894 Thorpe Market labourer on farm m. Mabel Roper served with the Norfolk Regiment awarded Distinguished Conduct Medal **Ernest** 1895 Thorpe Market labourer on farm **Ethel** 1897 Thorpe Market m. William Moy **Albert** 1899 Thorpe Market labourer on farm served with the Bedfordshire Regiment WWI **William** 1902 Thorpe Market
HURN **Alice** Lower Street	**1904** Received a book prize for best marks earned in each standard in late examinations standard IV	**James** 1862 Southrepps Yardman on farm **Caroline Brackenbury** 1863 Aldborough	**Horace** 1883 Southrepps teamster on farm **Frederick** 1885 Southrepps farm labourer **Sidney** 1884 Southrepps farm labourer **Alice** 1894 Southrepps m. James Pitcher **Florence** 1898 Southrepps **Ellen** 1900 Southrepps **Walter** 1904 Southrepps
HURN **Arthur** Thorpe Market	**1907** 6 years and 7 months when admitted 1906, 193 attendances 1907, 352 not transferred to Upper school	**John William** 1867 Thorpe Market Farm labourer **Julia Codling** 1868 Bradfield	**Robert** 1895 Thorpe Market carpenter served with the Norfolk Regiment killed in action France buried Thiepval Memorial **Louisa** 1898 Thorpe Market m. William Tranter **Herbert** 1899 Thorpe Market cowman m. Gladys Pipes served with the Labour Corps WWI **Arthur** 1901 Thorpe Market lorry driver m. Bertha Scott **Bertie** 1903 Thorpe Market builder's labourer m. Gladys Long **Charles** 1905 Thorpe Market roadman County Council m. Violet Risebrow **Leonard** 1907 Thorpe Market railway worker m. Kathleen Frost

HURN Albert Lower Street	**1916** Albert Hurn son of Leonard Hurn has received the Military Medal for saving the life of an officer. Albert was a pupil in this school	Leonard 1861 Southrepps Agricultural labourer **Ann Pitcher** 1862 Southrepps	John 1880 Southrepps farm labourer died 1909 aged 29 Clement 1882 Southrepps bricklayer emigrated to Canada m. Alice Walton Charles 1883 Southrepps railway guard m. Charlotte Gipson Leonard 1885 Southrepps bricklayer m. Louisa Nicholls Albert 1895 Southrepps estate labourer m. Daisy Leeder 1919 served with the Norfolk Regiment WWI awarded the Military Medal Florence 1898 Southrepps emigrated to Canada m. Herbert Allen Beatrice 1900 Southrepps emigrated to Canada m. Michael Creese Emily 1903 Southrepps m. Walter Briggs Maud 1908 Southrepps m. Wallace Peeke-Vout
JEFFRIES Harry Antingham	**1901** 5 years and 5 months when admitted	Unknown **Lillie Bond** 1876 Bradfield, Essex	Harry 1896 Mistley, Essex carter on farm
JONES George Suffield	**1879** Admitted to school	George 1841 Ireland Musician died 1874 **Georgina Browne** 1845 Woolwich	George 1870 Woolwich m. Elizabeth Jones Arthur 1873 Walworth, Surrey bank clerk m. Isabella Nichols Mother school mistress of Suffield School
JORDAN John Dorothy The New Inn Upper Street	**1899** John absent due to illness **1902** Dorothy 5 years and 9 months when admitted	Henry 1865 Southrepps Publican and farmer **Julie Dixon** 1867 Ridlington	Francis 1888 Aylsham small holder m. Ebbie Waterfield John 1889 Aylsham m. Daisy Dyball Henry 1892 Aylsham farm labourer m. Ellen Hylton Sidney 1894 Aylsham butcher served with the Royal Field Artillery in WWI m. Annie Hudson Stanley 1895 Southrepps butcher, served with the Cheshire Regiment killed in action 1918 no known grave, commemorated on Pozieres Memorial, France Dorothy 1896 Southrepps drapery saleswoman Archibald 1899 Southrepps Maud 1900 Southrepps m. George Booth Alice 1902 Southrepps died 1925 aged 23 George 1904 Colby James 1907 Norwich There were two other siblings unnamed who died
KERRISON Emily Julia Old Farm House Bradfield	**1878** Julia admitted to school 25th February Julia readmitted 16th September **1879** Emily and Julia absented themselves from school for three weeks to pick turnips	Robert 1841 Bradfield Agricultural labourer **Susan** 1834 Corpusty	Emily 1867 Bradfield m. Henry Witham Julia 1869 Bradfield m. Herbert Clarke Alfred 1874 Aylsham farm labourer m. Augusta Lambert Stanley 1888 Ingworth m. Rachel Hicks served with the Royal Engineers killed in action France 1918 buried Berles New Military Cemetery
KIMM Herbert Alice Bradfield Road	**1888** Herbert weak health and impediment to speech **1896** Alice to help in this room on alternate days for one month	Robert 1843 Deopham Relieving Officer and registrar of births and deaths **Sarah Porter** 1849 Thetford	Charlotte 1871 North Walsham m. John Smither John 1872 North Walsham railway station master m. Sarah Wright Mary 1875 North Walsham m. William Mendham Robert 1877 North Walsham boot maker and dealer m. Alice Ede Ernest 1879 North Walsham builders clerk served with the Norfolk Regiment m. Florence Blogg Herbert 1881 North Walsham grocers assistant m. Bertha Tooke Alice 1883 Southrepps teacher at the School left June 1900 died 1917 Francis 1885 Southrepps joined the Metropolitan police m. Alma Reed Albert 1888 Southrepps boot maker served in the Royal Artillery m. Eva Woods Cyril 1890 Southrepps Cyril died 1892

KNIGHTS Frederick Lower Street	**1891** Too backward to work with Standard I an arrangement is made to teach him letters and monosyllabic words, and to give him more reading	**John** 1841 Antingham Gardener **Elizabeth Moore** 1846 Salhouse, Norfolk	**Thomas** 1871 Hempnall market gardener m. Edith Larke **Richard** 1874 Swanton Abbot grocer m. Elizabeth Burton **Fanny** 1875 Swanton Abbot m. Frank Noy **Alice** 1880 North Walsham m. William Clitheroe **Caroline** 1882 North Walsham m. Charles Gotts **Frederick** 1882 North Walsham gardener m. Laura Allen served with the Labour Corps in WWI **Albert** 1887 Southrepps farm labourer emigrated to America
LARKE William Upper Street	**1902** W. Larke continued idleness **1903** Playing when master's back was turned to the class and insubordination and impertinence	**James** 1850 Southrepps Horse keeper on farm **Jane Silver** 1858 Bradfield	**Eliza** 1872 Southrepps **Frederick** 1874 Southrepps bricklayer m. Susan Clarke **Charles** 1876 Southrepps bricklayer m. Laura Reynolds **Benjamin** 1878 Southrepps agricultural labourer m. Violet Childs **Gertrude** 1880 Southrepps m. Elijah Craske **Bertie** 1885 Southrepps farm labourer m. Evangeline Gray **Albert** 1889 Southrepps farm labourer m. Frances Platford **William** 1891 Southrepps farm labourer **Lilian** 1892 Southrepps m. Gerald Risebrow
LARKE Donald Sandy Lane Southrepps	**1913** Donald Larke aged 7 is a very delicate child and has only made 154 attendances during the last school year Not transferred to the Mixed department	**Bertie** 1885 Southrepps Farm labourer **Evangaline Gray** 1887 Northrepps	**Donald** 1907 Southrepps window cleaner m. Edith Lawrence **Elsie May** 1909 Southrepps m. Edwin Cundick
LAURENCE Walter	**1881** The school book of Walter is at Roughton as he attends the examination of the school there	**Unknown** **Emma Laurence**	**Walter** 1873 Roughton Only record for him
LAWRENCE Mary Ann Antingham	**1881** Mary Ann left school	**James** 1841 North Walsham Agricultural labourer **Lydia Graves** 1841 Stalham	**Mary Ann** 1858 North Walsham **Elizabeth** 1860 North Walsham **James** 1862 North Walsham agricultural labourer m. Elizabeth Wiseman **Cook** 1864 North Walsham agricultural labourer m. Charlotte Gray **Mary Ann** 1868 North Walsham m. Arthur Timbers
LAWRENCE Arthur Antingham	**1895** Put down a class owing to weak health	**James** 1861 Antingham Agricultural labourer **Elizabeth Wiseman** 1864 East Ruston	**Anna** 1881 Beckham step daughter **Arthur** 1884 Antingham fettler m. Mildred Stannard **James** 1894 Antingham farm labourer
LUBBOCK George Katherine William Upper Street	**1883** Fees owing remitted **1889** William and Katherine put on non-paupers list	**Walter Lubbock** 1853 Southrepps died 1880 **Sarah Basey** 1855 Middlesex, London married William Temple	**George** 1873 Southrepps emigrated to New Zealand m. Grace Charlton **Katherine** 1877 Southrepps m. Harry Rowell **William** 1879 Southrepps emigrated to Australia m. Violet
LUBBOCK Ellen Bessie Thorpe Road Southrepps	**1891** Taken off non-paupers list by Guardians on account of bad attendance at school. As school fees were not brought Bessie was sent home for the week's money	**William** 1842 Southrepps Farm labourer died 1891 **Hannah Pull** 1845 Antingham	**Martin** 1866 Southrepps farm steward m. Mary Pearson **John** 1867 Southrepps agricultural labourer **Herbert** 1869 Southrepps platelayer on railway then horseman on farm m. Caroline Risebrow **Arthur** 1872 Southrepps agent for Insurance company m. Alice Reynolds **Alice** 1875 Southrepps housekeeper m. George Bullimore **Lambert** 1877 Southrepps coal carter in Cromer m. Ellen Holmes **Bessie** 1878 Southrepps died 1892 aged 14 **Ellen** 1881 Southrepps m. Albert Allen **Laura** 1887 Southrepps m. John Jarvis

LUBBOCK Alfred Thorpe Road Southrepps	**1902** Alfred was 5 years and 9 months when admitted	**Martin** 1867 Southrepps Farm steward **Mary Pearson** 1869 Methwold	**Lily** 1893 Southrepps died 1909 aged 16 **Alfred** 1894 Southrepps labourer on farm
MAYES Thomas Thorpe Market	**1878** Admitted to school	**William** **Elizabeth Hurn** 1834	**Thomas** 1870 Thorpe Market cabinet maker died in WWI 1918 Ipswich Military Hospital, served in Labour Corp m. Annie Rogers
MAYES Olive (Nora) Thorpe Market	**1902** 6 years and 2 months when admitted	**Thomas** 1870 Thorpe Market Cabinet maker **Annie Rogers** 1871 Gunton	**Olive** 1895 Thorpe Market died 1907 aged 12 **Lancelot** 1897 Thorpe Market lorry driver m. Florence Booth **Kathleen** 1901 Thorpe Market shop assistant
MOBBS John Bradfield	**1887** Received notice that John Mobbs has been absent being sick with brain fever	**John** 1837 Wingfield, Suffolk Foreman of bone mill **Emma Deville** 1849 Hageland, Hertfordshire	**Harry** 1870 Wenhaston, Suffolk labourer in bone mill m. Rosamond Cork **Frederick** 1872 Saxtead, Suffolk harness maker m. Mary Sheppard **William** 1873 Hageland jeweller's assistant **John** 1882 Fritton, Suffolk grocer m. Priscilla Page **Rachel** 1884 Bradfield servant m. Walter Fulcher **Robert** 1886 Bradfield emigrated to Canada **Charlie** 1889 Bradfield served with the Royal Navy and emigrated to Canada
MOY William Thorpe Market	**1886** Left to live in London	**William Rogers** 1826 Thorpe Market General labourer **Elizabeth Blogg** 1836 Suffield	**William** 1871 Southrepps
MOY William Upper Street	**1902** Striking a girl	**Herbert** 1864 Thorpe Market Stockman on farm **Edith Vince** 1867 Southrepps	**Maria** 1888 Southrepps m. Herbert Burton-Pye **Ursula** 1890 Southrepps m. James Saunders **May** 1893 Southrepps m. Harry Neave **William** 1895 Southrepps farm labourer m. Ethel Hurn served with the Norfolk Regiment WWI **Cyril** 1899 Southrepps general labourer m. Alice Gray **Alfred** 1900 Southrepps **Campbell** 1903 Southrepps **Herbert** 1905 Southrepps **Evelyn** 1907 Southrepps
MOY Elsie Antingham	**1907** Elsie was 6 years and 6 months when admitted 1906, 92 attendances 1907, 375 not transferred to Upper school	**Arthur** 1861 Thorpe Market Farm labourer **Eliza Whitwood** 1867 Antingham	**Bertie** 1887 Antingham farm labourer m. Florence Larke **Georgina** 1889 Antingham m. Christmas Dewing **Arthur** 1891 Antingham farm labourer **Selina** 1894 Antingham m. Samuel Ellis **Ernest** 1899 Antingham builders store keeper m. Louisa Brooks **Elsie** 1900 Antingham m. Sidney Gent **Ada** 1905 Antingham m. John Thornton **Frank** 1907 Antingham water miller and stone man m. Blanche Copping
NICHOLLS Upper Street next to the reading room	**1880** Fee arrears	**Josiah** 1843 Gimingham Agricultural labourer **Ann Bane** 1850 Southrepps	**William** 1870 Southrepps agricultural labourer m. Ada Risebrow **John** 1872 Southrepps gamekeeper m. Amelia Hurn **Ellen** 1874 Southrepps m. Frederick Colman **Mary** 1876 Southrepps cook **Elizabeth** 1877 Southrepps m. William Moore **Charlotte** 1878 Southrepps m. Frederick Vincent **Robert** 1879 Southrepps Jobbing gardener m. Marion Barber died 1915 serving with the Norfolk Regiment England buried Norwich **Jane** 1881 Southrepps servant

NICHOLS **Margaret** **Ellen** **William** Thorpe Market	**1905** Measles **1907** William 7 years 4 months when admitted very deficient intellect 1906 373 attendances 1907 311 not transferred to Upper school **1914** Doctor visited; Frederick must go to hospital for attention to eyes. Fred is very backward	**William** 1870 Southrepps General labourer **Ada Risebrow** 1871 Northrepps	**Margaret** 1898 Thorpe Market m. William Pearson in Yorkshire **Nellie** 1899 Thorpe Market m. Walter Bullimore **William** 1900 Thorpe Market **Bertie** 1903 Thorpe Market **Frederick** 1907 Thorpe Market
NOY **Donald** Thorpe Market	**1904** Received book prize for best marks earned in Standard I	**Frank** 1869 Great Yarmouth Railway signalman **Fanny Knights** 1872 Swanton Abbott	**Daisy** 1895 Thorpe Market m. James Reid **Donald** 1897 Thorpe Market m. Victoria Hall served with the Norfolk Regiment WWI **Helen** 1906 Thorpe Market m. Reginald Hedge
PAGE **Susannah** Antingham	**1880** Susannah Page is monitoress for present week	**John Page** 1826 Antingham Agricultural labourer died 1868 **Hannah Bean** 1835 Mundesley	**Robert** 1864 Antingham agricultural labourer **Susannah** 1867 Antingham m. Robert Roberts then William Hewitt
PARDON **Elizabeth** **Amelia** Upper Street	**1891** Both girls too backward to work with standard I Elizabeth found unable to work with her standard in arithmetic	**Unknown** **Jane Pardon** Unmarried 1837 Southrepps Agricultural labourer	**Amelia** 1884 Southrepps **Elizabeth** 1884 Southrepps m. Edwin Booth **Walter** 1885 Southrepps farm labourer m. Jessie Aldrich
PAUL **Ellen** **Emma** Bradfield	**1879** Ellen passed standard 1 in government examinations **1884** Emma absent with bad eyes **1888** Emma weak eyes	**William** 1841 Bradfield Agricultural Worker **Elizabeth Dixon** 1842 North Walsham	**George** 1862 North Walsham agricultural labourer **Charles** 1864 Bradfield agricultural labourer **Ellen** 1868 Bradfield m. Samuel Allen **Maryann** 1871 Bradfield died 1883 aged 13 **John** 1873 Southrepps agricultural labourer **Harriet** 1875 Bradfield died 1884 aged 9 **Emma** 1879 Bradfield cook **Edith** 1882 Bradfield m. Robert Moore **Matilda** 1887 Thorpe Market m. Egbert Foulsham
PAUL **Elizabeth** Bradfield	**1879** Transferred from Infant department	**James** 1843 Bradfield Agricultural labourer **Harriet Adams** 1845 Bradfield died 1882	**Edward** 1862 Bradfield agricultural labourer m. Harriet Cobitt **Walter** 1866 Bradfield agricultural labourer m. Martha Pull **Elizabeth** 1871 Bradfield housekeeper **Herbert** 1873 Bradfield farm labourer m. Ellen Lovick **Harriet** 1878 Bradfield
PAUL **Martha** **Alice** The Common Bradfield and Trunch Hall cottages	**1901** Martha prize for full attendance **1904** Alice won an attendance prize at 13 Alice received a book prize for best marks earned in each standard in late examination standard V **1907** Martha absent due to scarletina and measles	**Walter** 1865 Bradfield Farmer and dealer **Martha Pull** 1862 North Walsham	**Charlotte** 1881 Felmingham m. Herbert Codling in Islington **Susan** 1887 Bradfield cook in Lewisham, London **Lucy** 1888 Bradfield m. Samuel Parrott **Alice** 1890 Bradfield servant in Surrey m. Harry Platton **Gertrude** 1893 Bradfield kitchen maid Kensington, London **Kathleen** 1894 Bradfield working in same household as Susan m. William Parrott **Martha** 1895 Bradfield m. John Moore in Barnet **Dorothy** 1899 Trunch m. Herbert Turner
PAYNE **Bessie** Thorpe Road Antingham	**1879** Caned Bessie Payne for disobedience	**James** 1837 Alby Farm Bailiff **Sarah Slaughter** 1836 Colby	**Arthur** 1860 Colby railway porter **Eliza** 1863 Bradfield domestic servant **Clara** 1865 Bradfield m. Robert Whittleton **Catherine** 1867 Bradfield **Henry** 1868 Bradfield agricultural labourer **Bessie** 1872 Bradfield m. Ashley Shonk emigrated to America **Edward** 1876 Bradfield stockman on farm

PAYNE Antingham	**1884** Fined for non-payment of fees	**John** 1839 Alby Agricultural labourer **Sophia Lambert** 1839 Swafield Died 1884	**William** 1868 North Walsham **John** 1870 Alby died 1887 aged 17 **Robert** 1873 Alby plate layer on railway m. Emma Bunton **Herbert** 1878 Antingham farm labourer living with brother Robert **Arthur** 1880 Antingham
PAYNE Violet Upper Street	**1917** Violet is a child of very little intelligence	**Edgar** 1872 Overstrand Farm labourer **Ruth East** 1870 Letchmore Heath, Hertfordshire	**Lillian** 1902 Northrepps **William** 1904 Northrepps m. Gladys Hatt **Annie** 1906 Southrepps **Ernest** 1908 Southrepps died 1924 aged 16 **Edgar** 1909 Southrepps m. Gladys Atkins **Violet** 1910 Southrepps
PIKE Edward Upper Street family moved to Suffield	**1888** Edward Pike left the school having removed to another district	**Walter** 1858 Southrepps Farm labourer **Susannah Lusher** 1858 Ashill	**Eleanor** 1879 Southrepps servant **Ernest** 1883 Southrepps farm labourer m. Cecilia Pitcher **Edward** 1884 Southrepps seaman Royal Navy m. Maude Hill Haringey, London **Daisy** 1889 Southrepps died 1909 aged 20 **Emma** 1892 Southrepps m. Bertie Cousens **Robert** 1894 Colby chauffeur mechanic m. Annie Gregory in Camden **Lacey** 1897 Colby tailor served with the Norfolk Regiment killed in action 1915 in Balkans, buried Helles memorial Gallipoli
PITCHER Rebecca Alice Marjorie The Warren Lower Street	**1888** Rebecca weak health Alice weak health and dull **1891** Marjorie too backward to work with standard I **1902** Pitcher continued idleness	**James** 1856 Southrepps Gamekeeper **Rebecca Baker** 1860 Corpusty	**Mary** 1879 Corpusty m. Thomas Daniel Burton-Pye **Rebecca** 1880 Corpusty **Alice** 1882 Corpusty housemaid at the Grange, Sprowston **Beatrice** 1882 Corpusty servant **Marjorie** 1885 Corpusty emigrated to Canada m. Herbert Thompson **Cecilia** 1886 Corpusty housemaid m. Ernest Pike **Ethel** 1888 Corpusty house maid m. James Youngs **Herbert** 1891 Corpusty served with the Suffolk Regiment died Flanders 1916 buried Bouzincourt Communal Cemetery, Somme
POLL Charlotte Dairy House Gunton	**1879** Admitted to school 21st April	**Edmund** 1840 Blickling Dairyman **Harriet Hazel** 1841 Matlaske died 1883	**Arthur** 1865 Erpingham emigrated to America **Alfred** 1866 Erpingham died 1888 aged 21 **Charlotte** 1871 Erpingham looked after widowed father **Ernest** 1878 Erpingham carpenter m. Gertrude Gough
REYNOLDS Ivy Thorpe Market	**1902** 6 years and 2 months when admitted	**George** 1867 Northrepps Agricultural labourer **Emily Cushion** 1856 Bradfield	**Robert Cushion** (half-brother)1889 Southrepps agricultural labourer m. Helena Baxter **Ivy** 1896 Gresham domestic servant By 1911 they all appear to have changed their name to Watts
REYNOLDS Stanley Doris Upper Street	**1907** Stanley was 6 years and 9 months when admitted 1907, 177 attendances not transferred to Upper school **1911** Doris visited by the attendance officer	**William** 1875 Metton General labourer **Mary Ann Rogers** 1873 Southrepps	**Stanley** 1900 Southrepps market gardener m. Gladys Earle served with the London Regiment WWI **Catherine** 1903 Southrepps m. Raymond Knights **Doris** 1905 Southrepps m. Walter Pank **John** 1908 Southrepps builder m. Eleanor Harvey **Sidney** 1910 Southrepps master builder m. Annie Fuller
REYNOLDS Alice Southrepps	**1911** Alice Reynolds visited by the attendance officer	**Frederick** 1881 Fundenhall Farm labourer **Alice Bell** 1882 Southrepps	**Alice** 1905 Southrepps m. Bertie Claxton **William** 1908 Southrepps died 1920 aged 12
RISEBROW Ethel Upper Street	**1902** 5 years and 8 months when admitted	**Herbert** 1867 Northrepps Blacksmith **Harriet Turner** 1866 Worstead	**Alice** 1893 Southrepps laundry worker **Mabel** 1895 Southrepps m. George Smith **Ethel** 1897 Southrepps m. Stephen Fieldstead

RISEBROW **John** **Charles** Upper Street	**1905** John measles **1911** Charles to stay in Infants, two, three months over age but very slow to learn and could not possibly do Standard I work	**Francis** 1856 Northrepps Bricklayer's labourer **Emma Reynolds** 1872 Roughton	**John** 1896 Southrepps hall boy, served with the Sussex Regiment m. Edith Payne **May** 1900 Southrepps m. Harry Baker **Arthur** 1901 Southrepps m. Florence Flack **Cecil** 1903 Southrepps m. Rose Wigglesworth **Charlie** 1905 Southrepps m. Muriel Gedge **Cyril** 1909 Southrepps
ROGERS **Edith** **William** Upper Street	**1880** Edith admitted to Girls' school **1888** William obviously dull Weak intellect	**Edward** 1850 Suffield Farm labourer **Phoebe Larke** 1854 Southrepps	**Edith** 1874 Southrepps m. Thomas Knights **Edward** 1876 Southrepps agricultural labourer **William** 1879 Southrepps agricultural labourer living with his parents **Ellen** 1886 Southrepps m. Walter Brett
ROGERS **Lena (Selina)** **Elsie** Upper Street	**1918** Lena doctor's certificate giving exemption until September Lena to stay in Infant Dept result of irregularity Elsie 7 years 4 months will not be transferred to mixed dept. Will be very much benefitted by another year in the Infant dept	**William** 1873 Southrepps General labourer **Hannah Abel** 1876 Cromer	**Selina** 1905 Bradfield m. James McCann **William** 1908 Southrepps **Elsie** 1911 Southrepps m. Arthur Squires
SAUNDERS **Harriet** **Sophia** **Frederick** Lower Street	**1878** Harriet admitted 15th April **1879** Harriet school money owing 5s 4d excused by the board **1890** Sophie and Fred taken off non-paupers list **1891** Fred on 5th class register but not able to do II standard	**Frederick** 1845 Gressingham, Norfolk Farm labourer **Charlotte Paul** 1849 Bradfield	**Ann** 1869 Bradfield m. James Morter **Harriet** 1871 Southrepps m. Charles Bradfield **John** 1873 Hartlepool farm labourer **Susannah** 1876 **Sophie** 1879 Southrepps m. James Massingham **Frederick** 1883 Southrepps farm labourer **Gertrude** 1886 Southrepps m. Albert Stamp **James** 1888 Southrepps farm labourer m. Ursula Elizabeth Moy 1911, served with Royal Field Artillery in WWI
SAUNDERS **William** Lower Street	**1901–1903** W Saunders wilful mischief in class. Singing in class during change of lessons. Idleness in class. Talking in class whilst teacher was engaged elsewhere	**Unknown** **Unknown**	**William** 1892 Beckham Living with his grandparents Frederick and Charlotte Saunders
SELF **William** Southrepps	**1907** Willie was 6 years and 6 months when admitted 1907, 256 attendances not transferred to Upper school	**James** 1862 Worstead Farm Bailiff **Elizabeth Spanton** 1871 Tunstead	**Jessie** 1896 Erpingham m. Mackenzie Scotter **John** 1899 Erpingham m. Eva Irene Jermany served with the Cavalry Regiment in WWI **William** 1900 Erpingham **Gladys** 1903 Erpingham **Eric** 1906 Southrepps farm labourer m. Hilda Allen
SEXTON **John** Suffield	**1880** Admitted to school	**Edward** 1834 Thorpe Market Labourer **Sophia Smith** 1839 Colby	**Elizabeth** 1862 Suffield m. Daniel Todd **Caroline** 1864 Suffield m. Charles England **George** 1866 Suffield emigrated to Canada **Louisa** 1869 Suffield m. Walter Nash **John** 1872 Suffield asylum attendant emigrated to Canada m. Emma Pye **Sophia** 1875 Suffield m. Frederick Upton in Surrey **Alfred** 1878 Suffield mental health nurse m. Elizabeth Breacker **James** 1885 Suffield bricklayer m. Marion Dyball
SHEPHEARD **Lucy** Lower Street	**1885** Received a note from Mr Shepheard surgeon that Lucy is suffering from sore throat and unable to attend school	**John** 1854 Plumstead Farm labourer **Anna Barret** 1855 Norwich	**Alfred** 1876 Ingworth Police Officer m. Edith Joyce **Selina** 1879 Southrepps m. Elijah Hunt **Lucy** 1880 Southrepps m. Robert Emmett **Leon** 1883 Southrepps joined the Royal Navy m. Elsie Mantle **Laura** 1885 Southrepps m. William Vardigans **Mildred** 1887 Briston m. Robert Turbett **Kathleen** 1889 Briston **May** 1891 Briston **Ethel** 1902 Briston m. Cecil Hammond

SKIPPER Ellen Southrepps	**1911** Visited by the attendance officer	**Frank** 1867 Costessey Vermin killer **Alice (Susannah) Buck** 1876 Roughton	**Frank** 1899 Southrepps m. Daisy Humphreys, served with the Norfolk Regiment in WWI **Reggie** 1901 Southrepps served with the Royal Artillery in WWI court-martialled for theft **Ellen** 1905 Southrepps m. Ernest Shepheard **Blanche** 1906 Southrepps m. Frederick Cannell
SMITH (Mary) Louisa Upper Street	**1878** Admitted to school 15th February **1879** Passed Standard I **1880** Louisa monitoress for past week	**William** 1827 Northrepps Farm labourer **Phoebe Earle** 1829 Northrepps	**John** 1860 Northrepps farm labourer **Edward** 1863 Northrepps farm labourer m. Sarah Bulley **Charles** 1867 Northrepps farm labourer **Louisa** 1869 Northrepps m. James Doughty **Blanche** 1871 Northrepps m. Alfred Farrow **Thomas** 1875 Northrepps groom
SMITH Rhoda Warren Lane Lower Street	**1901** 1st prize for attendance	**Charles** 1865 Northrepps Gamekeeper **Emma Chapman** 1865 Hickling	**Ernest** 1894 Southrepps farm labourer served with the Norfolk Regiment died Dec 1915 Bulgaria, no known grave, commemorated Doiran Memorial, Greece **Rhoda** 1896 Southrepps died 1919 aged 23 **Roland** 1897 Southrepps farm labourer served with the Labour Corps in WWI m. Lottie Long **William** 1899 Southrepps **Blanche** 1902 Southrepps m. George Morris **Mildred** 1905 Southrepps m. James Codling **Rosa** 1907 Southrepps
STOREY William Lower Street	**1901** 2nd prize for attendance	**John** 1852 Southrepps Carpenter **Louisa** 1860 Southrepps	**James** 1891 Southrepps farm labourer **William** 1895 Southrepps grocer's assistant m. Edna M. Smith 1939, served with the Norfolk Yeomanry in WWI **Ellen** 1898 Southrepps m. Arthur Daniels
SUFFOLK William Bradfield	**1888** Found out that he was working with III standard since his illness should have been in IV	**James** 1852 Bradfield Carpenter **Betsy Richardson** 1853 Ovington died 1882	**William** 1877 Bradfield **Ernest** 1879 Bradfield blacksmith London m. Ellen Marks **Arthur** 1880 Bradfield maltster labourer **Sidney** 1882 Bradfield door porter
TEMPLE George Harry Alice Sidney The Common Bradfield	**1902** G. Temple inattention and impertience **1905** H. Temple of Bradfield and his sister are absent on account of measles **1913** Sidney did not enter school until he was six years of age and is exceptionally slow to learn and will not be transferred to the Mixed department	**Isaac** 1866 Bradfield Agricultural labourer **Ellen Sexton** 1872 Knapton	**George** 1890 Bradfield emigrated to Canada **Rebecca** 1893 Bradfield m. Fred Hewitt **Robert (Harry)** 1895 Bradfield served with the Lincolnshire Regiment killed in action Gallipoli buried Azmak Cemetery, Suvla **Gladys** 1897 Bradfield m. Orvis Wade **Alice** 1900 Bradfield m. Robert Deacon **Joshua** 1903 Bradfield cowman m. Ruby Cutting **Sidney** 1907 Bradfield cattle feeder on farm m. Ethel Storey
THAIN Rose Ethel Colins Farm House Antingham	**1890** Appointed monitoress to help in this school in the morning and in the Upper school during the afternoon. Went on to be a pupil teacher in the school **1896** R. E. Thain leaves this school today as her apprenticeship is at an end	**Robert** 1843 Repps Blacksmith **Eva Holman** 1844 Salhouse	**Rose Ethel** 1877 Great Yarmouth teacher **Ann** 1879 Great Yarmouth m. Douglas Bruce
THURSTON George Rebecca Antingham	**1879** Rebecca absented herself from school for three weeks to pick turnips **1880** Sent home due to measles **1880** Rebecca at home with the measles **1883** Sent Thurston back to the Infants having been admitted by mistake	**John** 1837 Antingham Licensed Hawker **Mary Bane** 1842 Southrepps	**George** 1870 Southrepps road labourer died 1906 **Rebecca** 1872 Bradfield m. Ernest Harwood **Frederick** 1875 Bradfield farm labourer m. Emma **John** 1877 Antingham farm labourer m. Clara Farrow **Walter** 1880 Antingham farm labourer m. Rosa Reynolds served with the Norfolk Regiment. 1900–04, served with the Labour Corps in WWI **Susan** 1881 Antingham m. James Bullimore **James** 1884 Antingham market gardener m. Maud Burton

THURSTON **George** Lower Street	**1917** George is a very delicate boy	**John** 1877 Antingham Farm labourer **Clara Farrow** 1881 Metton	**Herbert** 1900 Southrepps m. Alice Rump served with the Training Reserve Battalion in WWI **John** 1901 Southrepps builder's labourer m. Emma Medlar **Albert** 1904 Southrepps m. Violet Eastoe **Edith** 1908 Southrepps **George** 1910 Southrepps
TURNER **Harry (Henry)** Thorpe Road Lower Street	**1900–1903** Persistent truant playing. Continual laziness. Impertinence to teacher. Telling a lie. Wilful inattention. Disobedience and impertinence. Bullying girl on road. Continued idleness. Bullying girls on road. Leaving school at noon without permission	**Alfred** 1853 Roughton Agricultural labourer **Louisa Pooley** 1859 Skeyton died before 1901 census	**George** 1878 Roughton farm labourer **Robert** 1879 Southrepps coal miner Warwickshire **Gertrude** 1882 Southrepps **Frederick** 1884 Southrepps cattleman on farm **Hannah Matilda** 1886 Southrepps m. John Ruddick emigrated to Canada **Amelia** 1887 Southrepps **Jane** 1889 Southrepps died 1891 aged 2 **Harry** 1892 Southrepps
TUTHILL **May** Lower Street	**1910** May won a book prize	**Arthur** 1870 Yaxham Corn Merchants Manager **Alice Drury** 1873 Southrepps	**Mabel** 1896 North Walsham m. Walter Chambers **Hilda** 1897 North Walsham **Alice** 1898 North Walsham m. William Bell **Gwendoline** 1899 North Walsham m. Raymond Hunt **May** 1900 North Walsham m. Thomas Green **Edith** 1903 Southrepps m. Isaac Neave **Arthur** 1906 Southrepps **John** 1907 Southrepps carpenter m. Phyllis Bayes **Roy** 1910 Southrepps
WELLS **Adeline** Thorpe Road Upper Street Southrepps	**1881** Caned Caned for being late	**William** 1836 Southrepps Blacksmith **Mary Ward** 1839 Skeyton	**William** 1867 Southrepps agricultural labourer plumber and gas fitter London m. Ada Bull **Adeline** 1871 Southrepps **Selina** 1875 Southrepps m. Robert Clifferton **Daniel** 1877 Southrepps horseman on farm m. Sarah Bull **Samuel** 1879 Southrepps builder's labourer London m. Charlotte Piper served in the RFC in WWI **Percy** 1881 Southrepps Metropolitan police officer m. Mary Ann Eaton
WHITWOOD **Daniel** **Mary** **Reuben** Thorpe Market	**1880** Daniel sent home on account of the measles Mary produced Dr's letter to say she was free from contagious disease **1888** Reuben large head **1890** Reuben weak intellect	**John** 1848 Thorpe Market Agricultural Worker **Ann Childs** 1841 Antingham	**Daniel** 1872 North Walsham died in 1887 aged 16 **Mary** 1873 North Walsham m. Henry Gee **Ruth** 1874 Dilham living with widowed mother **Reuben** 1877 Thorpe Market farm labourer died 1915 aged 39 **Ned** 1879 Thorpe Market fisherman m. Ethel Bird **Albert** 1881 Thorpe Market Able seaman **Martha** 1882 Thorpe Market m. Ernest Bane
WHITWOOD **Mary** **Anna** **Agnes** **Jeremiah** Letter Box Cottage Antingham	**1878** Agnes transferred from Infants **1879** Anna passed standard I at the last Government examination **1880** Mary returned to school produced a doctor's certificate to state that she was free from contagious disease **1880** Jeremiah sent home on account of the measles **1881** Anna's and Jeremiah's fees will be paid by the Guardians	**Jeremiah** 1842 Antingham Agricultural Labourer **Mary Bullimore** 1844 Bradfield	**William** 1862 North Walsham military groom m. Rose Whippe **Arthur** 1864 Bradfield platelayer on the railway m. Anna Algar **Edith** 1866 Antingham m. Tom Oxley **Mary Ann** 1868 Antingham m. George Sythers **Anna** 1871 Antingham dressmaker **Agnes** 1872 Antingham m. Harry Yellop egg merchant in London **Jeremiah** 1873 Antingham beastman in Yorkshire m. Eva Good **Kate** 1875 Antingham m. Robert Keen in Hillingdon **Blanche** 1878 Antingham m. Charles Shepperd both baker's salesmen **Gertrude** 1880 Antingham m. Horace Simpson **Harry** 1882 Antingham waiter m. Ethel Harwood **Violet** 1884 Antingham m. James Hammond **Cecil** 1886 Antingham agricultural engine driver m. Gertrude Beane **Ernest** 1888 Antingham beastman Yorkshire m. Daisy Tuttle **George** 1891 Antingham police constable served in RFC WWI m. Rosanna Goodson

WHITWOOD **Sidney** **Charles** Antingham	**1907** Sidney 6 years and 8 months when admitted 1906, 268 attendances 1907, 359 not transferred to Upper school **1910** Charles seven years perfect attendance	**Harry** 1862 Antingham Gardener **Sarah Cock** 1861 Bradfield	**Reginald** 1889 Antingham assistant draper emigrated to Canada **Ernest** 1892 Antingham agricultural engineer served with the Army Service Corps WWI m. Elsie Gray **Ronald** 1895 Antingham farm servant served with the London Regiment killed in action 1918 France buried Longueval, Departement de la Somme **Charles** 1898 Antingham furnishing salesman m. Ann Coultas served with the Royal Field Artillery WWI **Sidney** 1901 Antingham died 1921 aged 20
WIGGETT **Mary Ann** Thorpe Market	**1878** 18th November received a Doctor's certificate that Mary is not in a fit state of health to attend school Again on the 4th April	**William** 1824 Rackheath, Norfolk Brick layer **Elizabeth Cooper** 1826 St Faiths Newton died 1865 **Rebecca Hardy** 1826 Hainford	**Rebecca** 1847 Southrepps m. Jonathan Swift **Mary Ann** 1868 Thorpe Market died 1891 aged 22
WIGGETT **Herbert** Church Street Southrepps	**1900** Disorder	**George** 1856 Thorpe Market Bricklayer **Clara McCullen** 1858 Plumstead died 1891 **Jane Flowerday** 1863 Antingham	**Bertha** 1879 Cromer m. Robert Coleby Northumberland **Ernest** 1880 Cromer blacksmith **Clara** 1882 Cromer m. Charles Baker **Walter** 1883 Cromer bricklayer **George** 1886 Cromer bricklayer/coal miner m. Margaret Shell Slater **Gertrude** 1880 Cromer m. Walter Hudson **Herbert** 1890 Cromer emigrated to Canada m. Lavinia Richardson **Maud** 1900 Southrepps (half-sister) m. John Ramsey
WOODHOUSE **Charlotte** **Hannah** **Eliza** Lower Street	**1879** Passed standard I Eliza transferred from the Infant room **1880** Eliza at home with the measles, on that account obliged to send home Charlotte and Hannah	**John** 1833 Haverland Farm labourer **Mary Ann Easton** 1822 Cawston	**Stephen** 1863 Southrepps farm labourer m. Sarah Bird **George** 1865 Southrepps farm labourer died 1896 aged 31 **Charlotte** 1869 Southrepps m. Frederick Knights **Hannah** 1871 Southrepps m. William Hopkin **Eliza** 1873 Southrepps housemaid Sheffield died 1903 aged 30

Index

Bold text *indicates a headed section on the topic;* bold numbers *indicate an item featured in an illustration. Entries in the Appendix are only listed if they also appear in the main body of the text.*

A

150th anniversary celebration 55, 112–3
    commemorative mugs presented 113
    memorable infants' performance 113
This is Your Life **112–3**
abolition of school boards 9
abolition of slavery 12, 126
Academy *see* North Norfolk Academy Trust
after–school activities 74
agricultural levy **28**
Agricultural Rates Act 1896 28
Agricultural Show **98**
Aldborough School 18
Allen, Miss Louisa 27, **57**, 133
all-weather clothing (Forest School) 19
Almey, William **112**
amalgamation of boys' and girls' schools 1881 28, 57, **59**, 77, 80, 116, 127
amalgamation of infants' and mixed schools 1924–5 51, **66**, 124, 130
Amies family 46–50
    Amies family photo **46**
    Amies, Elsie **49**
    Amies, George **47**, 118, 134
    Amies, Jessie **48**
    Amies, Katie **48**
    Amies, Louisa **47**
    Amies, Margaret **49**
    Amies, Mr William 24, 27–8, 46–7, **50**, 76–7, 85, 116–122, 126–7, 129, 134
    Amies, Mrs Louisa 47, 50
    Amies, William Jnr 49
Amies, Elizabeth 14
animal incursions into playground **56**
Antingham and Southrepps School
    aerial view **41**
    clock **32**
    founded 1826 2
    grade II listing 1
    hall **59**
    illustrated **2**, **16**, **31–4**, **38–41**, **54**, **81**, **83**
    layout plan **32**
    map of the School and surrounding land 1835 **30**
    pupils illustrated – often with staff **8–10**, **15**–6, **38–9**, **54**, **61**, **65**, **67**, **74**, **79**, **83**, 8–9, **94**, **100**, **112–3**, **115**
Antingham parish 1, 25–6, 28, 29, 31, **76**, 126
arithmetic 5, **7**, **23**, 25, 116–9, 123–5
Armistice Day 1919 **106**
art 10, 28
Ashmanhaugh **83**, 131
attendance data 68–9, 72, 74
attendance officer 15, 26–7, 67–9, 72
Ayden, Miss 85

B

babies' room 32–3, **39**, 103, 122, 128
Bacton **83**
Baker days 132
Baker, Ella **72**, 138
Balle, Miss Mary 60–1, 126, 133
Bane, Ernest **106**, 138
Bane, Florence **64**, 139
barns 51, 81, 83, 101–2, 129
beekeeping 55
Bell, Dr Andrew 5
    Bell system 6, 14
Bent, Miss Naomi 62, **64–6**, 70, 94, **101**, 103–4, **105**, 120–3, 130, 133
Bible as a teaching resource 5, 20
Birt, Mr Joseph (Headmaster) 14, 44–5, 126, 133
    letter of reference **44**
Birt, Mrs 14, 44
blackberry picking in school hours **99**, 129
blackcurrant picking, time off for 99
Blakeney
    birdwatching trip **54**
    Blakeney School 2
Blickling Hall 11, 31
    Pyramid mausoleum 31
blinds 116
board members 14–15
Board of Guardians 26
board room **32–3**, 95
board schools 1, 7–8, 12–15, 26–7, **29**, 45, 122, 126–7
    abolition 9
Bodham School 18
Boer Wars 95
books 13, 20–4, **58**–9, 116, 122–6
boules tournament 85
Bowles, Joanne 112
Boys' school 1, 14, 27–8 **32–3**, 47, 57, 67, 77, 80, 116, 126–7, **134**
Bradfield Hall farm 15
Bradfield parish 1, 25–6, **28**, 31, 126
bread riots 3
breakfast club 74
Brett, Miss Emily 57, 59, 69, 77, 126, 133
British and Foreign Schools 5–6
British Schools Museum vi, **5**
Bullimore, Frank 71
Burton, John 15
Burton, Sam **109**
Burton, Ted **109**
Burton–Pye, Major **106**
Burton–Pye, Sam **106**, **109**, 140
Burton–Pye, William **106**
Butler, Miss Mary 57, 133
bye-laws 7, 15, 26, 67, 128

C

caning 77–9, 142–4, 148, 154, 158
canteen 32, 41, 96–7
Carleton Rode School 2
carriage shed *see* stabling
census 1841 44
census 1871 60

census 1881 47, 147
census 1891 47, 60, 62, 133
census 1901 29, 158
census 1911 49, 133, 147
census returns 98
Chatby Memorial, Alexandria 138
chicken pox 90, 94
chilblains 68
child labour 4
Church's responsibility for education 28
Clarke, George 15
class sizes 10, 57, 64
classrooms 6, 32–3, 35, 39, 57, 103, **105**, 118–9, 124–5, 127–8, 132
    layouts 5–6, 14, 20, 33, 39
cloakroom 33, 38, 119–20, 122, 128
closure due to bad weather 129–32
closure due to illness 90–2, 93–4, 96
Clutterbuck, Mr 85
coal and coke, tender for **40**
coal shed 32, 39, **40**
Coatesworth, Mr David MBE 113
Code of Education (1862) 7, 25
Code of Education (1872) **7**
coffee room in Lower Street 13
Colby School 18
Collier, Mr 112
Colman family 24
compulsory education 4, 7–9, **15**, 26, 27–8, 127–8
compulsory medical and dental inspections 95–**6**
computer room **33**, 39
computers 33, 132
Cook, P 79
Cooke, Marion 85
Cookery 8, 28, 40, 42, 51, 80–2, 101, 128, 132
Corn Laws 3
Cossey family **72**, 141
Costessey School 2
country dancing lessons 85
County Education Officer 113
Covid–19 96
Crane, Mr Frederick (Acting Headmaster) 53, 130, 135
Craske, Edith **64**, 140
cricket team? 1914 **87**
crop rotation 3
Crowe, Anne 77, 142
currant picking, time off for 111, 130
Curry, Miss 80
cycle shed **32**, 40
cycling proficiency lessons 85

D

Dack, Miss Mabel 134
Dack, Mr Thomas (Headmaster) 53, 79, **107**, 130, 135
Dack, Mrs Margaret 53
Dagenham County High School evacuees 53, 107, 130
Dame schools 5

dance 53
Daniels, Mrs Anne 82
Davies, Fairfax (Poor Law clerk) 15
Davies, Rev. vicar of St Mary's Antingham and St Margaret's Thorpe Market 15, **76**
Day, Mrs Sue 18, 132, 136
DDT 84
den making (Forest School) 19
dental treatment 9, 95–6, 129
Devon trip 2008 **89**
Dickleburgh School 2
Diocesan Inspector 120–1
Diocesan Training Institution, Norwich 62
diphtheria 90, 94–5
discipline 62, 116–23
Dix, Harriet 77, 142
Dolphin, Rev. vicar of Antingham and rector of Thorpe Market 14
doors and doorway 33–5, **38**, 42, **59**, 101, 112, 116, 128, 132
drainage 40
dress–making evening classes 85
drill (PE) 87–8, 118
drill instructor coordinator 88
Drury, Reggie MM **104**, 143
drying room 19, 41
Duncan–Coates, Freja **89**
Dunham, Joan **87**
Dyball, Walter, death of 128

E

Earl, Edith **77**, 143
Earl, Mrs Ann 27, 45–6, 126, 133
East Ruston National School 46
Eastern Arts Association 18
Eastern, Robert **112**
Education legislation
    Academies Act 2010 10
    Education (Fisher) Act 1918 9
    Education (Provision of Meals) Act 1906 96
    Education (Forster Act) 1870 126
    Education (Provision of Meals) Act 1914 96
    Education Act 1833 6
    Education Act 1870 7, 15
    Education Act 1880 – nationwide compulsory education 7
    Education Act 1891 8
    Education Act 1902 8–9, 13, 29
    Education Act 1906 97
    Education Act 1907 95
    Education Act 1921 97
    Education Act 1944 9–10, 16, 40
    Education Act 1980 89
    Education Reform Act 1988 10
    Elementary Education Act 1870 67
    Elementary Education Act 1880 27–8, 67, 69
    Elementary Education Act 1891 28, 69
    Parochial Schools Bill 1807 4

Edward VII 12, 24, 128
    half day holiday for his visit to
    Norwich 76
Edward VIII 130
Elden, Mr John (Headmaster) 27,
    45–6, 126, 133
    Elden family graves 46
elections *see* polling station
electoral reform 12
electricity 43, 130
eleven plus 10, 132
Elizabeth II 1, 130–1
embroidery 80
emergency teachers' scheme 10, 16
emigration **47**, 60, 98, 133, 141, 144,
    146–7, 151–9
enclosure of common land 3
Erpingham School 18
Erpingham Union 28, 134
evacuees *see* World War Two
evening classes 85
exemption from attendance 8, 69, 127
exercise books **20**
extension built 1877 32–4
    repaired 1884 34–8
    surveyor's report 34, **35–7**

F
faggot yard (kindling) 40
Farrington, Mr A **50**, 134
Feast Day holidays 75
Federation of Small Schools; Northern
    Area Group 18
fees 4–5, 8, **15**, 25–28, 57, 67, 126
    abolition of 27–8, 69–70, 127
    arrears 26–8, 67
    prosecution for non–payment 27,
    155
felt slippers 84
fire door **38–9**, 131
fire guards 96, 105
First School, plans to become 18
flower shows 75–6
football **86**, 89
Forest School 18–9, 132
founding of **Antingham &**
    Southrepps School 4
Fousler, Mrs (school cook) 97
free school meals 96–7, 128
free school milk 9, 97
French language and culture 56, 85,
    131
Frost, Mr (Dagenham County High
    School) 53, **108**
Funding 25–29
    boys' school grant 126
    cost of original building of A & S
    School 25
    discipline grant 120–1
    education code 25
    English grant **25**, 119, 121–2, 127
    fee grants 8
    from parishes 26
    gardening grant 84
    geography grant 118
    Girls' school grant 126
    infant grant 26
    Infants' school grant 27, 126
    Judith Bartram Trust grant 136
    Local Education Authorities'
    responsibility for education 29
    maintenance grant 27
    merit grant 8, **25**, 28, 117–8
    needlework grant 117
    school fund 26
    small–population grant 29
    unspecified grants **58–9**, 80, 117, 127

Futter, John Stanley **64**, 144
G
galleries vi, 6, **14**, **21**, 24, 33, **35**, 39, 64,
    121–2, 127–8
garden 41, 51
gardening 51, **83–84**, 85, 88, 125,
    129, 131
    horticultural inspector 84
Gaze, Marjorie **64**, 144
geography 10, 21–2, 23, 28, **52**, 85,
    116–9, 123–5
George IV 1
George V 127, 129
George VI 130
George, Reggie **78**
German measles 90, **92**, 94
Giant Stride **86**, 128
Gibbons, Timothy MM (killed in action
    WW1) **104**, 144
Giddy, Davis MP 4
Gimingham **83**, 132
    school 2
Girls' school 1, 27–8, **32–3**, **39**, 42,
    57–9, 67, 77, 80, 116, 126–7, 133
Gladwin, Mr Harold (Headmaster)
    55–6, **88**, 131–2, 136
Godwin, William 4
Gotts, Cyril **106**, 145
Gotts, John **109**
Gotts, Mrs (school cook) 53
Gotts, Robert **106**, 148
Government jam–making scheme **99**
grammar **23**, 117–8, 127
grammar schools 9, 16–**17**
gramophone 124
Gray, George (fall from tree in
    playground) **86**, 127
Gray, Grace 69
Gray, Ivy **64**, 146
Gray, Kathleen **64**, 146
Gray, Theophilus 84, 146
Greenfield, Sidney MC 103–4, 146
Gresham Village School 18–9, 89
Gressenhall Museum vi, 1, 24
Grey, John **112**
Grimes, Neville **79**
ground source heat pump 41
Gunton
    Hall and estate 11–2, **13**, 43, **76**
    parish 1, **26**, 28, 126
    saw mill 3
    St. Andrew's Church 50
Gwyn, Rev. rector of St James
    Southrepps 15

H
half day holidays 70–1, 75–6, 98, 127,
    129
Hall Farm **3**
handicrafts 51, **81**, 83, 101, 131
    hut **32**, 40, **81**, **83**, 131
handwriting 21, 53, 118, 120, 123
Harbord family *see* Suffield family
Harbord, Honourable Miss Doris 88
Harbord, Rev. John(rector of St. James)
    Southrepps 13
Hardingham, Sid **109**
Hare, Mr John (Headmaster) 10, 43,
    53–5, 79, 93, 95, 130–1, 135
Hare, Mrs Mena (Paddy) 16, **33**, 53, **55**,
    130
Harrison, James 15
harvest holidays 35, 60, **75**, 90, 93, 99,
    129
Harwood, Emma 18, 136
hay making **99**
Headmasters living in the School

House 44–56
Heaps, Mr (handicrafts organiser)
    94
heating 34, 40, **43**, 56, 81, 104–5, 107,
    123, 129, 131–2
helping with the harvest etc. 68, **74**, **98**,
    110
Hemp, Miss 80
Hewitt, Charles **106**, 148
Hewitt, Dorothy **64**, 149
Hewitt, Henry 77, 148
Hewitt, James 69
Hewitt, John **106**, 148
Hewitt, Mr H 69
Hewitt, Sid 106, 109
Hewitt, Wilfred **106**, 149
Hill House **4**, 15, 108, 130
His/Her Majesty's Inspector (HMI) 9,
    14, 50, 85, 96, 104, 116–125
Hiscock, Elizabeth 45
history (the subject) 10, 20, 119,
    124–5
Hockering School 2
Holt Hall camping trips 89
HORSA: Hutting Operation for the
    Raising of the School leaving Age 10,
    32, 40, 130
horse chestnut gathering 129
Hurn, Albert MM 103–4, **106**, 151
Hurn, Arthur DCM 103–4, 150
Hurn, Ernest **64**, 142, 150
Hurn, Herbert **109**
Hurn, Reggie **109**
Hurn, Walter **109**

I
ice–cream van **87**
illegal employment 69
immunisation 95
industrial action by staff 132
industrial Revolution 3
Infants' department/school 1, 14, 27,
    29, **32**, 34–5, **38–9**, 41, 48, 51, 57, 59,
    60–6, 68, 77, 80, 91–4, **101**, 103–5,
    113, 116–24, 126–30, 132–3
influenza 76, 90, **93**, 129
interactive whiteboards 41
inter–school sports 89
Ives, George (farmer at Bradfield Hall)
    15

J
Jeffries, Harry **64**, 151
Jones, Mr Hector (Headmaster) 51–3,
    73, 75, 78, 81, **84**, 93, 101, 129–30,
    135
    glowing HMI report **52**
    resumé of teaching career **51**
    retirement **52**
Jones, Mrs Maud 51–2
Jordan, Dorothy **64**, 151
Judith Bartrum Trust **33**, 136

K
key stages 10
kiln room 33
kitchen 41, 97, 125
Klokskov, Nikki **112**
Knapton **83**
    school 2, 134
knitting 80, 118, 127

L
Lancaster, Joseph 5
late starting age **63**, **64**, **70**, 118
laundry lessons 28, 40, 51, 80–1, 101,
    129

Lawrence, David **109**
Learner, Mr (school manager and
    farmer) 15, **95**, 99
legal employment 69
Leman, Miss Gertrude 80, 122, 134
Library 33, 39, 42, 132
lighting restrictions in WW1 102
literacy rate 4
Local Education Authorities 9–10, 29, 41
log books 1, **14**, **21**, 24, 49, 67, **75–6**,
    80, **84**, **90–1**, **96–8**, **100–2**, 103–4,
    110, **113**, 114–5
London Zoo trip, 1939 53, 130
long–jump sandpits on the Common
    88, 128
Loos memorial, Belgium **102**
Lower Street coffee room 13
Lubbock, Alfred **64**, 153

M
MacDonald, Mr (School House tenant)
    56
McKenzie, Mr (Dagenham woodwork
    master) **111**
Machine Gun Corps 104, 141, 143, 146
Mafeking, celebration of relief 76
Maguir, Miss Rebeka 27, **60–1**, 126, 133
Malson, Miss *see* private school, Upper
    Street
Mathematics 10, **23**, 119, 124
Mayes, Olive **64**
meals–on–wheels 97
measles 90–2, **93**, 127–8
Meatyard, Mr Edward 16–7, 135
mechanisation of farming 3, 99
medical officer 69, 90–1, 93, 95–6
medical room 33, 95, 97, 130
medical treatment *see also* School
    Medical Service 9
meeting room **33**
men's reading room Lower Street 53
military hospital, request for temporary
    use of two school rooms 102–3
milk 9, 97
mini–buses 18, 89
Ministry of Education 51
minute books 1, **17**, 26–7, **40**, **42–3**, 56,
    66, 68, 70, **73–4**, 80–1, **88**, 96, 100,
    101–2, **105**, **109**
mixed school 29, **35**, **48**, 62, **66**, 91, 93,
    101, 117–24, 127–**8**, 133, 135
mobile classrooms 41, 132
Monitorial System 5–6, 14
Montesole, Mrs Liena 102
Moulson, Mr W clerk to the Board and
    attendance officer 15
Moy, Robert 69, 127
Moy, William **106**, 153
mumps 90, 94
Mundella code 8, 28
Mundesley **83**
    school 2, 89, 132
music 53, 85, 121, 123–4, 136
music room **33**, 136

N
National Archive, Kew 1, **36**
National School Museum (Wilderspin)
    14
National Schools 5–6, 14, 25, **44**, 46–7
National System of Education School 14
nature area 88
needlework 5, 43, 47, 80, 116–9, 121,
    123, 125, 131
netball 89
NHS 95–6
non–paupers list **28**

Norfolk Archive Centre 1, 81
Norfolk Education Committee 1, 13, 15–6, 43, 69, 70, **71–2**, 82, 84, 105, 107, 129
Norfolk Historic Buildings Group 2
Norfolk Museum Service 72
Norfolk Regiment 100, 103–4, 138–40, 143–145, 148–51, 153–5, 157
Norfolk Schools Cookery Book 82
North Norfolk Academy Trust 19, 74, 132
North Norfolk Small Schools Federation 89, 132
North Walsham 16, 85, 98, 131
    central school 16
    cinema 85
    Infants School 2, 75
    Secondary Modern School 18
    North Walsham Technical Education Committee 85
Northrepps 132
    school 2, 18, 40, 97

O
object lessons 6, **21**, 118–9
Ofsted 10
Oulton School 11
outdoor relief 26, 28
Overseas Club charitable collection 102
Overstrand 18, 132
    Overstrand Hall used as Auxiliary Hospital in WW1 **103**
    school 2, 18, 97
Owles, Mr Clement (school manager and farmer) 15
Owles, Mr George (school manager and farmer) 15, 99

P
Paine, Thomas 3–4
Pardon, Jane 98
Paris trip 56, 85, 131
parish School is located in, dispute over **29**
parishes served 1, 14, 25–6, 28, 126
    map ii
partitions 33, **39**, 128
Paul family 72, 154
Payne, Bessie 77, 154
Peacock, William 67–9
Pearson, Mr **106**
permission to leave school for employment **69**
pewter smelting (Forest School) 19
physical education (PE) 10, **87–9**
Pike, Robert **112**
Pit Street 4, 100–1, 108
Pitcher, Herbert **106**
play and **playtime** 6, 32–3, 39, 41, 86–7, 101, 124
    playgrounds 6, 14, 32, 35, 39–40, **56**, 86–7, 101, 103, 124–5, 127–8, 130, 132, 145–6
playgroup 32, 41, 132
Plumby, James – Poor Law clerk 15
Plummer, Ernie **109**
poetry learned by rote 7, 24
polio 90, 94–5, 130
Pollard, Mrs 18
polling station 76, 82, 127–31
Poor Law 15, 28, 62
porch 29, **31**, 32, **33**, 35, 132
potato lifting, time off for 99, 111, 130
poultry-keeping lectures 85
poverty 8, 26, 68
primary schools 2, 10, 16, 19, 83, 131
Prince of Wales see Edward VII
prison reform 12
private school, Upper Street 68–9, 126, 128

prizes for good attendance 70–3, 128
prosecution for non-attendance 15, 26, 67–9, 74, 127
PTA 19, 42, 132
Public Works Loan Commissioners 34
Punchard, George **109**
punishment book 1, **77–9**
pupil teachers 6–7, 9, 14, 21–2, 24, 47, 48–9, 117, 119–20, 133–135, 144, 157

Q
Queen's Scholarship exam 6, 133

R
RAF 104, 143, 148
reading 5, **7**, 25, 116, 118–9, 123–4
reading room 53, 100, 129
reasons for poor attendance 68
recreation ground, Upper Street **88**
Red Cross Sale 1918 107
Reepham School 53
Reform Act 1918 76
regular attendance defined 67
relieving officer 27
religious teaching non-denominational 8
Reynolds, Gray **78**
Reynolds, Ivy 64, 155
Reynolds, John **79**
Risebrow, Ethel 64, 155
Rix, Miss Lydia 57, 133
Roche, Liena Miss see Montesole
Rogers, William **106**
Roughton 16, **83**, 130, 132
    school 2, 16, 18, 40, 80–1, 85
Rubella see German measles
rural to urban population shift 3

S
sand trays 6
SATS (Standard Assessment Tests) 10
Saunders, William **78**, 156
scarlet fever (scarlatina) 76, **90–1**, 128–9
scavenger 40, 129, 131
school badges 19
school bus 132
School Common 110, 128
school garden 41, 51, 84, 125
School Health Service 9
School house (Headmaster's house) 42–3
    converted for school use 42
    Headmaster's garden **38**, 40, 55, 86, 130–1
    let to tenant 42
school leaving age 9–10, 16, 27, 40, 67, 127, 129–30
school meals 9, 41, **96–7**, 128, 130
School Medical Service 95–6
school nurse 91, 95
school office 39, 41, 43, 132
school roll 16, **18–9**, 27, 67, 108, 126
school secretary vi, 16, 39, 53
school team in 1940s **89**
science 8, 10, 18, 28
Secondary Modern Schools 9, 16, 18, 88
sewing **80**, 118, 122, 134
Sheringham High School 19
shooting parties 11–**12**, 128
simultaneous method 6
slates 6, 122
small-parish status 29
Smith, Adam (author) 4
Smith, Ernest **106**, 157
Snelling, Grace **73**
Soames, Miss Eleanor 62, 119, 127, 133
softball 89
Southrepps

Boys **106**
Commons 13, 19, 31, **81**, 86–88, 110, 128
fair 75–6, 128
Hall 24, 156
parish 1, 25–**6**, **28**, 31, 126
Parish Council 112
St. James's Church **11**, 13, 15, 55, **81**
Social Club, Lower Street 53
special needs 69
sports days **88**
sports field 88
sports hall (unsuccessful bid) 89
St. John's Ambulance Brigade 103
stabling 32, 126
staff car park 86
staff room 39, 43
staffing levels **58**–9, 64
Stalham High School 19
standards 7–8, 20, **23**–4, 80, 116–22, 124
    standard posts 6, 20
Stone, Miss Mabel 66
streaming 10
Suffield 11, 128
    school 2, 11, 151
Suffield family, including Harbords 11–13
    Suffield, Ladies 11, **12**–**13**, 14, 127
    Suffield, Lords 2–4, 11, **12**–**13**, 14, 25–7, 31, 44, 125–6
Sullivan, Rev. rector of St. James Southrepps 15, 81
Summertime Act 1916 **102**
Sunday Schools 5, 11, 76
Swafield School 2, 134
swimming lessons 88, 131–2
swing riots 3

T
TB see tuberculosis
technology 10, 18
Technology Schools 9, 16
Temple, Mr 84, 129
Templewood 112
tenant in School House see Macdonald, Mr.
textbooks 21, **22**–3, 24
The Ant magazine 85
"the college" 112
Thew, Rev. Frederick vicar of St Nicholas Swafield 15
Thiepval memorial, France 104, 140, 144, 150
Thorpe Market
    parish 1, 25–**6**, **28**, 31, 76, 126
    Parish Council 112
    St. Margaret's Church 31, 44–6
Thurston family 69, 157
Thurston, Peter 79
Tilney, Miss Harriet 48, 62–3, 119–20, 133
tithe system 28
toilets 32–3, **40**–1, 42, 81, 101, 103, 127–8, 132
transfer of school from Lord Suffield to Board 27
treats 76, 129
Trimingham School 2, 80–1, 138
Trollope, Miss Inez 62, 117, 127, 133
Trunch 72
    school 2
tuberculosis 95
Turner, David 79
Turner, Henry 77, 158
"Turnip" Townsend 3
turnips 3, 137, 141, 151, 157
Tyler, Peter **98**
typhoid 90, 94

U
uncertificated teachers 6, 135

V
vaccinations see immunisation
VE Day **110**
ventilation 33, **58**, **61**, 116, 118–9, 126–8
Vergerson, Antony 64
Victoria, Queen 12, 126–7
    diamond jubilee 128
    golden jubilee 127
    half-day for birthday celebration 76
Virol **95**

W
War Workers' Association sale of work 104
Ward, Edith 69
water for break times **43**
water pox see chicken pox
Watson, Bessie 120–21, 133
Watson family, Antingham 62
Watson, Mr E.W. **22**, 118–9
Watson, Mrs (Lower Street barn) 81, 101
Watts, Miss Ida 53, **114**, 135
weather, effect on attendance **68**
Welden, Mr Matthew (builder of 1877 extension) 34
well 43, 126, 128
Wells, Adeline 77, 158
Whitwood, Charles **73**, 129, 159
Whitwood, Jack **106**
whooping cough 90, 93–4
Wilderspin, Samuel vi, 6, **14**
Williams, Mark **112**
windows 31, **33**, **39**, 81, 83, 116, 119, 125–6, 131
Wolstonecraft, Mary 4
Wood, Mr builder of the school 31
Wood, Robert 69
Woods family 57, 59, 69
woodwork 40, 82–3, **111**, 125, 129–30
    class of 1937 illustrated **83**
Workers Education Association (WEA) evening lectures 85
workhouse 15, 26–7, 47
World War One vi, 9, 74, 88, **100**–7
    attendance certificates **106**
    casualties see Pupils Appendix 137–159
    combatants group photo **106**
    infants' school commandeered **100**
    demand for cost of straw used by soldiers 102
World War Two 53, 104, **107**–11
    air raid precautions **108**–9
    Christmas parties **109**
    declaration of war **107**
    evacuees 107–**11**, 130
    50th anniversary visit 1989 **111**
    Home Guard **110**
    Home Guard members photo **109**
    VJ Day **110**
Worstead National School 47
Wortley, Mr John (Headmaster) 14, 44–5, 126, 133
Wortley, Mrs 14, **45**
Wortley family graves **46**
writing 5–7, 25, 118–9, 124–5

Y Z
Yorkshire field trip 1987 18
zig-zag trenches on Common 110